2 4 AUG 2023

AFTER THE FALL

AFTER THE FALL

Crisis, Recovery and the Making of a New Spain

Tobias Buck

WEIDENFELD & NICOLSON

First published in Great Britain in 2019 by Weidenfeld & Nicolson
an imprint of The Orion Publishing Group Ltd
Carmelite House, 50 Victoria Embankment
London EC4Y 0DZ

An Hachette UK Company

1 3 5 7 9 10 8 6 4 2

A CIP catalogue record for this book is
available from the British Library.

ISBN (hardback) 978 1 4746 1007 0
ISBN (ebook) 978 1 4746 1009 4

Typeset at The Spartan Press Ltd,
Lymington, Hants

Printed and bound in Great Britain by Clays Ltd,
Elcograf S.p.A.

www.orionbooks.co.uk

To my parents,
who gave me all the books I ever wanted.
This one is for them.

'There is no oil, there is no tin, no gold, no iron — positively none,' said the functionary, growing vexed at such unreasonable rapacity.

'What do you want with it?'

'I am going as a journalist.'

'Ah, well. To the journalist every country is rich.'

Evelyn Waugh, *Scoop*

Contents

PROLOGUE

A crisis reveals

I arrived in Madrid in December 2012, in time to celebrate the bleakest Christmas the city had seen in a generation.

Capital and country were reeling from a series of economic shocks that had brought Spain to the brink of ruin. As I started to find my way around the city, I saw reminders of the nation's desperation everywhere. On days when I took my son to nursery school we would pass a long line of people – not all of them poorly dressed – waiting outside a church-run soup kitchen. Walking to my office in the morning, I would find that more and more shops had gone out of business. Inexplicably, the tiny store that sold and repaired mechanical typewriters held out, defying both technical obsolescence and the economic downturn. Then, one morning, I turned into Calle Hernán Cortés and found that it, too, had closed for good.

Part of my daily work as the correspondent for the *Financial Times* in Madrid was to survey the disaster zone that was Spain's economy. Six months before my arrival, a slow-burning banking crisis had suddenly blazed out of control, forcing the government to request billions of euros in rescue aid from its European partners. The roots of that crisis in fact reached back more than four years, when Spain's decade-long housing boom had dramatically turned to bust. But it was only in 2012 that the full extent of the economic calamity became clear. A big chunk of the nation's banking system was now in state hands, investors had taken fright and the flow of credit to households and businesses had dried up. Every week brought a new piece of horrendous economic data: the budget deficit was on course to exceed 10 per cent of gross domestic product – more than three times the level allowed under European Union rules. Debt was inching ever closer to 100 per cent of national output, prompting stark warnings from rating agencies and bond traders. Worst of all was the steady drumbeat of dismal news from the labour market. Jobless numbers had more than tripled since the start of the crisis – from 1.8 million in 2007 to just over 6 million when I arrived. The unemployment rate would peak a few weeks later at 27 per cent of the workforce, a number that seemed fantastical to outsiders but painfully real to Spaniards themselves. Youth unemployment, meanwhile, was estimated to be twice as high.

Standing behind those numbers were millions of people, every one of them with a different story of failure, injustice, disappointment, frustration and fear. I would meet and interview countless victims of the crisis over the years that followed – more than I can remember. But I never forgot my first: his name was Roque Marchal, a middle-aged carpenter whose business had been ruined by the downturn, and who was now no longer able to pay off his mortgage. We sat in a bar close to Madrid's Puerta del Sol, and he told me how scared he was of being evicted from his home. 'The letter could arrive tomorrow,' he said.[1] Marchal spoke only for himself, but in a few short phrases he managed to capture the mood of bewildered anxiety that had befallen the whole nation. 'All my life I considered myself middle-class, with my car and my house. I had a pretty good life,' he said. 'I never thought this could happen to me.'

Spain's crisis was not confined to the economy, however. It spread and mutated as the months and years went by, touching an increasing number of institutions, and other parts of Spanish life. What started out as a housing crisis became an economic crisis, then a banking and financial crisis, and – eventually – a political and constitutional crisis that threatened to tear up the country.

A crisis reveals, for good and for bad. There was, I found, much to admire about the way Spain confronted the great economic downturn. Even at the worst moments of the crisis, Spain never felt like it was staring into the abyss of social collapse. Families helped each other. Communities rallied. People continued to treat each other with the decency and empathy that make Spanish society – for all its tensions and problems – so admirably resilient. There was anger, to be sure, but it was directed at people you saw on television, not in the street. Spaniards cursed the corrupt politicians and reckless bankers who had created this mess, and those merciless austerians in Brussels and Berlin who told them how to get out of it. But I never saw a bad word directed at the young West African migrant who sold pirate DVDs outside my house, or the foreign lady begging outside the local supermarket. Neighbours would greet them every morning, like people who belonged to the *barrio*. Madrid, and the country at large, came through the crisis with reserves of solidarity and grace that were at times hard to fathom, and harder still to forget.

The refusal to turn against migrants and minorities, the unspoken commitment not to look for scapegoats among the weakest in society, was remarkable in the context of political developments elsewhere in Europe. No less surprising was the absence of a populist far-right party in Spain at a time when such groups were surging into parliaments and governments across much of Europe. At the height of the crisis, Spain looked

3

like a ripe target for the far right: it was home to millions of unemployed and millions of recent migrants, while faceless European officials were taking critical and painful decisions about the country's economic future. Yet Spain remained, until very recently, deaf to the siren calls of anti-immigration and anti-European political parties. Over the course of the past two decades, millions of migrants from Latin America, Asia, North Africa and Eastern Europe found a new home in Spain. Most were made to feel not just safe but welcome. Whether this will remain the case in the years ahead is hard to say. Towards the end of 2018, there were unmistakable signs that the far right was finally starting to gain a foothold in Spanish politics, in the form of a new nationalist party called Vox. Fuelled by popular anger over Catalan separatism and the recent rise in migrant arrivals, Vox managed to win more than 10 per cent of the vote in Spain's general election on 28 April 2019, shattering the notion that the country was somehow immune to the far-right surge taking place across Europe. The rise of Vox caused plenty of soul-searching in Spain. But it also seemed clear that the party enjoyed far less support than its extreme right peers in other European countries. Nor was there much evidence to suggest that the vast majority of Spaniards were abandoning their traditional backing for the European Union, or their broadly supportive attitude towards migrants.

Spain also managed to make – after much initial confusion and hesitation – bold reforms and brave changes to deal with the economic crisis itself. Recession gave way to recovery, and that recovery has been stronger and more durable than anyone predicted at the nadir of the crisis. The pain and dislocation wrought by the great downturn were terrible, and the effects will linger for years to come. But in economic terms, at least, Spain is no longer viewed as a basket case, but as proof that reforms can work – and that countries can learn from the policy mistakes of the past.

Spain's crisis, however, also unveiled fragilities and fissures that could not be fixed by economic recovery alone. All the country's institutions were put to the test in the years after the 2008 crash, along with some long-held assumptions that Spaniards made about themselves. Few survived without damage. Spain's political system, for example, had been dominated for decades by the Socialists (PSOE) and the Popular party (PP), alternating flag-carriers of the establishment. Today, after three elections in four years, Spain's parliament is fragmented and divided as never before. Recent governments have lacked the strength to win all but the most basic votes in the legislature. A seemingly unending string of corruption scandals eroded support not just for individual politicians and parties, but for the system as a whole. The banking sector was dismembered, too: of the fifty-five lenders that were vying for business in 2009, only ten were still around in 2017.[2] Support for the royal house was shattered, forcing the abdication of King Juan Carlos in 2014. The judiciary, the police, the media – they all bled trust and confidence in the years of the great recession. But even these losses seem trivial (and recoverable) when set against the greatest challenge facing Spain today: Catalonia.

The Spanish region on the border with France would come to occupy more and more of my time and attention. After decades of relative harmony, relations between Catalonia and the central government took a marked turn for the worse during the years of the recession, giving rise to a powerful independence movement and – eventually – a full-blown constitutional crisis. The true extent of the political disaster brewing in Catalonia became clear to many only on 1 October 2017, the day the Catalan regional government tried to hold an independence referendum in defiance of the Spanish constitution and clear rulings from the courts and authorities in Madrid. Thousands of Spanish police officers were sent to the region to stop the voting, but they were hopelessly outnumbered. The images that went round the world that day were calamitous for Spain: they showed helmeted riot police storming into voting stations, Spanish batons crashing down on heads and bodies, and Catalan protesters kicked and dragged across the ground by Spanish officers. Everyone watching the events unfold that day could see that something had gone terribly wrong – for Spain and for Catalonia alike.

The violence-scarred referendum on 1 October would prove hugely significant. It set in train a series of events that led rapidly, inexorably, to a declaration of independence by the Catalan parliament twenty-six days later, and a no-holds-barred constitutional clash between the separatists and the Spanish government. It led to the arrest of Catalan independence leaders, and the flight of the Catalan president to Belgium. It also sparked an uncommon outburst of nationalist sentiment in the rest of the country, as Spaniards flew their country's red-yellow-red banner from windows and balconies in untold numbers, offering a silent riposte to the countless independence flags fluttering across Catalonia. Barcelona and Madrid, those two great cosmopolitan cities, were suddenly awash in the primary colours of patriotism. The vote also led, eventually, to the suspension of Catalan autonomy and a new balance of power in the tension-filled region. Indeed, within less than eight months both Catalonia and Spain were under new political leadership, but the tensions never disappeared. The political, social and economic effects of the Catalan clash kept on coming, a remorseless cascade of blow and counterblow.

The origins of the secession campaign are complex, and reach back in time beyond the start of the crisis. But the separatist surge cannot be understood without the economic frustration caused by the downturn, and the broader longing for a new beginning – a decisive break with a country that many Catalans felt had nothing left to offer. It was part of a slow erosion, a gradual unravelling, of the structures, habits and traditions that held Spain together in the years after the death of the dictator Francisco Franco. The Catalan crisis was the most alarming expression of that unravelling because it threatened to tear apart the very shape of the country, but also because it tapped into anxieties buried deep in Spain's collective conscience. In his 1844 *Handbook for Travellers in Spain*, Richard Ford described Spain as a 'bundle of local units tied together by a rope of sand'.[3] It was an observation that would be repeated and paraphrased down the ages, but the idea was always the same: that Spain was a country uniquely fragile and lacking in unity, a collection of regions, cultures and nations that could be held together only by force or by virtue of a common national project. That common national project undoubtedly existed after the end of the Franco dictatorship in the late 1970s, when Spaniards everywhere wanted democracy, freedom and – eventually – membership of the European Community. Where was that common vision and desire now? To some, the surge of Catalan separatism in the years after 2008 suggested that Spain was succumbing to that old illness of fragility and fragmentation once again. For the first time in generations, a break-up of the country seemed thinkable.

As grave as the situation in Catalonia was, however, there was always another side to the Spanish story. Amid the political drama playing out on the streets of Barcelona, it was easy to forget that one of the deadliest separatist campaigns in modern European history was drawing to an end in another strife-torn corner of the peninsula. The Basque Eta group declared an end to its gruesome decades-long killing spree in 2011, sparking jubilation in the tormented region and across the rest of Spain. In the years that followed, the story largely disappeared from the international media: we chronicle death and murder even when they are routine, but not the absence of death and murder, no matter how remarkable. Yet here was a tale of hope that should have inspired not just Spain but the world. It showed that a society riven by hatred and fear can forge a new path after all, and that political extremists can silence a peaceful majority only for so long.

The Spanish crisis was, finally, also a crisis of confidence in Spain itself. The country had worked so hard to close the gap – political, economic and social – with the rest of Western Europe. In the years since the death of the dictator Franco in 1975, it became a model democracy, stable and deeply committed to European integration. Once a bastion of social conservatism, it became one of the most progressive nations in the West, abolishing the death penalty ahead of France, and becoming one of the first countries in the world to legalise gay marriage. Spain also became rich, almost as rich as the average European country (and richer than the Italian cousins across the sea, a small but especially pleasing statistical achievement).[4] The crisis forced that long process of convergence into reverse. Spain was poor again. Spain needed help again. And young Spaniards were leaving the country to find work abroad, just as their grandfathers had done in those humiliating decades of isolation and stagnation before the dictator's death.[5] A whole country woke up as if from a dream: We thought we were rich, but we weren't. We thought we were like the others, but we aren't. We trusted our leaders, but they failed us. We trusted our banks, but they betrayed us. As the novelist Antonio Muñoz Molina wrote in his memoir of the

8

crisis (echoing Karl Marx), 'everything that was solid dissolved into air'.[6] In a desperate attempt to offer a different narrative, the government installed a high commissioner for the *Marca España*, or 'Brand Spain', who was charged with travelling the world and explaining why things were really not all that bad.[7] The idea was to shift perceptions abroad, but if anyone needed reassurance it was Spaniards themselves. As far as I could tell, the initiative made little difference.

The fear of falling behind is an especially potent one in Spain. It echoes historical traumas from which the nation has never quite managed to escape. This is a country that has to look back 500 years to its *siglo de oro*, or Golden Age. The centuries since have been marked by decline and defeat – the loss of Spain's South American empire, the terrible violence of the Napoleonic wars, the humiliating defeat in the 1898 Spanish-American war, and endless cycles of weak government, putsch and repression. Between 1812 and 1931 alone, the country passed no fewer than eight different constitutions.[8] Then, in 1936, a group of generals around Francisco Franco launched a military coup against Spain's Republican government, plunging the country into a bloody, bitter Civil War that lasted three years – and whose poison continues to seep into Spanish politics and society today. It ended in victory for Franco, who ruled Spain with an iron fist for another thirty-six years. At the time of his death, Spain formed part of Europe in geographical terms only. It was backward, poor, repressive, entirely cut off from the politics and culture of countries to the north. It was Franco's tourism minister, Manuel Fraga,[9] who promoted the slogan 'Spain is different'. It certainly was, but not in a good way.

Among Spanish intellectuals and writers, the lament over Spain's exceptional – and exceptionally tragic – history is almost a genre unto itself. As the Spanish poet Jaime Gil de Biedma wrote in 1962:

> Of all the histories of History
> without a doubt the saddest is that of Spain
> because it ends badly. As if Man,
> finally tired of struggling against his demons,
> decided to entrust to them the government
> and administration of his poverty.[10]

José Ortega y Gasset, the Spanish philosopher and essayist, put it more succinctly still, capturing both the idea of Spanish backwardness and the nation's desire to form part of European normality in the famous phrase: 'Spain was the problem and Europe the solution.'[11] The line dates from 1910 but to some Spaniards it never lost its relevance. At the height of the crisis, it rang especially true. Spain needed European money to sort out its banking system, European advice to get its economy back on track and European backing for the difficult structural reforms pushed through in 2012 and beyond. But whether in the days of Ortega or in the days of the crisis, Spain's search for European redemption was always about more than everyday politics and economics. Here was a country that, for all its progress and achievements, never seemed quite sure of its place in the world, a country forever in doubt, always measuring itself against the outside world and more often than not finding itself wanting. I know no nation that criticises itself so frequently and so mercilessly. In my time as a correspondent in Spain, I was told over and over again that *this* – this crisis, this scandal, this election result, this whatever – would never happen in other European countries. Only in Spain could politicians be so corrupt and bankers so venal. Only in Spain would judges and prosecutors let them off the hook.

In part, I found this lack of national swagger refreshing. A country that is willing to criticise itself is a country willing to improve and to learn from others. Spanish newspapers would print long articles examining the political culture in Denmark, the vocational training system in Germany, Britain's universities and Finland's schools. Its politicians would promise reforms aimed at turning bits of Spain into Scandinavia, or South Korea or even China. Other nations could learn from Spain how to eat and how to play football. In most other regards, however, it was Spain that needed to change, to adapt, to reinvent itself. But could it? Should it?

I was not sure at the time, and I am unsure today. Spain's weaknesses were evident, and never more so than at the height of the crisis. But I also felt that too little was made – especially by Spaniards themselves – of the country's remarkable strengths and advantages. I admired the openness and tolerance of Spain, the everyday friendliness, the way people looked out for each other, the curiosity and creativity that were on display wherever one looked, from the kitchens of Catalonia and the Basque country to the winemakers of Rioja and the start-up labs in Madrid, among architects, writers and film-makers but also in the media and – ultimately – even in the world of politics. The crisis was, for many, a chance to try out new things and explore new ways of leaving their mark on the world. I also thought there was much to admire about the surge in grassroots political activity in Spain after 2008, most notably in the case of the massive anti-austerity protests that shook the country in 2011. Whatever one made of the goals and policies that animated these and countless other demonstrations, it was clear that millions of Spaniards were determined to make their voice heard.

Even at the height of the crisis, they did not retreat into the shell of private misery. If they had to suffer, they refused to do so meekly.

This book is a portrait of Spain during and after the crisis, but the observations and conversations it contains are, I hope, more than momentary snapshots. I have not consciously set out to develop a thesis. But writing and reading the chapters that follow, it was hard not to notice certain recurrent themes and motifs. One was Spain's long struggle towards normality – the normality of a European country at ease with itself and its history. It comes up when we look at the legacy of Franco, and what to do with his brooding mausoleum in the mountains above Madrid. It surfaces again in the blood-stained lands of the Basque country, where a society traumatised by terror is struggling to turn the page. Another theme that crops up throughout the book is the sense of an ending, the feeling that a distinct phase in Spanish history is coming to a close. The seemingly stable framework that emerged after the country's celebrated *transición* from dictatorship to democracy in the late 1970s seems broken. A new framework, however, has yet to emerge – leaving Spain today with a strange blend of old and new, of things that have not quite disappeared and things that are not yet fully formed. The political system is a case in point, with two establishment parties struggling to defend their turf against a trio of political newcomers, and neither side emerging triumphant. The relationship between Spain and the regions – and Catalonia in particular – is another. Here, too, things cannot stay as they are, unless Spain wants to risk a cataclysmic descent into open conflict.

These are some of the issues and stories that dominate the chapters that follow. Some will be told from the vantage point of Madrid, Spain's sprawling yet laid-back capital, home to the government and parliament, the courts and banks, Europe's perennial football champions and one of the most exquisite art collections anywhere in the world. But no picture of contemporary Spain can ever be complete without leaving the capital and exploring the country's endlessly diverse and fascinating regions. More than any other state in Western Europe, Spain is a mosaic of different regional and even national identities. Catalonia and the Basque country – where locals have preserved their own language and tend to see themselves as distinct nations – are the most obvious examples. But even in other parts of Spain, such as Andalusia and Galicia, the sense of distinctiveness and distance from the country's Castilian core is palpable. Here, unlike in Catalonia or the Basque country, the vast majority of people do feel Spanish. The two identities simply exist in parallel, often in harmony but occasionally in conflict.

We will head east to Valencia, to tell the story of how Spain slid into crisis and what it did to get out of it. We will head south, to the sun-burnt fields and cities of Andalusia, and north to the industrial heartlands of Catalonia and the Basque country. We will take detours through Spain's vast, empty inland empire – to regions that count among the least populated in all of Europe, but that are filled with stories all the same.

There are, of course, no easy conclusions, and no obvious answers to the questions facing Spain after the crisis. But I spent more than four years looking for them nonetheless, in interviews and conversations with politicians, business leaders, academics and many of the brightest minds in the country. More often than not, however, I learnt more about Spain in places that were far from the national capital and other big cities. Over the course of my reporting, I interviewed hundreds of people – some for hours in their homes and offices, others briefly, in the street or in bars and cafés. I met a surgeon in the Catalan hill country, who insisted that Spain would always be a foreign country to him; a nurse in Seville, still waiting for a job after many years; a Peruvian barman in Madrid, wondering why all his compatriots are heading home; a fisherman in Galicia, writing poems about the sea; a mayor in the Basque country, delighted that the killers have gone, and that he is still standing. To them, and to all the others, I owe an immense debt of gratitude.

CHAPTER ONE

Another country

Oriol Junqueras was letting his hands do the talking. I watched as he threaded the fingers of his left hand into the fingers of his right hand, over and over again, pushing hard and turning his palms upwards. It looked laborious, and it was meant to be. Junqueras, a big man with big hands, was using his fingers to tell a centuries-old story of conflict, nationalism and identity: one hand was Catalonia, the other was Spain. And, as hard as he might try, one would never quite fit into the other. 'This is a very old phenomenon,' he told me, finally untangling his hands. 'These are two political communities that have great difficulty finding one another. Neither recognises itself in the other. They have different priorities. They have different visions.'[1]

A prosperous region of 7.5 million people, Catalonia has been part of the Spanish state for centuries. Yet many Catalans regard themselves as a nation apart, with a language, culture and history that is intimately related to Spain but different all the same. At times, the region has been the target of severe repression, not least during the dictatorship of Francisco Franco, who banned the use of Catalan. That changed when Spain returned to democracy four decades ago. Today, Catalonia forms one of the country's seventeen 'autonomous communities' with powers over matters such as education, health care and welfare, and a police force of its own. Spain's constitution vaguely recognises the rights of 'nationalities and regions' within the Spanish state, but stops short of recognising Catalonia's claim to nationhood. Despite occasional rumblings of discontent, the whole arrangement was – until recently – broadly accepted by Catalans and Spaniards alike.

Junqueras, however, believed that Catalans and Spaniards never truly belonged together. They were different nations, he told me, held together only by Spanish law and Spanish force. 'Catalonia wants to decide its own future – its political future. And it is faced with a state that says: You can't take those decisions. We will take them for you,' he said. 'So this is ultimately a question of democratic dignity, and of political dignity.'

We were speaking in his office, high above the elegant Rambla de Catalunya in central Barcelona. A veteran politician who had fought all his life for an independent Catalan state, Junqueras seemed more tense than on our previous meetings. I had interviewed him on several occasions during my time in Spain, and was always struck by his insight and boundless appetite for stories and information. A well-placed barb against the Spanish government would be followed by a long digression on army food rations during the Second World War. A devout Catholic as well as a committed leftist, his speech was punctuated by deep sighs, broad grins and occasional biblical references. The leader of Esquerra Republicana, a left-wing pro-independence party, Junqueras had served until recently as mayor of his small home town outside Barcelona. Now, he was one of the most powerful men in Catalonia, the finance minister and vice-president in the regional government. More importantly, Junqueras was one of the architects of the campaign to establish a Catalan breakaway state from Spain – against the explicit will of Madrid, and in defiance of clear rulings from Spain's constitutional court. We were speaking on a searing hot day in early May 2017, as the region was gearing up for an illegal independence referendum on 1 October. We both knew that some kind of clash was unavoidable. But we had no idea of the price that he and others would pay for their stance. Six months after we spoke, Junqueras found himself inside a Spanish prison cell, pending a trial for rebellion and sedition.

His fall from grace was remarkable, but so was everything else that happened in those tense, wild months before and after 1 October. The cause of secession had moved – in the space of only a few years – from the fringes of Catalan politics and society right to centre stage. Here was the defining challenge for Spain and its leaders, and a crisis unlike any the country had seen since its return to democracy in the late 1970s. It was a crisis, moreover, that resonated across Europe and beyond: the Catalan quest to form a breakaway state echoed campaigns in countries as diverse as Britain, Belgium, Ukraine and Canada, all of which had faced or were still facing a separatist challenge to the union. Tension between Catalonia and the central government in Madrid had existed for much of Spanish history, yet the latest flare-up was also, in many ways, new and shocking. The regional government that Junqueras belonged to was the first in more than eighty years to advocate secession from Spain. The same was true of the regional parliament, where pro-independence deputies were in the majority. But the change was perhaps most evident on the streets. In the years since 2012, Catalonia has held some of the largest political demonstrations in Europe, with hundreds of thousands of marchers calling for secession every year on 11 September, Catalonia's national day. On other days, Catalans expressed their views on balconies and windows, tens of thousands of which were covered with the distinctive red-yellow-and-blue *estelada*, the lone-star flag of Catalan independence. To know the political allegiance of a city, village or street in the region, all you had to do was look up: the more *esteladas* fluttered in the wind, the more local support for secession.

If Catalonia ever does become independent, historians will probably look to 13 September 2009, and the event that took place that day in Arenys de Munt, as one of the sparks that started the secessionist fire. A hillside town of 8600 inhabitants, Arenys can be reached by train and bus from Barcelona in little more than an hour. The trip is spectacular. For much of the journey, the rail tracks run right alongside the glistening azure waters of the Mediterranean and long stretches of sandy beach. Looking out towards the sea, I thought that there could not be many places in the world that afford a better life than Catalonia: the beaches of the Costa Brava in the summer, the peaks of the Pyrenees in the winter, and the glories of Barcelona all year round. Whether in economic or gastronomic terms, in architecture or football, the region seemed blessed like few others. Yet the discontent was evident. With every kilometre and every stop along the way, the number of *esteladas* increased. By the time I sat on the bus for the last stretch of the journey, there was an independence flag hanging on every second tree that lined the road.

Arenys de Munt is a quiet, prosperous kind of place, with an unemployment rate below the already low Catalan average. It is also a bastion of the secession movement. At the time of my visit, of the thirteen local councillors, no fewer than eleven were committed to independence.

The local sentiment was made manifest in 2009, just a year after the bursting of Spain's housing bubble, when Arenys became the first town in Catalonia to hold an independence referendum. 'The police had to close the entrance into town because so many people wanted to come. There was a river of people coming up from the train station. They couldn't vote. But they wanted to see us vote,' recalled Josep Manel Ximenis, a local activist and former mayor of Arenys.

As he thought back to that day, a smile crossed his tanned face. He remembered it all: the crowds, the demonstrators, the journalists and camera teams; his fear that something – anything – could go wrong, ruining years of work. And the moment when, after the voting was done, he climbed on to the podium to read out the results: 2861 votes cast, more than 96 per cent in favour of independence. It felt, to Ximenis and many others, like they were making history. 'What more can you ask for, than to experience that kind of moment?' Ximenis said, as we sipped coffee on the deserted town square of Arenys. 'We broke through the barrier. And we broke through the fear. All of a sudden, people said: If those people in Arenys can vote, why not me?' For Ximenis, the vote was a deeply personal affair. All his life, the cause of Catalan independence had been viewed as the cause of outsiders, dreamers and fanatics. 'We were always in the minority, and never more than 15 per cent of the Catalan population,' he said. 'We had the reputation of being a bit crazy – aiming for something that was impossible to achieve, for Utopia.'

Like many of the people I spoke to in Arenys, he told me that he saw Spain as a different country: 'I have been disconnected from Madrid for many years. To me, what happens in Madrid has the same importance as what happens in Paris. What concerns me is my society, my country and my capital [Barcelona]. I work to improve them – not other things.'

Born in Barcelona in 1962, Ximenis grew up in a Spanish-speaking home. Both his parents came to Catalonia from other regions of Spain, part of a vast influx of migrants from poorer regions such as Andalusia and Extremadura hoping to find work in Catalonia's thriving factories. Even as a child, Ximenis said, he felt a strong bond with the land that surrounded him. When he was sixteen, his cousins took him to a meeting of a small pro-independence party. 'They said what I had been thinking for some time. So I became an *independentista*,' Ximenis recalled. From one day to the next, he spoke only Catalan, even with his own parents and siblings. He became a banker, but a midlife crisis led him to abandon his career and dedicate his life to politics – and the struggle for independence.

The Arenys referendum was the product of a long chain of conscious decisions and improbable coincidences. The idea was first raised at a meeting of local activists in 2006, shortly after the town held a referendum on the mundane issue of whether or not to pave the tree-lined avenue that runs down the middle of Arenys. 'Someone said: "Now that we have worked out all the steps you have to take to hold a *consulta* [local referendum], why don't we do a *consulta* on Catalan independence?"' said Ximenis. 'Everyone laughed.'

The laughter did not last long. The plan to hold a referendum triggered a backlash in other parts of Spain, and invited a sharp response from the government at the time. Far-right demonstrators travelled from the rest of Spain to protest the event. But the vote went ahead regardless, inspiring other villages and cities across Catalonia to follow suit. Over the next two years, another 553 municipalities would organise similar ballots. More than a million Catalans reportedly took part in the symbolic *consultas*.[2]

The steady stream of mini plebiscites – informal as they may have been – helped to plant the idea of independence in the collective conscience, and suggested a seemingly simple path to get there: just vote. In some cases, the impact was instant.

'I always thought independence was impossible. And I always thought that we could come to an understanding with Spain – that we could live in one state without renouncing our identity,' Marta Encuentra, another local activist from Arenys, told me. 'The day that I realised that independence was possible was 13 September 2009, when we voted here. I remember looking at my husband that day and saying: "Is it possible? Is it possible that we can make it?"' She clicked her fingers, like a hypnotist trying to bring round someone in a trance. 'It was like that. Suddenly, the people were waking up.'

After decades during which Catalan support for independence rarely exceeded 15 per cent, secessionist sentiment started climbing rapidly in 2009. By 2012, according to the closely followed surveys by the Catalan Centre for Opinion Studies, support for independence had risen to 34 per cent.[3] The following year, it reached an all-time high of 48.5 per cent.[4] The share has fallen back slightly since then, but it remains far above the historic average – and within striking distance of the level that independence campaigners need to win a referendum.

There is no single factor that explains this rapid rise. But Spain's harsh economic crisis, which erupted just a year before the Arenys referendum, certainly played a key role. The collapse of a decade-long construction boom was followed by a protracted recession, mass unemployment, austerity and a banking crisis – dealing a brutal blow to millions of Spaniards, and to their faith in the country's leaders and institutions. In Catalonia, tensions came to a boil in June 2011, when anti-austerity protesters surrounded and blocked off the regional parliament, forcing ministers to reach the imposing building by helicopter. The government, led by Artur Mas, the regional president, faced intense pressure. Within a few months, however, all that rage and fury on the streets would find a new outlet: Spain.

'The people who protested against the Generalitat [Catalan government] that summer were the same people who joined the independence movement in the months that followed. The protest was deflected in a new direction,' said Javier Cercas, a Barcelona-based novelist and prominent critic of the independence movement.[5] 'The fundamental fact here is the crisis. What happened in Catalonia is the same thing that happened in Europe, and that happened in Spain. We suffered a crisis like in 1929, a crisis that changed the world. It brought us Trump and it brought us Brexit.' Miquel Iceta, the cherubic leader of the Catalan Socialist party, offered a similar diagnosis when I visited him in the regional parliament: 'People are afraid. They are uncertain. So they think if they close themselves off in small communities they will be protected.'[6]

Most supporters of independence agreed that the crisis helped loosen the ties that once bound Catalonia and the rest of Spain. Yet they insisted that there was a far more powerful reason driving middle-of-the-road Catalan voters towards the independence camp: the stubborn refusal of Madrid to take seriously Catalans' growing frustration with the status quo.

The man who embodies these frustrations more than anyone is Artur Mas. The president of Catalonia from 2010 to 2015 was the dominant political figure in regional politics in the years leading up to the great political clash. Today, however, he finds himself shunted to the margins: in early 2017 a Barcelona court formally barred him from holding public office for two years, over his decision to defy a ruling by Spain's constitutional court in 2014. Mas was one of several Catalan leaders penalised for his role in the separatist struggle – and the list grew steadily longer as the years progressed.

His new-found role as a political renegade struck some as ironic. As leader of the centre-right Convergència i Unió party, Mas for many years followed the traditional Catalan approach to Spanish politics, which meant supporting the government of the day in Madrid in exchange for financial or political concessions towards Catalonia. The aim was not rupture, he explained to me, but to 'put fish in the basket' – accumulating small incremental gains for Catalonia. In 2006, moreover, Mas signed off on a grand accord – the so-called *estatut* – that was designed to reorder the relationship between his region and the Spanish state. It granted new powers to Catalonia, and made Catalan the 'preferred' language in public offices – but also clearly reiterated the region's status as a part of Spain.

The *estatut* was approved by the Catalan and Spanish parliaments, and by the Catalan population in a referendum. Then, in 2010, key aspects of the documents were struck down by the Spanish constitutional court, for violating the country's basic law, which proclaims the 'indissoluble unity of the Spanish nation'. The uproar in Catalonia was immediate.

Sitting in his Barcelona office, Mas described the ruling, and the political campaign that preceded it, as an 'act of betrayal'. In his view, the *estatut* would have solved the rapidly building tensions between state and region – over funding, over education, over the status of the Catalan language – for at least a generation. As president of Catalonia, Mas made one final attempt to strike a deal with Madrid. In the summer of 2012, at the height of the Spanish financial crisis, he presented a plan to Spanish prime minister Mariano Rajoy that would have given Catalonia far greater financial autonomy. Like other wealthy Spanish regions,

Catalonia is obliged to transfer a sizeable share of its tax revenues to financially weaker parts of the country. Just how much it loses is a matter of fierce dispute, but even conservative estimates put the number at close to €10bn a year.[7] Mas was trying to respond to the perpetual Catalan complaint that 'Spain robs us', but his timing was poor. Rajoy, who was battling a banking meltdown and soaring deficit at the time, said no.

The overarching narrative – shared by Mas and many of his allies and supporters – was one of increasingly frantic Catalan attempts to find accommodation with Spain, met at every turn by Spanish rejection. For them, the death of the *estatut* marked a turning point, final confirmation that Catalan demands for more autonomy, more rights and more money would never be fulfilled inside Spain. 'People like me, we moved from a position where we were confident that the Spanish state could be transformed, that it could become a modern and pluri-national state, to a different conviction,' said Ferran Mascarell, who headed the Catalan government delegation in Madrid from 2016 to 2017. 'I now believe that it is impossible to change the Spanish state from the inside.'

Supporters of independence often display confidence – if not certitude – that a majority of Catalans share their secessionist dream. 'Don't look at the polls, look at the people,' Ximenis, the organiser of the Arenys referendum, told me. 'In every Catalan, inside, there is an *independentista*.'

The truth, however, was that while there was a large majority in favour of an independence referendum, neither polls nor actual election results had ever shown a clear majority in favour of secession. The high point so far came in 2015, when 48 per cent of Catalan voters backed pro-independence parties in regional elections. The votes were enough to secure a majority of seats in the regional parliament, but fell short of the stated goal, which was to convert a normal regional election into a quasi-referendum – and then to win it. The outcome was repeated in the regional ballot in December 2017, when pro-independence parties again won 48 per cent of the vote.

The fact that Catalan independence leaders saw the need for a referendum in October 2017, and held one at great political cost, highlighted an uncomfortable truth for the movement. Even after all these years of campaigning and voting, leaders like Junqueras were not preparing their country for independence – they were still trying to establish that voters actually *wanted* independence. For some Catalans, the October referendum would be the fourth time they were asked to vote for secession, having already gone to the polling stations in a local referendum like the one held in Arenys, in a region-wide informal independence ballot held in November 2014 and in the 2015 regional elections, which were billed as a 'plebiscitary' ballot. It was hard to escape the conclusion that the secession campaign was running to stand still.

To some, that sense of stasis was just another indication that Catalonia would never manage to break away from Spain. 'There will be no independence,' Teresa Freixes, a professor of constitutional law at Barcelona's Autonomous University, told me bluntly in the weeks leading up to the referendum. 'Independence is not viable politically, economically or socially. And legally it is just not possible. You can't simply hold a referendum and proclaim independence – a state has to be recognised by the UN. And without recognition we would be just like the Western Sahara, or the Palestinians, or Northern Cyprus. Is that seriously what we want?' In addition to her academic role, Freixes was also the co-founder and president of Concordia Civica, one of several anti-independence groups that sprung up in the years after 2012.

Their goal was to counter the separatist narrative, and to give voice to the large but disparate part of Catalan society that wanted to stick with Spain. Their efforts, however, proved only partly successful: even among Catalan opponents of secession, the uncompromising political course set by Madrid was deeply unpopular; few wanted to be seen marching for Mariano Rajoy – the country's unpopular prime minister until 2018 – or behind the banner of Spain.

Freixes' own family had been Catalan for generations (one of her ancestors was Francesc Macià, who proclaimed an independent Catalan state in 1931) yet she took a dim view of the recent surge in separatist sentiment. More than anything else, she voiced alarm at the popular claim that the will of the Catalan people – however defined – must take precedence over the articles of the Spanish constitution. 'There is no law without democracy and no democracy without law,' she said.

Like most experts on the Spanish constitution, she believed there was no legal way for Catalonia to break away from Spain without a major overhaul of the 1978 basic law and establishing an explicit clause permitting regions such as Catalonia to secede from Spain. But changing the constitution required large majorities in parliament and the senate, as well as a nationwide referendum. The hurdles were high, and patience in Catalonia was low. The independence movement had made clear that it did not seek change within the system, but a break with the system – the sooner, the better.

For many Spaniards, however, it was not just the constitution that made Catalan independence unthinkable. When they looked to Catalonia, they saw an integral and irreplaceable part of the country – a stretch of land and coast, people and cities, factories and monuments that Spain simply could not do without.

Catalonia accounted for 16 per cent of Spain's population and almost a fifth of the economy. Losing the region would deprive the country of an economic powerhouse and a vital source of tax revenue. Catalonia was home to many of Spain's largest corporations and best research institutions, its second-biggest seaport and airport. The capital, Barcelona, was one of the world's great cities, drawing in almost twice as many tourists as Madrid. No fewer than five of the eleven starting players who won Spain the World Cup in 2010 were Catalan.

Scotland's contribution to the UK, by contrast, both in terms of population and economic output, was much smaller. There was another crucial difference: even if Scotland had said yes to independence in 2014, few people thought that Wales or Northern Ireland were likely to follow down the same secessionist road. In the case of Spain, the situation seemed different. Most importantly, the Catalan independence campaign was being watched with intense interest in the Basque country, traditionally the main focus of secessionist tensions in Spain. Hardcore Catalan separatists also made clear repeatedly that their vision of Catalonia was not limited to the area covered by the Spanish region of that name. Visitors to the party headquarters of Esquerra Republicana, the party led by Junqueras, would find a map in the foyer depicting the historical *Països Catalans* (Catalan countries), which included the Balearic Islands and the region of Valencia – along with bits of southern France and a sliver of Sardinia. Recovering these territories was – unsurprisingly – not part of anyone's political agenda, and neither was it likely to be in the future. But that map hinted at a potential for destabilisation that reached far beyond the borders of Catalonia. 'Scotland is about creating a new country. Catalonia is about creating a new country that is expansionary and that has territorial aspirations in all directions,' Lluís Bassets, a Barcelona-based columnist for *El País*, told me. All this helped explain the vehemence of Madrid's refusal to even entertain the idea of a referendum. For a country that had spent centuries shedding vast chunks of its overseas empire, losing Catalonia was simply unimaginable. The deepest, darkest fear of policy makers in Madrid was encapsulated in a blunt warning made by Alberto Ruiz-Gallardón, Spain's former justice minister, in 2012. 'It is often said that Catalonia is to Spain like a limb to a body, and that you can amputate it and the body goes on living. The truth is that Spain does not understand itself without Catalonia... What is being proposed is not that we amputate a limb, it is that we dissolve our nation,' he told *ABC*, the right-wing Spanish daily.[8] He added: 'The separation of Catalonia would put an end to the Spanish nation.'

We will look at the tumultuous, tension-filled months that followed the October referendum in the next chapter, but this is a drama without denouement or conclusion. The situation in Catalonia remains volatile and unpredictable, and will likely remain so for years to come. What is undeniable, however, is that the the story of Catalonia and its push for independence is part of a much wider story. In more ways than one, the Catalan campaign is symptomatic of a broader awakening of national and nationalist sentiment across Europe: nations that until recently seemed content to hitch their fate to that of larger entities and blocs are clamouring to stand alone once again. Flags are making a comeback, as are demands for higher walls and harder barriers to shut out the world. There is, at least in Europe, a sense of fragmentation both within and between countries. The seams that stitched together a broken continent are starting to unravel – not everywhere, but in enough places to give pause for thought.

The Catalan independence movement fits the broader pattern, but it does have its peculiarities. It remains, for example, staunchly pro-European and keenly internationalist. Supporters hail from almost all political camps, from religious conservatives to far-left anarchists. Yet the parallels are also striking, not least the degree to which the political shift has been fuelled by Europe's recent crisis, and the economic pain and social dislocation it wrought. 'The economic crisis has brought us populism and nationalism – magical solutions for a complicated situation that is indeed desperate for many people,' Inés Arrimadas, the young leader of the anti-independence Ciudadanos party in Catalonia, told me.[9] 'In other countries they say: "Everything is the fault of Europe." Here in Catalonia they say: "Everything is the fault of Spain."'

Looking beyond the immediate political drama, however, the struggle for Catalonia is clearly also a struggle for the future of Spain. Indeed, even harsh critics of the Catalan independence movement often insist that Spain must change – and change profoundly – if it wants to keep the centrifugal forces at bay.

For Spain, every *estelada* hanging from a Barcelona balcony is a reminder of its own historic failure to forge a single nation from the different tribes and tongues that populate the peninsula. The story of the relationship between Spain and Catalonia is indeed a complex one, going back centuries: a powerful medieval principality, Catalonia had formed a dynastic union with the crown of neighbouring Aragon since the twelfth century. In 1469 the marriage of Isabella of Castile and Ferdinand of Aragon brought Catalonia formally within the new kingdom of Spain. For many Spaniards, it is that year and that union alone that matter: in their view, Catalonia has been part of Spain ever since. Any claim to independence, they argue, is therefore not just unconstitutional but ahistoric. In truth, however, the picture is a little more complicated. The kingdom that emerged as a result of Isabella and Ferdinand's marriage was a so-called 'composite monarchy', an amalgamation of different territories. Those that joined the union by marriage not conquest owed allegiance to their ruler but they also enjoyed – at least nominally – parity of status with the political unit they joined.[10] In the case of Aragon (and Catalonia), that status was epitomised by the famously mealy-mouthed oath of allegiance sworn by the Aragonese to the Spanish ruler: 'We who are as good as you swear to you who are no better than us, to accept you as our king and sovereign lord, provided you observe all our laws and liberties; but if not, not.'[11] Those separate laws and liberties would survive for centuries, as would crucial Catalan institutions of self-governance. More important still, Catalans – and Basques – kept alive not just their language but also a sense of separate identity that endured war and suppression and that burns perhaps brighter than ever today.

For some Spaniards, who dream of a monolithic nation state *à la française*, this is a fact that is hard to accept. For others, it is an opportunity to overhaul old structures – both mental and constitutional – and turn Spain into a state that provides more room for different identities and nations, even the Catalan one. The challenge is not a new one, nor is it unique to Spain. But rarely has it presented itself with greater urgency than in Spain in the years after the great crisis.

To report on the Catalan conflict from both Madrid and Barcelona in the years leading up to the October referendum was at times an unsettling experience. As a German-born British journalist with two passports and a partner from Spain, I found it hard to understand the appeal of nationalist movements, or the dream of living in a country of my own. I had two, and had spent the past decade living happily in neither. My son had three, leading to long discussions about which national football team he would ultimately decide to play for. The idea of hanging a national flag from my window seemed absurd, whether in pursuit of a new state or in defence of an old one. My previous posting in the Middle East had also made me wary of those neat, polished versions of history in which my side always did the right thing and the other shouldered all the blame.

At the same time, I thought it was wrong to deny people the right to define themselves as a nation. As much as I disliked the lachrymose version of Catalan history told by some *independent-istas*, it was evident that Catalans *did* have a history, tradition, culture and language that set them apart. If they saw themselves as a nation, who was I to dispute that claim? What that meant for the political future of Catalonia and Spain was, of course, a separate question. But it made no sense to cut short any debate about Catalan political demands – as some in Spain did – by simply rejecting their claim to nationhood in the first place.

To me and many of my colleagues, travelling from Madrid to Barcelona often seemed like stepping from one bubble into the other. There was an overriding sense of two combatants who exulted in their own strength and righteousness, without so much as glancing across the ring to the opposing corner. There was little effort to analyse and understand the other side's motivations, frustrations and desires. Neither was there much effort to expose their own historical narrative to critical scrutiny, and ask whether long-ago victories, defeats and humiliations could really be wielded so glibly in defence of political positions today.

On the Spanish side, politicians never tired of the assertion that Spain had been a nation state, united and content, for more than five centuries. The secessionist narrative, in contrast, told a simple tale of the Catalan desire for liberty meeting Spanish repression, over and over again. Yet both versions – centuries of national harmony versus centuries of repression – fell short, according to Joan-Lluís Marfany, a Catalan-born historian at the University of Liverpool who has written widely on Spanish and Catalan nationalism.

'History would be better left alone and out of the current [Catalan] question. It is being used by both sides to the detriment of both history and of the political situation,' he told me in the weeks before the October referendum. The problem, Marfany explained, was that both sides were looking at distant historical events through the lens of contemporary politics, and 'project[ing] back in history a kind of relationship that is anachronistic'. He added: 'History does not move in a steady direction. It is full of twists and turns.'

He was right, of course. But with political passions running high on both sides, such pleas for subtlety and restraint fell on deaf ears. Every nationalist movement needs a historical narrative to validate its political claims, and the Catalan one was no exception. This was no sterile exercise for academics and politicians, but something that touched on everyday life. Indeed, the effort to link Catalan history (or a version thereof) with today's political struggle extended even to the terraces of the most popular Catalan institution in the world: Futbol Club Barcelona.

Barça has long claimed to be, as the official motto says, *més que un club* (more than a club). In the years of Franco, supporting the team's famous blue-and-garnet colours offered a rare opportunity to openly defy the regime, which was closely linked with Real Madrid, the hated rival in the Spanish capital. More recently, home matches of FC Barcelona have been used by supporters of Catalan independence to advertise their cause; the *estelada* is often prominently displayed (much to the annoyance of European football authorities).

During one of my reporting trips to the Catalan capital, I took an evening off to see Barça play Sevilla FC, and experience the strange amalgamation of politics and football for myself. The Camp Nou is a glorious place – the biggest stadium in European football – but on a cold wet night in November, its wide, open terraces offer little shelter from the driving rain. I watched, shivering, as some of the finest players in the world marched onto the sodden pitch below. The home side's starting line-up included stars such as Andrés Iniesta, whose goal in the 2010 final won Spain the World Cup, Luis Suárez, the insatiable Uruguayan striker, and – of course – the sublime Lionel Messi. The tempo and precision of Barça's game were on full display, as the team pushed and probed in search of their first goal (Barça would win 2-1). After a quarter of an hour, however, my eyes were drawn away from the pitch and towards the vast stadium clock to my left. The digits showed that 17 minutes had passed, then another 14 seconds. Suddenly, from the stands below, a chant went up that had nothing to do with football, and that quickly spread across the ground: *In! Inde! Independència! In! Inde! Independència! In! Inde! Independència!*

As in every home match, the fans had waited for the pre-cise moment – 17 minutes and 14 seconds into the game – to bellow their support for independence. The importance of the four digits was understood by everyone familiar with Catalan history. To Catalan separatists and die-hard Barça fans alike, the year 1714 had become a defining historical moment, the point at which Spain showed, irrevocably, that it could deal with Catalonia only when it was defeated and subjugated. On 11

September 1714 the city of Barcelona fell to the troops of Philip V, the first Bourbon king of Spain, after a bitter year-long siege. The battle was part of the protracted and notoriously complex War of Spanish Succession that lasted from 1701 to 1714. It pitted supporters of the Bourbon claim to the Spanish throne against defenders of the Habsburgs from Austria. Fearful that the famously authoritarian Bourbons would revoke their privileges and political rights, the Catalans sided with the Habsburgs. But when Europe's powers tired of war, the Spanish crown was ultimately awarded to the French king, leaving Barcelona at the mercy of Philip's troops. Defeat was followed by repression, as the new ruler set about dismantling Catalan political and cultural institutions – including the ancient Catalan Corts, or parliament.

Such was the way of life – and war – at the time. *Vae victis*, woe to the vanquished. Philip was a monarch in the absolutist mould, as were most kings and rulers on the continent in the early eighteenth century. In the grand narrative of European history, the conquest of Barcelona was little more than a footnote. Not so in Catalonia. 'It was never forgotten. It was never erased from Catalan consciousness,' said Marfany. By the late nineteenth century, the region and its booming capital were in the grip of a new movement of national awakening, the Renaixença, which was determined to revive the Catalan language and culture and the glories of the past. It was then that the great defeat of 1714 became anchored as a cataclysmic moment in Catalan history – and celebrated as the Diada, Catalan national day, as it is today. For many Catalans, as Raphael Minder observes in his recent book on the conflict, the defeat 'has become the historical wrong that needs to be challenged for Catalonia to assert its nationhood'.[12]

Marfany did not dispute the relevance of 1714 as a crucial

date in Catalan history. But he felt uncomfortable with the way the events of that year were being used and portrayed in the current conflict. I asked him what he made of the view that there was a link – a certain historical continuity – between the assault on Catalan liberties in the wake of the 1714 defeat and the Spanish approach to Catalonia today. 'A very simplistic parallel,' he responded. 'There is this essentially nationalist view of history according to which you have two nations – Catalonia and Spain – and there is a confrontation that Spain wins, leading to the oppression of Catalonia. But at the time there was no Spain in the terms of today, and there was no Catalonia in the terms of today.'

The uses and abuses of history were part of a much broader effort to draw a sharp dividing line between Catalans and Spaniards where previously there had been a blur. It was a joint endeavour, though one that was pursued with greater determination and ambition on the Catalan side. In one of my last conversations with Mas – he was already out of office – I was surprised to hear him frame the conflict as one that was, at least in part, about the Castilian and Catalan character. 'The Castilian is a person who comes from the land, from soldiering or from the church. They were landowners, farmers, soldiers and monks.'[13] The Catalan tradition, he went on, was different: 'The Catalan character is based on the codes of commerce and industry. That leads to negotiations, pacts, agreements. The Castilian is different. The Castilian wins or loses. But he does not negotiate.' Mas concluded: 'There is a huge difference of mentality that clashes – and that has always clashed.'

This was a view I would hear over and over again. Junqueras, for example, spoke of the Catalans' distinctive 'anxiety for liberty' that set them apart from Spain. The basic idea was always the

same: Catalonia was presented as the open, tolerant, sophisticated, and truly European element trapped inside a reactionary,
corrupt and backward-looking Spain. As Robert Hughes pointed
out in his peerless book on Barcelona, this game of Castilian and
Catalan stereotypes had been going on for ever:

> By tradition, when Catalans reflect on themselves they get
> absorbed by the differences that set them off, individually, and
> as a 'nation', from the rest of Spain... Thus when Catalans
> looked at Castile, they saw sloth, privilege, and a morbid
> tendency to inwardness, bred of long years of aristocratic
> effeteness; a taste for oppressing others, particularly Catalans,
> a lack of practical sense. The image of the Castilian as the
> occupying leech, taxing the lifeblood out of Catalunya, was
> standard in Barcelona from the seventeenth century to the
> death of Franco in the late twentieth.
>
> When Castilians looked at Catalunya, they had their
> say too. Catalans were dull. They were pedantic and resent-
> ful by turns, usually both; too addicted to material things
> to understand the classic austerities of Castile, let alone its
> spirituality; and inordinately self-satisfied with their patch of
> Mediterranean earth – a polity of grocers, barking in a bastard
> language. No Catalan, in their view, could see beyond the
> pig in his yard, the fat angel sent to earth by God to supply
> Catalans with daily viaticum of *butifarra* [sausage] and ham.[14]

Like many national and regional stereotypes, these clichés
contained some grains of truth: as a port city close to the
French border, Barcelona was indeed a more cosmopolitan and
polyglot place than other parts of Spain, including Madrid.
But the Catalan capital was no stronghold of the independence movement. On the contrary: elections, polls and surveys

all showed that voters in Barcelona were far less supportive of secession than the Catalan hinterlands. And yes, there was a strong tradition of civic engagement in Barcelona that was not matched in Madrid. But the latter was the national capital – and had previously been the capital of an empire. The two cities had different histories, traditions and economic circumstances, just like Washington and New York or London and Manchester. And, of course, there was an aesthetic tradition in Castile that centred on austerity – just look at the monumental simplicity of the Escorial palace outside Madrid, in contrast to the exuberant playfulness of Antoni Gaudí's buildings in Barcelona. But was any of this really relevant? Were these ideas not so riddled with exceptions and contradictions that they were rendered almost meaningless? And was that cultural and social gulf – insofar as it existed – really any deeper than that separating Bavaria and Prussia? Naples and Milan? Texas and Vermont? More importantly, did it make Catalan independence any more desirable or reasonable? To an outsider, probably not. But what mattered here were perceptions and self-perceptions, the stories that people told one another about themselves, and that they believed. These stories – of Catalan uniqueness and Spanish backwardness – were told often, and often believed. And that meant they mattered, because they provided a powerful historical base note to the political grievances of the day.

In their assessment of contemporary events, both sides often displayed ignorance and mutual misunderstanding. In the Spanish capital, even on the eve of the October referendum, I heard decision-makers describe the independence movement as a 'soufflé' that would collapse any minute now. The metaphor seemed almost comically inaccurate: even a well-crafted soufflé deflates after no more than ten minutes. The Catalan version had remained solid for almost a decade. Then there was the conviction, aired privately but frequently in the Spanish capital, that the conflict could be resolved quickly if only the Spanish government had the courage to crack down hard on the law-breakers in Barcelona. A spell in prison for the ringleaders, and surely calm would be restored. That view, too, failed to stand the test of time. Within weeks of the October referendum, Catalan self-rule was suspended and the entire Catalan government was either in prison or in self-imposed exile. Yet there was no sign that the separatist fervour was about to subside. If anything, the tough measures taken by Spanish judges and officials inflamed passions even further.

On the other side, many independence supporters seemed determined to ignore any information that might have disturbed their narrative. One popular view, forever nourished by pro-independence media outlets, was that foreign governments would rush to recognise a new Catalan republic once the deed was done. Another hard-to-shake conviction in the run-up to the referendum was that a breakaway state would suffer no economic damage. Few outside the secessionist circle of trust shared those views, yet they were repeated endlessly, suggesting that independence was not only desirable in the long run, but relatively cost-free in the short term. Here, again, the weeks and months that followed the October referendum would prove instructive: not one foreign government offered sympathy or solidarity for the Catalan campaign, let alone recognition of a new Catalan state. The indifference came as no surprise to anyone who had sought out the views of these governments. Yet many inside the independence movement were reliant on information from the biased – but highly influential – pro-independence Catalan media. They were living, as Teresa Freixes, the professor, told me contemptuously, 'in a fictional world'.

That world was especially intact in places such as Arenys. Josep Manel Ximenis told me with serene confidence that there would be a 'queue' of countries lining up to recognise Catalonia once the region declared independence. Joan Rabasseda, the current mayor of Arenys, said he was convinced the independence movement was within touching distance of its goal. 'There is not a lot of road left,' the mayor insisted. 'We are close. We are close.'

Comfortable in their respective bubbles, both sides also made a habit of underestimating the strength and resolve of their opponent. As they prepared for the inevitable clash in October 2017, officials in Madrid and Barcelona seemed equally certain that their opponents would lose their nerve and swerve out of the way at the last minute. The Catalans could not imagine that Spain would dare to crack down on peaceful voters. In Madrid, there was confidence until the end that the referendum would simply not take place. It was a dangerous assumption to make, if only because so many in the Catalan independence movement seemed earnestly to desire a full-on confrontation. In their view, the arrest of Catalan independence activists or a similar heavy-handed response from Madrid would be the best – and perhaps the only – way to draw international attention to the conflict. That attention was indeed forthcoming, at least for a while. But it was far from clear whether the Catalans had taken a step closer to independence, or were in fact moving further away.

For Javier Cercas, the writer, the build-up to the referendum was marked by 'brutal irresponsibility'. He explained: 'Isaiah Berlin said the first virtue of a politician is a sense of reality. If you press a button you must know what light will go on. You must know what will happen next. To press a button without knowing what will happen next – to provoke a clash without knowing what will happen next – is the maximum expression of irresponsibility.'[15]

One of several prominent intellectuals to have come out forcefully against secession, Cercas believed that Spain must, ultimately, provide a path to independence all the same. 'The Spanish state cannot be a prison. If certain conditions are met, there should be an exit path for those who aspire to independence.' But he also made clear that such a path could only open up when a region – or nation – had shown over a long period of time that independence was indeed the choice of the majority. 'If you have 70 per cent or 80 per cent of Catalans who want independence then Catalonia will be independent. There is no question,' he said.

That moment, clearly, had not yet come. But the ties binding Catalonia and Spain had weakened, worn down by years of neglect, indifference and political calculation. The border separating the region from the rest of the country – invisible though it still was – was hardening all the time. Spaniards who were asked to move to Barcelona for a job thought twice. Catalans travelling in the back of a Madrid taxi opted to speak Spanish not Catalan. For some, like Miquel Iceta, the Socialist, the conclusion was evident: Spain and Catalonia had to come to an accord – not too different from the one enshrined in the ill-fated *estatut* – as soon as possible: 'A deal today is easier to do than in ten years. And in twenty years, it might be impossible.'

I sensed that some of the most ardent *independentistas* were thinking in those terms already. People like Oriol Junqueras, for example, whose languid movements and slow delivery always made him seem like a man who could bide his time. He said he was committed to the referendum, but I wondered whether he saw the looming clash not as the decisive battle but as yet another skirmish in a struggle that would last for generations. I remembered a previous conversation with Junqueras, in which he had told me about the day, more than forty years ago, when he had watched thousands of people cross the bridge over the Llobregat river and stream into the town of Sant Boi just outside Barcelona. It was 11 September 1976, the first public celebration of the Diada, Catalonia's national day, since the Franco dictatorship banned the event almost four decades before. Junqueras was only seven years old. He had waited a long time for Catalan independence. For a man with a sense of history, what were a few more decades? As we left his office, squeezed into the tiny elevator, and slowly made our descent to the ground floor and the blinding light of a Barcelona summer's day, he offered a strange blend of resignation and defiance. 'We will try,' he said. 'We will try. We will try. We will try.'

Junqueras was not making empty promises. A few months later, they tried – tried as they had never tried before. The 2017 referendum was a watershed moment in the history of modern Spain. It led the country into a crisis from which it has yet to emerge. And Junqueras from the pinnacle of Catalan power to the confines of a Spanish prison cell.

CHAPTER TWO

Autumn in Catalonia

The streets are blocked, the trains have stopped. The flower kiosks on Las Ramblas are closed in the middle of the day. Further down the famous avenue, I turn into the Mercat de la Boqueria, the great bustling food market of Barcelona, and find its narrow alleys deserted except for a few disappointed tourists. Everything is closed – shops and schools, restaurants and universities. Normal life in Barcelona has come to a halt. In the heart of the city, young people are walking in the middle of the road, waving the *estelada*, the lone-star flag of Catalan independence. The atmosphere is festive, but it carries an angry edge. On Via Laietana, where tens of thousands have gathered to call for Catalan secession from Spain, the crowd passes the headquarters of the national police. Hundreds of middle fingers are raised towards the building. In chants and on placards, the crowd demands: 'Out with the forces of occupation'.

It is Tuesday, 3 October 2017 – day two after a Catalan independence referendum that has pushed the city, the region and the country to the brink of a political explosion. The separatists have called for mass demonstrations and a general strike, and hundreds of thousands have followed the call. It feels like the end of something, but the protesters in the street think otherwise. Further down the Via Laietana, I stop a couple walking dreamily in the middle of the road, draped in the *estelada*. 'This is the beginning,' Nestor Sastre, a sixty-year-old teacher, tells me.[1] 'This is only the beginning.'

The tourists stroll and gawp at the city's architectural wonders just as they do every other week. For the people of Barcelona, however, the days are filled with tension, expectation, hope and fear. I meet Valentí Puig, a Barcelona writer, in the lobby bar of the Hotel Majestic on Paseo de Gracia. He tells me the city has been gripped by 'vertigo' – that strange feeling when all it takes is one small step to know whether you will fall or fly.

Rumours chase rumours. News bulletins struggle to keep up with events. In Girona, an hour north of Barcelona, protesters have occupied the train station and blocked the high-speed line to Paris. FC Barcelona issues a press release, saying the club has decided to join the strike. All over the region, police are trying to clear motorways that have been occupied by demonstrators. On Tuesday night, the king speaks on television. Many expect him to deliver a message of conciliation, but his words are harsh. He chastises the Catalan government for breaking the law, and denounces its recent actions as 'irresponsible' and 'unacceptable'. On Wednesday night, the Catalan president responds, denouncing the king and the Spanish government. On Thursday, the principal Catalan banks announce plans to move their domicile to other parts of Spain. Barcelona, it seems, is no longer a safe address for a company with nervy depositors and worried shareholders. The city is awash in speculation: Will the cash machines run out of money? Will the Catalan government declare independence? Will Madrid have the region's leaders arrested?

The city's business and financial elite grow more despondent by the day. 'The people are pushing, they are pressing,' one well-connected business leader tells me. He fears that only a few of the young demonstrators are aware of the dangers that lie ahead, the potential for escalation, including violent escalation. 'This is what always happens in revolutions: the people are not aware of the consequences. They see the aspirations, even the noble aspirations. But they don't see the consequences. They don't see the risks.'

For many Catalans, these are days of anguish. There is mounting pressure to take sides – for independence or against, for Spain or for Catalonia. Accusations of treason are flying in all directions. In response, Llàtzer Moix, a journalist and architecture critic, writes a sad, angry column in *La Vanguardia*, insisting on his right not to take sides. 'Everyone pressures us but few offer what we now need most urgently: an exit from the Catalan labyrinth.'[2] That exit, however, has rarely felt more distant. Supporters of Catalan independence sense they are closing in on their goal – a unilateral declaration of independence, and statehood at last. The 1 October referendum, they argue, has given them the mandate – no, the imperative – to press ahead. This is not the time for tactical delays and diplomatic caution. Manel Escobet, a senior member of the Catalan National Assembly, the pro-independence grassroots movement, sums up the prevailing mood in those fraught, pulsating days. 'The ones who move are the ones who make history,' he tells me. 'We are very close to seeing our dream come true.'

For one side, the biggest shock on referendum day is the brazenness with which Catalans choose to defy Spanish law. The other side is aghast at the violent intervention of the helmeted policemen from Spain. And some notice another thing: that Catalonia's own police force, the Mossos d'Esquadra, spend much of the day on the sidelines. In some instances, Catalan officers openly confront their Spanish colleagues; in others, they simply refuse to carry out the orders from Madrid. Of all the questions swirling around Catalan conversations after referendum day, few are as pertinent as these: how much authority has the Spanish government already lost in the region? And will it have the nerve to reclaim it, by flooding Catalan cities with thousands of police officers from other parts of Spain?

Ada Colau, the left-wing mayor of Barcelona, steps up to the podium a few days after the landmark vote, with an appeal for calm and dialogue. She urges European authorities to intervene and mediate, warning that further escalation could destabilise not just Barcelona and Catalonia but Spain and Europe as well. At the same time, Colau tries to calm foreigners and locals anxious about the state of her city. 'The city of Barcelona has overcome bigger challenges than this one in its history,' she says. Given the city's turbulent and bloody past, this does not sound like much of a consolation.

At night, the narrow lanes of Barcelona's Barrio Gótico resound once again to the clanging of pots and pans from thousands of windows and balconies. Known as a *cacerolada*, the infernal anonymous protest by pro-independence locals has been going on for weeks, every night at 10 p.m. The tourists rush out from their restaurants and stare into the sky, as the air around them fills with the discordant sound of a city on the edge of something momentous.

How quickly it all happened.

I had spent years covering the slow, halting approach to the cataclysmic events of October 2017, returning to Catalonia again and again in an attempt to understand the conflict, and find out how it might end. There had been endless talk of the *choque de trenes*, the train crash between Catalonia and Spain, that was forever about to happen but never did. And then, all of a sudden it did. The smouldering wreckage of a centuries-old relationship was on full display in the streets of Barcelona – and everywhere else in the region. Looking at the protesters, I noticed how many of them carried independence flags that were brand new. They had been unfolded for the first time, the original creases from the packaging still on show. Their owners were not veterans but converts, drawn to the cause of independence by the shocking events that had taken place two days earlier.

The referendum of 1 October was always intended to mark a moment of departure – the clearest expression yet of Catalan defiance against the Spanish state. It was obviously illegal under the terms of the Spanish constitution, which proclaims the 'indissoluble unity of the Spanish nation' and makes clear that 'national sovereignty belongs to the Spanish people'. To remove the last shred of doubt, Spain's constitutional court had issued a formal ruling on 7 September ordering the Catalan government to halt all preparations for the referendum.[3] On previous occasions – most notably in the run-up to an 'informal' independence ballot in November 2014 – Catalan leaders had made an elaborate effort to show that they were trying to stay within the formal remit of the law. The fact that they ultimately failed to do so was beside the point. What mattered was that they were still – at least in public – committed to respecting the letter of the Spanish law and the verdict of the Spanish judiciary. In 2017, however, that pretence was abandoned. The legal basis for the referendum was a law passed by the Catalan parliament. As far as the Catalan government under president Carles Puigdemont was concerned, that would suffice. To hell with Spanish judges.

As the referendum date drew nearer, Madrid decided to send police reinforcements to the region. Together with the Mossos, the Catalan regional police, they would be tasked with upholding the law. The message from Mariano Rajoy, Spain's prime minister, was clear, and had been repeated endlessly: 'There will be no referendum.'[4] By all accounts, he was confident that his prediction would survive the day. But, as so often in the past, the men and women in the Moncloa government compound outside Madrid were acting on poor intelligence. They had underestimated the organisational capabilities of the Catalan separatists, who had managed to stash away thousands of ballot boxes and millions of ballot papers. They had underestimated the readiness of Catalan mayors and school principals to open polling stations across the region in defiance of the law. And they had – crucially, disastrously – underestimated the willingness of millions of Catalans to show up at those stations, and cast their vote. All across the region, riot police bludgeoned their way into the voting stations to confiscate ballot boxes. But the numbers were against them. Again and again, they were confronted by unarmed protesters blocking their way. The policemen used their truncheons, they used pepper spray and, in some instances, they even fired rubber bullets.[5] And so Spanish authority suffered a double defeat that day. The first was the complete failure of Spanish police to prevent the referendum from actually going ahead: by the end of the day, two million Catalans had cast their vote, according to figures released by the Catalan government, with more than 90 per cent voting in favour of independence.

Those numbers require some perspective. Even taking the Catalan government statistics at face value, the turnout was just over 40 per cent. Once again, the number of those who voted was smaller than the number of those who stayed away. But the separatists had proven their ability to mobilise vast numbers of supporters despite the rulings from Madrid and the threat of police violence – an impressive feat of both organisation and determination.

The second loss for Madrid was more consequential still: a stream of images showing policemen beating and kicking, civilians bleeding and screaming, and of ballot boxes snatched from the hands of ordinary citizens. The images went around the world in an instant, and Spain would pay a steep price for the actions that they captured. Those who were caught up in the violence would not forget. In the weeks that followed, I spoke to many Catalans – to those who had voted and those who hadn't – who summed up their experience with the same words. The violence of 1 October, they said, marked a 'before and after'.

Spain's government argued that it was merely defending the constitutional order against a quasi-insurrection. But Anna Gabriel, for one, was having none of it. The police actions, she told me, were a 'savage and brutal attack against an entire people'. A prominent separatist politician and a senior leader of the far-left Popular Unity Candidacy (CUP), she was certain that the violence on 1 October would backfire on Madrid: 'Many people who were not in favour of independence now say that they no longer want to form part of a Spanish state that confronts political problems like this. In political terms, people are saying: Is this what the Spanish state has to offer?'[6] Spain, Gabriel argued, was not only a country with 'fascist roots' but also one that refused to acknowledge its own failure as a unitary state. 'If you need so much brute force to defend the unity of the state, isn't it evident that this unity does not exist?'

I had come to see Gabriel in her modest shared flat in the Barcelona neighbourhood of Graciá a few days after the vote. The first thing that caught my eye when I entered was a poster of Hugo Chávez, the former Venezuelan leader, and a table stacked with political brochures. The joint living room was small and spartan, devoid of books and personal objects. As late afternoon turned into evening, it grew steadily darker inside the flat, yet Gabriel made no attempt to turn on the lights. In the room next door, one of her flatmates was hanging up the washing on a clothes rack.

These humble surroundings were a world away from the

ornate medieval palaces that house the Catalan president and his ministers. But there were many – not least inside the Spanish government – who believed that the rhythm and pace of Catalonia's escalating political conflict with Madrid were being dictated not by the official Catalan leadership but by Gabriel and her pro-secession party. The CUP had burst onto the political scene just two years before, when it won ten parliamentary seats in the 2015 Catalan regional election. The party made every one of those seats count. Without its support, the more mainstream separatist parties had no majority in the regional parliament. The CUP showed its muscle for the first time in early 2016, when it refused to back Artur Mas for another term in office as regional president of Catalonia. In a last-minute compromise, the pro-independence parties settled on a largely unknown former journalist whose most senior post to date was that of mayor of Girona. Carles Puigdemont became the new president of Catalonia, and the man tasked with steering the Catalan independence process through its decisive – and most dangerous – moments. He was acceptable to the CUP because he was – unlike Mas – a life-long supporter of independence. The fact that Puigdemont was a relative novice, untainted by political battles and scandals of old, also helped. At heart, however, his views were just as incompatible with those of the CUP as those of Mas had been. In fact, the CUP's views were incompatible with those of pretty much any mainstream politician or party in Europe in the twenty-first century: it was opposed to Nato and the EU, and called for public control over key sectors of the economy, from telecommunications and energy to transport and infrastructure.[7] Gabriel herself had caused a storm of controversy a year before we met, when she had advocated that children should not be raised by their parents but by a collective 'tribe'.[8] She was radical, determined and utterly convinced of the correctness of her hard line. Like all CUP deputies, she gave most of her salary to the party. 'Look how we live,' she told me. What she meant was: We are not afraid of losing our posts, positions and salaries if it helps the cause.

Her party's role as kingmaker had given Gabriel and other CUP leaders the power to shape the Catalan political process – and to insist on a hardline stance that called for a unilateral declaration of independence from Spain as soon as possible. The fact that the CUP's pronouncements were seen as crucial in the days following the referendum said much about the broader shift inside the independence camp. In the four decades since Spain had returned to democracy, the cause of secession had mostly been the preserve of radicals and outsiders. That changed a decade ago, as moderate nationalist politicians and voters started adopting the call for independence. Beginning with Mas, support for secession and a referendum became the official policy of the Catalan government. But in the wild, chaotic days of October 2017, the focus was on mobilisation not negotiation. 'This is a process without a steering wheel and without brakes,' explained Oriol Bartomeus, a political scientist at the Autonomous University in Barcelona. The mainstream nationalist parties might have been formally in control of government, he argued, but they were no longer in control of the street. Here, it was groups like Gabriel's CUP that were in charge, along with grassroots movements such as the Catalan National Assembly. 'They are the ones ensuring that the process continues,' Bartomeus told me.

Despite its radical roots and position, the CUP had so far made common cause with the more centrist, business-friendly elements of the independence movement. But Gabriel was frank about her party's ultimate goals. 'For us, independence is not an end in itself. It is an instrument to change the rules of the game and the material conditions of life for the majority of the people.' She acknowledged that even an independent Catalan republic was unlikely to back the CUP's radical brand of social- ism. But she pointed to recent examples of progressive Catalan legislation on issues such as police tactics and energy poverty as a sign that a new state could tilt markedly to the left. And if Spain decided to answer a unilateral declaration of independence with the arrest of senior leaders and a takeover of the regional government? 'Of course there is fear. It would be frivolous to say that we are not afraid that the tanks will return,' Gabriel told me before I left. 'But what should we do? Nothing? Stay at home, paralysed?'[9]

Talking to Gabriel in her gloomy flatshare, I was reminded once again that the Catalan independence movement was no monolithic bloc. It was a force united in pursuit of independence as an abstract ideal, but divided on two elementary aspects: how to get there, and – once established – what an independent Catalan state should look like. In the days after the violence- scarred ballot, unity was assured by the mere shock of the events that had taken place. But it did not take long for the fissures to resurface. The four weeks that followed the referendum were marked by an escalating confrontation not just between Barcelona and Madrid but also between the different strands of the Catalan independence movement. The all-important ques- tion facing Puigdemont and his colleagues was this: should they treat the referendum result as they had promised they would – as a binding declaration of their will by the Catalan people? If so, they had to follow through and declare independence. That was what people like Gabriel were demanding. It was also the only move that seemed to match the high-flying rhetoric and revolutionary spirit pervading Catalan politics in the weeks that followed the referendum. The mood was summed up in a new battle cry: *Independencia ya!* Independence now!

The response from Puigdemont was more cautious. On 10 October the Catalan president addressed the regional parliament with a strangely ambivalent message. 'I assume the mandate that Catalonia becomes an independent state in the form of a republic,' he said, prompting prolonged applause from pro-independence lawmakers.[10] But then he added: 'I propose suspending the effects of the declaration of independence to undertake talks in the coming weeks without which it is not possible to reach an agreed solution.' The language was as awkward as the policy: the Catalan government was trying to put the ball into Madrid's court, holding out the threat of an independence declaration in the hope that Mariano Rajoy might offer some new process of negotiation. It seemed – even at the time – like a grave miscalculation, especially given the nature of the opponent he was facing. Rajoy had suffered severe criticism for his handling of the referendum crisis. Now the veteran tactician was back in his element. Sensing an opportunity to sow division in the separatist camp, Spain's prime minister turned the pressure back on Puigdemont. He simply asked the Catalan leader whether he was serious or not. Rajoy told his opponent to clarify whether or not he had declared independence – a clarification that, he knew, would not be simple to make.

Back in Barcelona, both in public and behind the scenes, the independence camp debated furiously. Hardliners could not understand what Puigdemont was waiting for. The eyes of the world were on Catalonia. This was the moment to strike.

Cooler heads pointed to the obvious pitfalls: they knew the international community would never recognise a breakaway Catalan state, especially not after an illegal referendum in which six out of ten Catalan voters had stayed at home. They also knew that the Catalan government had failed to lay the groundwork for an independent state. The past two years were supposed to have been dedicated to building up the institutions and structures of a new country, from a Catalan tax authority to a parallel government administration. These institutions, however, were not yet in place. If Catalonia did declare independence, who would collect the taxes and pay the civil servants? Then there was the question of the personal consequences that senior leaders such as Puigdemont and his cabinet ministers would face if they went ahead with a full-blown declaration of secession. Madrid had repeatedly made it clear that it would use the full force of the Spanish law to go after Catalan leaders, should they declare independence. In the recent past, separatist politicians had faced prosecution and punishment for acts that were far less serious than the one being contemplated now. A declaration of independence, they knew, would almost certainly land Catalan decision-makers in a Spanish prison cell. Finally, there was the problem of Article 155 of the Spanish constitution, which was also known as the nuclear option. This article gave the Spanish government huge leeway to bring recalcitrant regional governments back into line. At the extreme, it would allow Rajoy to suspend the rights of self-government in Catalonia, and to effectively rule the region from Madrid. And if those rights were lost, when and how would Catalonia get them back? It was a question that gave at least some pro-independence politicians in Barcelona pause to think. They realised what was at stake – all the freedoms, powers and advances that the region had achieved since the end of the Franco era four decades ago.

The pressure on Puigdemont was brutal. He tried to win more time, writing a letter to Rajoy on 19 October that reiterated his decision to suspend 'the effects of the popular mandate' and urged the prime minister not to invoke Article 155. But Rajoy simply repeated his demand: clarify whether you are declaring independence or not, and face the consequences.

The tensions between Catalan leaders reached a climax in the week leading up to Friday, 27 October, culminating in twenty-four hours of political whiplash that would prove fateful for Puigdemont in particular.[11] The Catalan president, it turned out, had made a decision: there would be no declaration of independence. Instead, he would call a fresh regional election, in a bid to renew the separatist mandate and capitalise on the popular anger with Madrid. It was, considering the circumstances, probably the correct decision. Here was a chance to finally achieve the goal that had eluded the independence movement all those years: to win at least 50 per cent of the popular vote – a true majority. Would that impress Madrid? Probably not. Would it stave off the threat of Article 155 and prosecution of Catalan leaders? Again, probably not. But there was a good chance that a snap election would close what had always been the weakest link in the Catalan argument. Puigdemont could show that there really was an indisputable majority for independence. Calling an election would give direction to the wave of popular anger and emotion that was ricocheting across Catalonia, but without breaking off all channels of dialogue with Madrid. The people demanded action. Given the personal and political risks, holding another election seemed like an obvious way to manage what was fast becoming an unmanageable situation.

But when news of the impending announcement filtered out on the morning of Thursday, 26 October, the outcry was fierce – much fiercer than Puigdemont had anticipated. The Catalan president was instantly branded a traitor on social media, including by some of his own political allies. One prominent independence leader changed his profile picture on Twitter to a portrait of Puigdemont upside down – a reference to an ancient insult inflicted on Philip V of Spain. Gabriel Rufian, a famously combative member of the Spanish parliament for Esquerra Republicana, also took to Twitter. His message simply read: '155 pieces of silver'. Lawmakers from Puigdemont's party threatened to resign if the president went ahead with the planned election announcement. The accusation of treason could now also be heard from the square in front of the Palau de la Generalitat, the presidential palace in central Barcelona. There, a group of pro-independence students had gathered to call for secession. As rumours started swirling of a possible Catalan climbdown, a new chant went up from the crowd: 'Puigdemont, traitor!'[12]

A harder, more ruthless man than Puigdemont would perhaps have shrugged off the pressure. A more experienced and confident man might have seen these threats and insults for what they mostly were: mere shouting in the street and social media 'noise'. But Puigdemont was neither hard nor ruthless, neither experienced nor – considering his position – especially confident. He was a small-town mayor, an ex-journalist, thrust into a political hothouse that would probably have made more formidable men wilt. And Puigdemont wilted. He again sought to obtain some kind of reassurance from Madrid. If he called elections instead of proclaiming independence, would Spain back off from its threat to invoke Article 155? No such reassurance was forthcoming. Now even key associates, such as Oriol Junqueras, the vice-president, started backing away from Puigdemont. According to some accounts, Junqueras, the leader of Esquerra Republicana, signalled that his party would have to leave the government if there was no declaration of independence. The unity of the independence camp – which had held fast for so long – was starting to unravel. Stunned by the ferocity of the response, Puigdemont decided to backtrack. When he appeared in front of the press, it was not to announce a new election, but to declare that last-ditch talks with Madrid had failed to deliver the 'guarantees' sought by the Catalan government.[13] It would now be up to the Catalan parliament to determine the next step.

The next day, the Catalan parliament met to vote on a historic resolution. The chamber was half-empty, after most anti-independence deputies decided to boycott the session. Their absence did not change the result: 70 out of 135 deputies voted in favour of a unilateral declaration of independence. For the third time since 1931, Catalonia had declared itself a republic, in open defiance of Madrid.[14]

There is one thing you have to know about Puigdemont, Carles Porta told me: 'He is afraid of blood. He hates blood.'[15] We were sitting in a bar in Barcelona, a few weeks after the 27 October showdown. I had asked to meet Porta, a prominent film-maker and writer and a close personal friend of the Catalan president, to learn more about the man at the centre of the political storm. He had known Puigdemont since their student days three decades ago. The point about the blood, Porta explained, did not mean that the president was a coward – not at all. It simply meant that he was a politician who did not thrive on confrontation, who derived no pleasure from the pure exercise of power: 'He has never fired anyone in his life. He always adapts and co-opts.'

Porta was one of the people who went to see Puigdemont during that fraught Thursday when the president decided to call an election, only to backtrack and push for a declaration of independence instead. Porta had advised him to stick with his decision and choose the less radical step, but the pressure from others was stronger, eventually forcing a man who believed in the virtue of patience into a rushed decision. 'Puigdemont has been in favour of independence all his life,' Porta explained.

'He believed in independence but for him there was no rush. He believed in building a large majority for independence. He also believed that independence was good for Catalonia and for Spain.' Puigdemont was convinced that Madrid would sooner or later come to see things the same way. 'It was not he who was in a rush. It was not he who promised independence in eighteen months,' Porta said, before adding wearily: 'The rush has caused a lot of damage.'

It certainly had. As we were speaking, Puigdemont was no longer in Barcelona. Nor was he Catalan president. His ministers were no longer ministers. Some had fled with Puigdemont to Belgium, to escape arrest and prosecution in Spain. Others, including Junqueras and the leaders of the two main pro-independence grassroots movements, were in jail, awaiting trial for rebellion. The damage, however, went far beyond the fate of individual politicians and activists. Madrid had indeed invoked Article 155 of the Spanish constitution, and taken over the day-to-day government of Catalonia. The region was not only not independent – it had lost all the powers of self-government granted by Spain's democratic constitution. Not since the dark days of Franco's dictatorship had Catalans been more dependent on Madrid.[16]

Porta, like many Catalans, had expected Spain to crack down hard on the independence movement. What had taken him by surprise, though, was the indifference of Europe.

'One thing is clear. We were naive to think that we could get a republic simply by saying we want a republic. Many things are missing, and the most important element that is missing is Spain. They don't want it, and they won't want it,' Porta said. 'Rajoy holds the key towards solving this but he doesn't want to solve this. He wants Catalonia to remain a powder keg.'

*

The town hall of Girona in northern Catalonia presented a sombre image when I visited the city in early November. The flags on the rooftop had been lowered to half-mast. The façade below was decked out with black ribbons, and a huge black banner cascaded from a top-floor balcony. The display was meant to convey outrage at Spain, and support for Junqueras and the nine other Catalan independence leaders who were in jail. But the black ribbons and lowered flags also signalled a broader shift in sentiment.

I had come to find out how local activists and politicians felt about the chain of events that had occurred since the referendum. I wondered in particular how they were dealing with a simple, undeniable fact: Catalonia had declared independence yet it was not independent. To me and many other outside observers, it seemed like the high-risk political gamble made by Puigdemont and Junqueras had not paid off – not for them and not for the country at large. But what did hardcore separatists think? Were they demoralised? Or had the drama and the setbacks of the past few months served only to deepen their commitment?

I found Girona in a strange, unsettled mood. Independence activists insisted that their historic goal remained within reach, and that they were as determined as ever to fight for independence and statehood. But they also made no effort to hide their disappointment at the recent turn of events. Some of that disappointment was directed at their own camp, and its apparent failure to mobilise and prepare for the turbulent days following 27 October. Above all, there was deep and bitter disappointment that Europe had failed to side with the Catalans, and that Spain's crackdown on the independence leaders had provoked so little condemnation in Berlin, Paris and other European capitals. 'What surprises me is that Europe doesn't give a damn,' Marta Madrenas, the mayor of Girona and a member of Puigdemont's pro-secession Catalan Democratic party (PDeCat), told me.[17] 'The Spanish state is violating fundamental rights and collective liberties. Are those not founding principles of the EU? Does no one care about this?'

It was the same exasperation that I had heard Porta voice back in Barcelona. The mayor, along with most independence activists I spoke to, struggled to understand why European governments and the European Commission didn't share their view of Spain as an oppressor. Many also realised that the gulf in perception posed a serious challenge to a movement that had long seen foreign pressure on Madrid as the only way to shift Spain's uncompromising stance. Mobilising European political and public opinion had been the cornerstone of Catalan efforts to push Madrid towards granting a referendum. Yet European leaders had rushed to the support of the Rajoy government in numbers that gratified the Spanish leadership and appalled the Catalan independence camp. 'We were hoping for a Europe of democratic values, a Europe that defends human rights, defends non-violence and that defends its citizens rather than its institutions. But what we have seen until now is silent complicity [with Spain],' said Ádam Bertran, who co-ordinated the activities of the Girona branch of the Catalan National Assembly (ANC).

We sat on a terrace in the magnificent old town of Girona – a maze of cobbled streets and shady squares, crowned by an imposing Gothic cathedral. It was not hard to see why US film crews loved to use the location as a medieval backdrop, or why locals were so proud of their city and its traditions. Halfway through my conversation with Bertran, we found ourselves silenced by a noisy procession led by a giant statue of a mule, accompanied by fireworks and a band. The march was part of an annual feast in honour of Saint Narcissus, who served as bishop of Girona in the fourth century, and is often depicted surrounded by a swarm of flies. Apparently, this curious attribute went back to the time when Girona was occupied by French troops in the thirteenth century: the invaders were attacked and eventually driven away by swarms of aggressive flies emanating from Narcissus' crypt. In Catalonia, it seemed, one was never too far from a quaint tale about foreign oppressors defeated by local ingenuity. Once the parade had passed, Bertran told me that the moment had come for the separatists to reflect. 'At this moment, now that they have detained the people who were leading the process socially and politically, we have to ask ourselves where we stand,' he told me. 'We have to reorganise a bit, we have to think about our strategy and about the kind of support we have and the support we don't have.'

There was little time for introspection, however. When Rajoy made his move against the separatist government of Puigdemont in October, he had not only invoked Article 155 to oust the elected Catalan leader and his cabinet; he also called a snap regional election for 21 December 2017. It was a signal to Catalan voters that the Madrid diktat was only temporary, as well as an attempt to break the secessionist stranglehold on Catalan politics. Rajoy's hope was that a demoralised independence camp would fail to secure another parliamentary majority, clearing the way for a new non-separatist regional government. The challenge for independence supporters was clear: to keep their campaign alive, they had to win the December election, and they would have to do so with much of their political leadership either in jail or in exile.

Looking beyond election day, an even bigger challenge loomed. Even if they did manage to secure another majority, most independence leaders knew that they faced a brick wall. The referendum and declaration of independence had failed to deliver the result they had hoped for. But what alternative tools and strategies did they have at their disposal? Catalans insisted that a shift towards violent action or armed struggle would never be an option. But neither was there much hope that the Spanish government would shift its stance voluntarily and allow Catalonia to hold a mutually agreed, binding independence referendum.

The activists in Girona were clearly aware of the conundrum, and they struggled to formulate a response. Despite her disappointment with the European reaction, Madrenas, the mayor, remained convinced that a solution to the conflict could come only through international involvement. 'We have to move the world,' she said. 'We have no other weapon.'

As the December election day drew nearer, Catalonia was gripped by a weary blend of resignation and determination. Hopes of a breakthrough, a decisive shift in favour of one camp or the other, had faded with each poll. All the turmoil and drama of the past months had failed to shatter entrenched positions and convictions on either side, and Catalonia was just as divided as before. 'Nothing will change on Thursday [the day of the election]. Catalan society finds itself in a structural stalemate,' Esther Vera, the editor of *Ara*, a pro-independence Barcelona newspaper, told me a few days before the vote.[18] The region, she added, had split into two opposing blocs that saw little room for compromise and that remained fiercely determined not to let the other side win. 'Our situation is one of stable instability,' Vera concluded.

That absence of great expectations turned out to be well founded. As I watched the results come in on election night in Barcelona, I realised that this would be like every other Catalan vote I had watched over the years: a messy stalemate that would confirm the hyper-partisan views of pro- and anti-separatists alike. Although the night did produce some surprises. The two most important Catalan independence parties had decided to run not on a joint list, as they had in 2015, but separately. Puigdemont was leading the PDeCat campaign from Brussels, appearing at rallies up and down the region via live feed from the Belgian capital. Junqueras, meanwhile, was visible on posters and banners urging voters to back his Esquerra Republicana party. Yet he was stuck in a prison cell in the Estremera detention facility south-west of Madrid, unable to campaign even on a television screen. For much of the campaign, polls had suggested that Esquerra was on course to emerge as the bigger of the two parties, raising the possibility that the next Catalan president would sit behind bars. In the end, Puigdemont and PDeCat staged a remarkable recovery, narrowly beating Esquerra into third place. The biggest party in the new Catalan parliament, however, would come from the unionist camp. Inés Arrimadas, the leader of the firmly anti-independence Ciudadanos party, pulled off a stunning victory, winning 25.4 per cent of the vote. For the first time ever, the most voted-for party in a Catalan regional election was not nationalist.

I rushed to the luxury hotel in Barcelona where Ciudadanos – meaning 'Citizens' – was holding its victory celebrations. Party leaders were thrilled with the result, but their main focus seemed to be not on Catalonia but on the rest of the country. The Catalan result, they felt, had opened the path for Ciudadanos to try to replace prime minister Mariano Rajoy's Popular party as the dominant force in Spanish politics.

Their ability to change the situation in Catalonia, meanwhile, would be limited. The pro-independence parties had won a majority of seats in the parliament, just as they had two years before, putting them in a strong position to form yet another separatist government. The fact that they had failed once again to win more than 50 per cent of the vote did not seem to bother them (in fact, the separatists' share of the vote had marginally declined, from 47.8 per cent in 2015 to 47.6 per cent). As in the past, there was enough in the election result to allow both sides to claim some kind of victory.

Having watched the conflict for so long, I found the December ballot strangely frustrating. It felt to me as if Catalans had spent three frantic months trapped inside their labyrinth, running into dead ends and walls along the way, only to end up in the very same place where they had started: as a nation divided against itself, with no resolution in sight.

More than ever before, I found it hard to envisage an event or scenario that might break the Catalan stalemate in the years ahead. Would a new government in Madrid make a difference? Could a new regional president in Barcelona bring change? I was sceptical, and so was everyone I knew. Indeed, barely six months later, both the government of Spain and the regional government in Catalonia would be in new hands. The rhetoric changed, but neither of the two newcomers – prime minister Pedro Sánchez in Madrid and regional president Quim Torra in Barcelona – seemed able to shift the fundamental dynamics of the conflict. This should not have come as a surprise. Short of an agreed referendum, what could Spain offer that might possibly satisfy the separatists? As Catalan leaders like Mas had told me over and over again, the kind of political deal that might still have been possible in 2012 – more money and more autonomy for Catalonia, but within the framework of the constitution – was simply no longer acceptable to the independence camp. Neither did I see much hope for a 'third way' – the solution favoured by moderate intellectuals and politicians in Barcelona and Madrid, and that prime minister Sánchez seemed to be leaning towards. They were determined to avoid a historic rupture, but also regarded the status quo as untenable. Most advocated some form of 'asymmetrical federalism', a constitutional overhaul based on the acceptance that not all Spanish regions were the same, that some parts – such as Catalonia and the Basque country – wanted and deserved a greater level of autonomy than others. A reform of Spain's constitution, some thought, should also lead to the explicit recognition of Catalonia as a nation within the Spanish state. Spain had to become a pluri-national state in law, they argued, because it was a pluri-national state in fact. To preserve Spain as a single state it had to stop pretending to be a single nation.

On paper, the model made sense. In reality, however, a constitutional reform along those lines seemed impossible to implement. What kind of Catalan leader could sign off on a deal designed to cement the region's status as an integral part of Spain, no matter how great the gain in rights and funding? For many Catalans, this was no longer about money and legislation. This was about a new beginning. And what kind of Spanish leader could sell such a compromise deal to the rest of the country, a deal that implied fewer fiscal transfers to poorer regions such as Andalusia and Extremadura, and that confirmed Catalans in their belief that they deserved special treatment? For many Spaniards, the very idea of granting further concessions to the Catalans seemed absurd. The current mess, they argued, had come about precisely because Madrid had been too generous in the past. Spain had allowed the Catalans to run their own public broadcast and radio network, and to subsidise Catalan-language newspapers, thereby creating a powerful pro-independence media machine. Spain had also granted the Catalans autonomy over the school curriculum, allowing Barcelona – in Spanish minds at least – to expose every child in the region to nationalist sentiment five days a week. The solution to the conflict, therefore, could never be more autonomy for Catalonia, but less.

Was it conceivable that the Catalans might simply climb down at some point, resign themselves to the union with Spain and move on? I found that difficult to believe. Supporters of Catalan independence had travelled too far for too long to simply turn around now. Everything that had happened since the referendum – the violence, the imprisonment of their leaders, the ousting of the Catalan government – had served to harden their resolve. Many of the emotional bonds with Spain that still existed prior to 1 October 2017 were burnt in the traumatic aftermath. What is more, many *independentistas* chose to live in a self-contained information bubble, in which a fascist Spanish government was forever at fault and the Catalan independence campaign was always marching to glory. Their worldview had survived even the setbacks and humiliations of October and November 2017. It was hard to see what might shatter it now.

At the heart of the conflict was a pernicious balance of power that made it fiendishly difficult to move forward. Neither side was so weak that it felt the need to rethink its fundamental position. But neither side was strong enough to impose itself on the other. Spain could not order an end to separatist sentiment in Catalonia, and Catalonia could not force Spain to let it go. The Catalan independence movement lacked the allies abroad and the levers at home to break the stalemate. Most importantly, it still lacked the clear, unequivocal support of a majority of its own citizens.

The weakness of Madrid was less easy to spot, but it was daunting all the same. Madrid's weakness was time. Looking towards the future, the hard reality for Spain was that the currents of history and demography were running – slowly, imperceptibly – against the union. Polls made clear that younger Catalans, who had been schooled in Catalan and often had less contact with the rest of Spain than their parents' generation, were among the most enthusiastic backers of independence. One typical survey, published in 2018 by the Catalan Centre for Opinion Studies, found that only 28 per cent of Catalans above the age of 65 wanted an independent state. Among voters aged between 18 and 24, the share was 46 per cent.[19]

Julia Vernet, a twenty-one-year-old philosophy student at the Autonomous University in Barcelona, was a case in point. 'I didn't have to think a great deal about becoming an *independentista*. It was very intuitive,' she explained, during a break from her lectures in a noisy café in Barcelona's Raval district.[20] In her free time, Vernet served as leader of the youth wing of the Catalan National Assembly. Though half her family hailed from other parts of Spain, she was raised and educated in Catalan, and felt increasingly disconnected from events in the Spanish capital. 'I feel Catalan and I want a state that represents me. When I watch the Spanish news I don't feel represented. There is an abyss between politicians in Spain and myself – we speak different languages, and in different registers.'

This generational divide was – to some degree – unsurprising. Older people are generally more risk-averse; younger people have less to lose. The young chase political utopia; the old dream of preserving the past. In the case of Catalonia, there was another important reason that explained the gap. In the 1960s and 1970s, Catalonia's population was swelled by arrivals from other parts of Spain, who were looking for work in the factories of the industry-heavy belt around Barcelona. They spoke Spanish at home and Spanish at work, and kept close ties with their friends and relatives in other parts of the country. Their children and grandchildren, however, went to Catalan schools, and were taught in Catalan. While their *abuelos* were reared on Francoist claims of a unitary Spanish state, they learnt a different kind of historical narrative – one that was based on the idea of a separate Catalan nation. The danger for Madrid was that Catalans' attachment to Spain, their invisible bonds of familiarity and kinship, would grow steadily weaker with the demise of the older generation.

In the long run, this generational shift is likely to impose itself on the conflict with ever greater force. How many votes will the separatists need to force a break with Spain? Fifty per cent? Sixty per cent? Will two-thirds be enough? No one knows. But a tipping point surely exists. There will be some level of support, some threshold, at which the demand for independence becomes simply unstoppable. And there are good reasons to believe that we are slowly, erratically, moving towards it. Miquel Iceta, the leader of the Catalan Socialists, once told me about a remark made to him by a fellow Socialist: 'In Catalonia, they bury them with the *senyera*, and baptise them with the *estelada*.' The *senyera* is the official red-and-yellow flag of Catalonia, and denotes constitutional allegiance to Spain. The *estelada* is the flag of Catalan independence. The old dies, the new lives. One flag is lowered, the other one is raised.

There, in one elegant image, is the existential challenge facing Spain. It is a challenge that has surfaced again and again throughout the long, tortuous history of Catalan–Spanish relations. In its current form, however, it is inseparable from the dramatic political and economic upheavals of the past decade. The Catalan conflict is many things, but it is also a child of the crisis that started in 2008 and tormented country and region alike over the years that followed. One of the harshest recessions in the country's modern history left nothing and no one untouched. Some places, however, suffered more than others. And one such place could be found just down the coast from Barcelona: in the city of Valencia.

CHAPTER THREE

The great hangover

As you leave Valencia's old town and head east towards the port, you come face to face with two decades of Spanish economic history frozen in concrete, steel and glass.

First come the gleaming spikes and waves of the City of Arts and Sciences, a €1.3bn complex that includes an opera house, science museum, cinema and Europe's largest oceanographic aquarium. The buildings are the work of star architect Santiago Calatrava, whose futuristic bridges, stations and museums can be found in cities around the world. His designs, which are prone to run over-budget and tend towards the repetitive, have often courted controversy – and nowhere more so than in his home town. Built at the height of Spain's property boom, the sprawling City of Arts and Sciences came to symbolise the reckless ambition of the time. Vastly exceeding the expected cost of €300m,[1] it blew a hole in the regional budget that haunts the Valencian government to this day.

Next up is the Formula One racetrack, built during the same period, but abandoned after just five races. It runs right past another relic of Valencia's great sporting ambitions: a string of buildings that were used – again for a brief period only – as a base for the America's Cup sailing teams. Despite their enviable location overlooking the yacht harbour, most fell into disuse after the last race in 2010. Now, at last, there are signs of life:

one building is home to a business school. Another has been converted into a gastronomic centre.

Boom and bust, recession and recovery – Valencia embodies the recent story of Spain like no other place. When times were good, this was the city that borrowed more rashly, built more lavishly and invested more foolishly, than any other. When the property bubble burst in 2008, Valencia fell hard. What makes the case of the Mediterranean city so remarkable, however, is not the nature of its folly but the scale. A decade after the end of Spain's great construction boom, modern ruins and half-ruins are scattered across the nation's cities like confetti after the parade: some towns built extravagant museums and oversized hospitals, others built stadiums and racetracks, some built underused airports, while others built functionless towers. Only Valencia built them all.

'The entire economy was built on bricks and mortar,' Mónica Oltra recalled.[2] An opposition leader for the left-wing Compromís party during the boom years, she became the vice-president of the Valencia regional government in 2015. Oltra spent long years in the political wilderness, a lonely voice against the excesses of the region's former rulers, forever ridiculed and humiliated by her opponents. She became known for appearing in parliament dressed in T-shirts emblazoned with anti-corruption slogans. The habit so annoyed the grandees of Valencia's Popular party that the conservative-controlled chamber passed a by-law forbidding T-shirts with political slogans. When I met her, in the spring of 2017, Oltra was sitting in a vast ministerial office in one of Valencia's many medieval courtyard palaces. Political success had not mellowed her opinion of the boom years, and the politicians and business leaders who failed to see what was coming. 'It was like being at a party of drunks,' she told me. 'People thought it would never end.'

At the time of my visit, the hangover from that party was finally receding – both in the city and in the rest of the country. After three years of impressive economic growth, Spain reached a crucial milestone in mid-2017, when the economy finally surpassed the pre-crisis level of gross domestic product. A decade after Spain slid into a long and bitter recession, the country was back where it had been before the great fall.

For some – not least the Spanish government and Europe's political establishment – it was a moment of relief and vindication. In their view, the recovery of the Eurozone's fourth-largest economy showed that the unpopular austerity policies pushed through at the height of the crisis worked. Despite causing initial pain, Spain's decision in 2012 to reform the labour market, overhaul the banking system and cut the deficit paved the way for a return to growth. It was a message that Madrid had been broadcasting with growing confidence as the recovery progressed: countries *could* reform their way out of an economic crisis, despite being locked into the single currency. The sick child of Europe had taken its medicine, and come through.

There was, of course, another view. Critics, mainly from the political left but also from parts of academia, argued – and still argue – that the country's recovery was not just incomplete but that the price of austerity and reform had simply been too high. The unemployment rate had indeed fallen sharply from its 2013 peak of 27 per cent, but four years on it was still at 19 per cent, far above the pre-crisis level (and the European average). Nor was there any prospect of a quick improvement. Even the upbeat macro-economic scenarios published by the Spanish government foresaw a jobless rate well above 10 per cent in 2020. Other statistics showed that the country was still in a far worse place than it had been at the end of the boom: poverty and inequality, for example, had increased dramatically. Those who did find work were now far more likely to be poorly paid and on short-term contracts than before the crisis. Instead of holding down one steady job with decent pay and conditions, millions of Spanish workers were now forced to jump from employer to employer, often signing five, ten or even fifteen contracts every year. According to official data, more than a quarter of all employment contracts signed in 2016 offered only a week of paid work, or less.

Unemployment was falling, and would fall further still. But Spain discovered that it was now dealing with a different kind of social crisis – the emergence of a class of working poor. The rise of a new Spanish 'precariat' mirrored developments that were visible across Europe and North America, and that reflected trends such as globalisation and the speedy replacement of entire professions and procedures by robots and information technology. In the case of Spain, however, these trends became manifest at the very moment when millions of workers were suffering the fall-out of the great crash. The government, meanwhile, had successfully slashed the deficit from more than 10 per cent of GDP to less than 4 per cent, but the nation's finances continued to bear the scars of the crisis. They will do so for years, perhaps decades, to come: Spanish government debt stands at close to 100 per cent of gross domestic product, up from 40 per cent before the crisis.

The lost decade – and the debt accumulated along the way – will weigh heavily on Valencia in particular. Almost a quarter of the government's annual budget is used to service the region's vast debt. 'We are paying for a lot of broken plates,' Vicent Soler, the regional budget minister since 2015, told me.

Amid the debris of the downturn, however, optimists could perceive the outline of a new economic model for Spain. The country had used the extraordinary political and economic circumstances of the crisis to finally address some of its long-standing weaknesses. The once decrepit banking system was now on a sounder footing, companies had become more competitive, exports were flourishing and the over-reliance on the construction sector was gone. 'It's too early to declare victory,' Javier Andrés, a professor of economy at Valencia University, told me. '[But] Spain is growing again, and it is creating jobs. It has shown that it can change.'

The origins of the crisis are today broadly understood: when Spain joined the European single currency in 1999, it seemed like the gates to economic heaven had been flung wide open. A country with a history of high inflation and high interest rates was suddenly able to borrow at dramatically reduced rates. The average rate at which Spanish banks lent money for the long term stood at 12 per cent in 1992. By 2005, it had fallen to 2 per cent.[3] The consequences were entirely predictable. Bank loans and mortgages became cheap, so Spaniards started taking out more of them.

The arrival of the euro sparked a credit and property boom that neither the European Central Bank nor the Spanish government seemed to be able or willing to stop. Spain – along with Eurozone countries such as Ireland and Greece – became victims of an underlying flaw that had haunted the single-currency area from the outset: in a currency territory as vast and disparate as the Eurozone, the ECB's interest rates were always going to be too high for some and too low for others. As Spain's economy was booming, Germany was battling with recession. Both had to make do with the same interest rate, however, which was arguably too low for Madrid yet still too high for Berlin. Neither was there a mechanism to even out the gaping economic disparities or share the financial risks between

Eurozone countries through, for example, financial transfers from richer to poorer states, joint debt instruments, a common deposit insurance system or common unemployment guarantees. The Eurozone was a monetary union, and a monetary union only. Hopes that the arrival of the single currency would spur the creation of a fiscal and economic union proved mistaken. When the crisis hit, countries such as Spain came to realise that they – and their vulnerable banking systems – stood alone. As my colleague Martin Sandbu writes in his book about the crisis: 'The periphery found itself abandoned by financial markets and fell into an economic black hole.'[4]

In Spain, moreover, the credit boom coincided with the arrival of millions of migrants from Latin America, Eastern Europe and North Africa, further fuelling demand for homes and second homes that eventually reached fantastical proportions. The country's housing stock grew by 5.7 million units over the course of the boom, increasing the total number of homes by almost 30 per cent.[5] House prices increased by an average of 10 per cent every year, creating vast amounts of paper wealth in a society that boasts one of the highest shares of home ownership in the world. Even after a decade of frantic building, the thirst for new properties did not flag: in both 2006 and 2007, Spain built more homes than the US, which had a population almost eight times larger.[6] The impact on the labour market was no less stunning: at the peak of the boom, 25 per cent of all male Spanish workers were employed in construction.[7]

Looking back, the foolishness of it all seems obvious. A giant real-estate bubble was inflating all over Spain, yet no one – or at least no one in power – seemed to notice or care. Fearful of losing out to their rivals, banks offered ever more generous terms to homebuyers. Confident that the good times were here to stay, homebuyers took them. Regulators and politicians, meanwhile, did what regulators and politicians usually do in the warm, happy glow of an economic boom. They convinced themselves that this time it really was different; that even after fourteen years of uninterrupted growth there was no need to fear for the Spanish economy; that there were sound reasons why house prices were shooting up, while companies and households were falling ever deeper into debt, and Spain's current account deficit was swelling ever further. Between 2000 and 2007, the Spanish economy grew by an average rate of 3.8 per cent every year, boosting GDP by more than a third.[8] As ever, there was no shortage of explanations for this miracle: some pointed to the (indeed substantial) windfall that Spain had received as a result of monetary union. Others pointed to the country's startling demographic boom, or to the way that once-staid Spanish banks and companies were buying their way into fast-growing markets around the world. Concerns about the state of the Spanish banking system were brushed aside with references to the innovative provisioning regime pioneered by Spain's central bank.[9] Even in a slowdown, the nation's lenders would surely be sufficiently strong to withstand the blow.

Still, the warning signs were there for anyone to see. Between 2000 and 2007, the debts amassed by Spanish households and non-financial companies rose from 94 per cent of GDP to 191 per cent.[10] Someone would, at some point, have to pay all this money back. Mortgage lending grew by 20 per cent every year during that period, and lending to property developers by 29 per cent.[11] This money, too, would have to be repaid eventually. Salaries were rising at a blistering pace, and productivity was falling sharply compared to other European countries. Someone would, at some point, decide that Spain was no longer a good place to do business in.

Given the nature of the single currency regime and the

divergent realities of the Eurozone, it was always going to be hard for a country like Spain to avoid a credit and construction bubble. But governments and regulators took far too long to realise what was happening, and longer still to come up with a political response. Years were wasted with vacuous reassurances that the economy, the banks and the housing market were doing fine. More time was wasted with a pointless stimulus package that poured yet more money into unnecessary public works and infrastructure projects. The bubble burst in 2008 but it was only in 2012 – with the banking system in meltdown and public finances spiralling out of control – that Spain finally became serious about reforming its financial sector and pushing through much-needed structural reforms. Even then, much of the pressure for change came not from within the system but from international institutions like the European Commission and the International Monetary Fund. It was European money that was used to recapitalise the Spanish banks, and a European memorandum of understanding that set out what Spain had to do to end its crisis.

In Valencia, the housing boom had been even more exuberant than in the rest of the country. Here, politicians had not just looked the other way as the bubble grew – they had done everything in their power to make it grow faster. Starting in the late 1990s, regional and local governments had placed an all-in bet on the construction sector and they used every lever at their disposal to help the industry along. Building regulations and zoning decisions were tailored to the needs of big developers. Both the Valencia region and the city itself provided land, infrastructure and billions in public funding to keep the cement mixers whirring.

This policy was personified by two leaders who came to dominate Valencian politics in the boom-and-bust years: Francisco

Camps, the slick regional president, and Rita Barberá, the luxury-loving mayor of the city of Valencia. Both were veteran members of the conservative Popular party and perennial vote winners. But even inside their own party, rumours about corruption and outrageous mismanagement had been circulating for years. Indeed, for many Spaniards, the abiding image of the Valencian power duo was taken in November 2009, with the national and regional economy already in freefall. It shows the two politicians driving an open-top Ferrari – she in dark sunglasses, he in a casually unbuttoned shirt – around a racetrack, waving to the crowds like nouveau-riche royalty. The racetrack, incidentally, was Valencia's *other* racetrack, built just outside the city and opened in 1999. The Formula One racetrack was constructed right next to Valencia's seafront and opened less than a decade later. It was a quintessentially Valencian decision: why settle for one racecourse when you can have two?

Much the same logic was at play in the decision to build a second stadium for Valencia CF, the local football club. Since 1923, the team had played its home matches in the atmospheric Mestalla, a 55,000-seater stadium close to the centre. In 2007, just as the crisis was about to bite, work started on the New Mestalla stadium, a modern arena with a capacity for 75,000 spectators. Two years later, the project was abandoned, leaving the city and the club with a hulking concrete shell that continues to rot in the sun and may ultimately have to be torn down. Both Camps and Barberá would eventually fall from grace in spectacular fashion, hounded by corruption prosecutors and the alleged financial sins of their past. Camps resigned from office in 2011, two years after he was first declared a formal suspect in a sprawling corruption probe (he was eventually acquitted but remains under investigation in several other corruption cases). Barberá was kicked out by voters in 2014 and heading for her own corruption trial when she died of a sudden heart attack in 2016.

Whatever help Valencia's political elite was able to provide to developers and construction groups, none was more important than bank funding. And, thanks to a historical quirk of Spain's banking system, there was plenty of that funding to go round. That quirk was the existence of large, publicly controlled regional savings banks, or *cajas*. Poorly run and poorly supervised, forever in thrall to the government of the day, the cajas provided the rocket fuel for Spain's building boom, and nowhere more so than in Valencia.

Evidently, that was not the role that the founders of Spain's caja system had in mind. The country's savings banks mostly date back to the late nineteenth and early twentieth century, when they were set up to provide rudimentary banking services for working-class families, and to look after their meagre savings. Crucially, the cajas were closely tied to a particular region or city, and formally barred from offering their services in other parts of Spain. The profits they generated flowed into foundations that funded welfare programmes and the arts. The mighty Caixa foundation in Catalonia, for example, controls Caixabank, the nation's third-biggest bank, along with stakes in some of Spain's largest companies. But it also ranks as one of the most generous charities in the world, dispensing more than €500m a year to the arts and sciences, the sick and the poor.[12] Starting in the 1970s, however, the cajas' historic shackles had been steadily loosened. From 1992 onwards, they were free to operate anywhere in Spain – a change that set off a manic scramble for territory and market share across the country. There was, however, one problem, as asserted in a 2013 report by Jesús Fernández-Villaverde and colleagues:

[The] growth of this sector was not accompanied by improvements in governance. In their past as small, local institutions, the cajas never had an incentive to improve their corporate governance. Cajas did not have shareholders: instead, they were governed by a board selected by the regional and local governments, employees and clients. These boards were the perfect target for takeovers by low-human-capital managers with the right political alliances and who could finance politically motivated projects.[13]

The most notorious case of financial vandalism caused by the caja system occurred in Madrid, the home of Bankia. Forged through a merger of seven separate cajas in January 2011, Bankia was floated on the stock market only six months later. It was big – with loans and assets worth €341bn, a third of Spanish GDP – and it was brash, led by the urbane, ultra-ambitious Rodrigo Rato, a former managing director of the IMF.[14] Rato had served as finance minister during the early years of Spain's economic boom, and was seen by many as the frontrunner to succeed José Maria Aznar as prime minister. In the end, he had to console himself with a high-paying career as Spain's man of international finance. Speaking to invited guests who had come to watch the bell-ringing ceremony at Madrid's imposing stock exchange, Rato hailed Bankia's listing as a 'strategic decision aimed at making the bank stronger and consolidating its leadership position'. In truth, he had just presided over the greatest destruction of value in Spanish corporate history. Bankia was an amalgamation of seven deeply troubled lenders, merged on the assumption that the less bad institutions could somehow tide over the catastrophically bad ones. As Spaniards learnt too late, the country's banking regulators thought the plan was madness but decided to let the lender float on the stock market regardless. Court documents released in 2017 included excerpts of internal emails in which senior Bank of Spain regulators described Bankia as a 'money losing machine' with 'severe and growing problems of profitability, liquidity and solvency'.[15] Two months later, in July 2011, Bankia started trading as a publicly listed company at a price of €3.68 a share. Some 350,000 retail investors – many of them Bankia customers who were talked into buying the shares by their branch managers – had bought into the initial offering. Within less than a year, they saw the value of their holdings wiped out. The bank went on to post an annual loss for 2012 of €19.2bn, the biggest loss in the country's history. Rato's personal fall from grace was completed in February 2017, when a Madrid court sentenced him to four-and-a-half years in prison for misappropriation of funds during his time as Bankia boss.[16]

Merged into Bankia was one of Valencia's own savings banks – Bancaja, a credit institute notorious for providing funding to some of the most financially ruinous schemes in the region. The new airport in Castellon? Funded by Bancaja. The Terra Mítica amusement park in Benidorm? Funded by Bancaja. The City of Light film studios in Alicante? Funded by Bancaja. The list went on and on, and the pattern was always the same: a bank controlled by the regional government lent hundreds of millions of euros to vanity projects that were politically desirable yet financially and operationally unviable. The result: an airport that was formally opened in 2011 but had to wait four-and-a-half years for the first plane to land,[17] a film studio that was shuttered after seven years and a crippling scandal over illegal state-aid payments,[18] and a leisure park that absorbed €425m in public funds and eventually had to be sold to private investors for just €65m.[19]

'The cajas played an important role because of their connections with political power,' Soler, the regional minister, explained.

'They provided funding at the most generous conditions in the market – and sometimes at conditions that were beyond anything the market would give … They operated like the tentacles of the regional government. They reached where the government couldn't reach.'

Valencia's three state-controlled lenders – Bancaja, Caja Mediterráneo and Banco de Valencia (which was no caja but part-owned by Bancaja) – offered lucrative side jobs and favours to politicians and ex-politicians.[20] The seamless transition from the world of politics to that of banking was epitomised by José Luis Olivas, who left his role as president of the regional government to become chairman of Banco de Valencia and then chairman of Bancaja, all within the space of just two years. He had no experience in banking.[21] Olivas was given an eighteen-month prison sentence in 2017, after a court found him guilty of falsifying documents – one of numerous Popular party grandees in the region to end up in jail.[22]

The real money, however, was being made elsewhere. According to Oltra, the shiny new public projects were often little more than the anchor investments for the commercial and residential zones that sprang up around them. The city built the museum and concert hall and aquarium, while private developers built the vast apartment blocks around them. 'Why did they build all this? To encourage urban speculation in the areas around these new emblematic buildings,' Oltra told me. 'What mattered was not the infrastructure but developing the plots of land surrounding these buildings.' The unspoken assumption was that demand for new housing would grow for ever, as would the population, as would tax revenues, and investments, and loans, and favours. Those favours came in the form of luxury gifts (Barberá had a notorious weakness for Louis Vuitton handbags), cash in envelopes and off-the-books funding for political campaigns.

The real problem, however, was not the stupidity and greed of local politicians. The problem was that these politicians had at their disposal a tool that turned that stupidity and greed into a systemic risk for the economy, whether in Valencia or in Madrid. That tool was the local caja (or, in the case of Valencia, two cajas and a partly caja-controlled local bank), with millions of customers and clients, and balance sheets worth many hundreds of billions of euros.

When the bubble burst, all but a handful of cajas – Caixa being a notable exception – were blown apart. Bancaja had been merged into Bankia, which was eventually rescued and went on to absorb €22.4bn in public funds.[23] Caja Mediterráneo received public funds worth €5.2bn and was sold to Banco Sabadell for the symbolic price of €1. Banco de Valencia was folded into Caixabank, but only after the state agreed to provide an asset protection scheme and guarantees worth €5.5bn. Valencia's folly cost the nation dearly.

Local politicians had little incentive to urge restraint, if only because so many of them stood to benefit personally from the boom. For more than two decades, both the city and the region were firmly in the grip of Spain's centre-right Popular party. With few checks on their power, and a compliant local business scene, PP mayors, ministers and presidents engaged in an orgy of waste, corruption, embezzlement and illegal party funding. 'The plunder of state coffers became institutionalised,' local journalist Josep Torrent wrote in 2012.[24] The kick-backs and pay-to-play affairs that engulfed Valencia are too numerous and too Byzantine to describe in detail, but even amid the torrent of scandals some stand out. I was curious to know which of the many misdeeds had shocked Monica Oltra the most. She responded in an instant: 'Blasco.'

*

The rise and fall of Rafael Blasco, a veteran politician who served as a minister in the Valencia regional government for the better part of thirty years, is indeed singular – as is his ideological trajectory. He started out as a member of Spain's Communist party, then joined the Socialists and ultimately ended up as a senior leader of the conservative Popular party (which had replaced the Socialists as the dominant party in the region). In his final government job, Blasco served as regional minister for co-operation and development. He decided to abuse his post in spectacular fashion – by funnelling into his own pocket donations that were destined to help some of the most desperate human beings on the planet. Among other things, he used almost all the €1.8m in funds earmarked for social projects in Nicaragua to buy properties and garages in Valencia, leaving just €43,000 for the impoverished Central American country.[25] The pattern was repeated with funds destined to help Haiti after the devastating 2010 earthquake, and with money that was intended to help child victims of sexual abuse in developing countries. The sums of money involved, Oltra explained, were not as large as those that were squandered or pilfered in other Valencia scandals. 'But the fact that he robbed from the poorest, from the most desperate…' She broke off. 'It pains me. It shames me.' Blasco is currently serving a long prison sentence, which seems to get longer with every new case brought against him. And he is far from being alone: after a cautious start, Spanish courts have sent many of the PP's most prominent leaders in the region to jail.

There was nothing that Valencia, or Madrid for that matter, could do about low interest rates. But the combination of mismanagement, hubris and greed, coupled with a banking system that lent according to political not financial criteria, proved disastrous. As the bubble continued to inflate, it touched on the lives of more and more people: teenagers left school to work on building sites without even the most basic qualifications; orange farmers whose families had tended their groves around Valencia for generations pulled up the fragrant trees to build apartment blocks; owners of small and medium-sized companies abandoned their businesses to sell real estate. Valencia, a region that had once prided itself on its manufacturing industry, succumbed to the dream of *dinero fácil* – 'easy money'.

'There came a moment when the speculator was the clever one and the industrial entrepreneur was the stupid one,' Vicent Soler told me. 'The son would tell his father: "I can make in six months more money than you made in twenty years." It was terrible. We had a culture of entrepreneurship here in Valencia. We always had the agricultural sector but starting in the 1960s it became more diversified. We had companies making toys, textiles, furniture, ceramics, metalwork. There was an industrial base. But then came the temptation to go for the easy money instead of investing in business and innovation, and analysing what the market needs. This is the worst legacy of the crisis – we lost a part of our culture.'

Spain's long, cruel recession finally ended in the third quarter of 2013. The recovery seemed fragile and anaemic at first, supported almost entirely by rising exports. But, gradually, the improvement spread into other areas of the economy. Profits recovered, allowing companies to invest in plants and machinery once again. The labour market finally turned around in late 2013, allowing at least some Spanish households to start spending again. Demand had been pent up for years. Now, at last, Spaniards were buying new cars and kitchens, and spending money on holidays. As critics were quick to point out, the tentative revival was firmly supported by factors outside Madrid's control, from low oil prices and low interest rates to the unprecedented stimulus provided by the European Central Bank. The decline in the value of the euro gave an additional boost to a Spanish export sector that was already riding high. But those tailwinds were also blowing into the sails of Italy, Greece, France and most of the other Eurozone countries. Yet few could match the buoyancy of Spain's recovery. In 2015 something remarkable happened: the Spanish economy grew by more than 3 per cent, faster than any other large Eurozone country. The same happened in 2016, and again in 2017. Even more important than the headline figure, however, was the composition of Spanish output. In the years before the crisis, the volatile construction sector accounted for more than 10 per cent of GDP. In 2016 that share had fallen to 5 per cent. Between 2009 and 2017, Spanish exports of goods and services rose from 22 per cent of GDP to 34 per cent.[26] The country's exports also became more diversified, with more companies in more sectors selling to more countries, including fast-growing markets such as Asia.

The export boom reflected, among other things, the country's recent gains in terms of its competitiveness. Spanish labour costs fell 15 per cent between 2009 and 2017,[27] the result of years of wage restraint as well as the new flexibility granted to companies by the 2012 labour market reform. Spain's motor industry, in particular, appeared to be emerging from the downturn with a renewed sense of vigour and dynamism. And, as it happened, one of the most imposing symbols of this revival was to be found on the outskirts of crisis-scarred Valencia.

Ford's vast manufacturing plant was opened in 1976, and today occupies some 270 acres of ground. I visited the factory during the first months of Spain's economic recovery, when examples of renewal and resurgence were few and far between. This one, however, was impressive: inside one of the immense production halls, I watched a chorus of industrial robots perform a high-precision ballet. A brightly painted robot picked up a chunk of metal bodywork, spun it around and came to a halt. The next robot swivelled towards it, sending a shower of sparks into the air as it began to weld at dizzying speed. The fiery pirouette was repeated dozens of times as the slice of metal, now visible as the side of a passenger van, glided through the hissing and stamping chain of fifty-two robots.

The new assembly line had been in operation for just two months. It was part of a €1.5bn expansion of the Valencia plant that saw the US carmaker install two additional assembly lines, build a massive new paint shop, buy 262 industrial robots and – most importantly – hire 1420 new workers. The decision to expand the plant was taken in 2011, at a time when the Spanish economy was still hurtling towards the precipice. But Ford, along with other carmakers, had seen something that would take outsiders far longer to realise: Spain's appalling unemployment record had given companies the upper hand in negotiations with workers and unions. The quality of the local workforce was never in doubt. Now the price was right as well. Ford was paying the newly hired workers 16 per cent less than its older employees. Unusually for the car industry, where historically nine out of ten labour contracts were for permanent jobs, all the new recruits signed temporary contracts. More important still, the whole workforce agreed to make working practices more flexible. The Valencia plant sent its workers home when there was little to do but demanded extra hours when the production lines were humming. Additional workdays could even be shifted from one year to another. 'The car industry has become one of the solutions to the Spanish crisis,' José Manuel Machado, Ford's president in Spain, told me.[28] The numbers proved him right.

In 2012, Spanish factories made 1.98 million cars and trucks. But output rose steadily – along with jobs and exports – finally reaching 2.85 million in 2017. Within the space of just five years, Spanish factories had increased their production by a third. The surge was vindication not least for the tough decision taken by union leaders at the height of the crisis: instead of maximising the rights of veteran workers, they tried to preserve jobs and expand overall employment by agreeing to employer demands on wages and working practices. As Mariano Cerezo, the federal secretary of Spain's MCA-UGT metal workers' union, told me in Madrid, this approach was based on one simple insight: 'There are no workers' rights without work.'

Away from the factory floor, another important sign of Spain's economic progress showed up in the current account, the measure of a country's balance of trade and overseas income with the rest of the world. In the boom years, Spain ran annual current-account deficits of as much as 10 per cent of GDP – a level that economists regard as a sign of acute vulnerability. This meant that Spain required vast amounts of foreign capital to finance its domestic demand and investment needs. The moment that foreign investors lost faith in the Spanish economy – as they did in the wake of the 2008 bust – the country was starved of capital, forcing abrupt and sweeping cuts to investment and consumption across the whole economy. Now, the numbers told a different story. 'For the first time in our recent history, we have a recovery that is not associated with a deficit in the current account. The economy has been growing strongly for more than two years and still we have a significant surplus,' explained Raymond Torres, chief economist at Funcas, Spain's savings bank foundation.

Possibly the most important area where Spain had broken with the past was in banking. Messy and costly as it seemed at the time, the country's 2012 banking bailout and recapitalisation package turned out to be vital for the recovery. 'Spain did a textbook bank rescue,' said Ángel Ubide, a managing director at Goldman Sachs and a former senior fellow at the Peterson Institute for International Economics. 'They shut down the banks that couldn't survive and recapitalised the ones that could. And then they moved all the bad assets into a bad bank.'

The overhaul killed off the cajas, which were either folded into larger private banks or forced to become normal lenders, free from political influence. But the reforms came at a price: contrary to initial government promises, the vast amounts of public money that were injected into the sector – €60bn according to calculations by the Bank of Spain[29] – had to be largely written off. In a report released in June 2017, the central bank forecast that Madrid would recoup at most 20 per cent of its investment. In other ways, however, the great Spanish bank rescue was successful: it allowed markets and businesses to regain trust in the broader banking system relatively quickly.[30] Balance sheets were cleaned up, bad loan ratios fell and loan loss provisions started to decline. Most importantly, credit started flowing to the private sector and to households once again. Official data showed that even small and medium-sized enterprises (SMEs), which had long struggled to get new loans, were able to borrow at decent rates. In 2013, one in three Spanish SMEs cited access to finance as their most pressing problem. Within three years, that number had fallen to one in ten. Analysts looking to explain the difference between Spain and Italy in terms of recent economic performance usually cited credit flow and the banking system as key factors. 'The banking issue was crucial, and it was the root of the crisis,' said Luis Garicano, a professor of economy at the IE Business School in Madrid, and an adviser to Ciudadanos, the centrist Spanish party. 'If you don't restructure the financial system – as Spain and Ireland did after the crisis – it is very difficult to have a real recovery.'

Away from hard economics, I noticed other signs of positive change – evidence that Spain was no longer willing to accept the political and financial excesses of boom-time Valencia. Elections at local, regional and national level all showed that voters were less tolerant of political corruption, and more reluctant to hand the country's establishment parties the huge majorities they had grown accustomed to. In the years after the 2016 election, Spain has been ruled by a succession of minority governments at the national level, which have been forced to build consensus even for marginal issues. Elsewhere, the PP and the Socialists have had to take on coalition partners, limiting the scope for any abuse of power. Some of the country's darkest corruption black spots, such as Valencia, have come under entirely new management.

Political rhetoric changed accordingly, as did priorities. Before the bust, the talk among Valencia's leading politicians was all about 'putting the city on the map'. When I visited the city, in contrast, regional ministers spoke in low-key terms about the need to strengthen the industrial base, and ways to help small and medium-sized companies tap into foreign markets and access new technologies. After the reckless hubris of the past, it all seemed thrillingly unexciting.

Indeed, if there was cause for optimism in Valencia, it had much to do with the new men and women in power. Politicians such as Oltra seemed to embody the collective catharsis experienced by voters in the city and surrounding region. The way they spoke, thought and behaved could not have been more different from the slick salesmen who inhabited Valencian politics in the years before the great crash. That was especially true for one of the last people I went to see in the city – a young politician from the Socialist party who had become deputy mayor in 2015. Barely into her thirties, Sandra Gómez now occupied a stately office in Valencia's imposing city hall. Her own story of rapid political success offered a poignant contrast to the fate suffered by so many of her generation. As we will see in the next chapter, young Spaniards in their twenties and thirties were among the biggest losers of the crisis. They were too young to have benefited from the boom years, and too old to have escaped the downturn, which hit them with full force. Gómez knew her generation was in bad shape, but she was also convinced that young Spaniards had learnt some existential lessons. They had learnt to be sceptical of easy promises and alluring shortcuts, to mistrust establishment politicians and unchecked power. They recognised the value of hard work and a good education. Maybe – just maybe – they would be better placed to avoid the follies that had almost sunk the city of Valencia.

'There is more awareness of how difficult it is to find work if you are not prepared. Everyone knows that you have to study, that you have to train and that you have to work hard,' Gómez told me. 'I think my generation, the one that lived through all of this, we will not make the same mistakes.'

CHAPTER FOUR

Left behind

A month before his sixteenth birthday, Francisco Perdones decided he had finally had enough. He was tired of school, tired of learning things that simply would not stick in his head. Other boys, not much older than him, were already earning good money at Emiliano Madrid, the big metalwork factory just outside town. They had money to buy motorbikes and cars, and rounds of drinks at the local nightclub on Friday nights. Times in Spain were good, everyone was making easy money – and Francisco wanted his share of it. The final straw came when his teachers forced him to repeat a year because of his poor marks. 'My brother was already working at Emiliano Madrid and he told me there was a vacancy,' he recalled. 'So I left school. I didn't even think about it.'[1]

For a youngster living in Cebolla, a small town in the central region of Castilla-La Mancha, it was an easy decision to make in the late 1990s: Spain was climbing the foothills of a decade-long construction boom, and the windows and steel frames made by Emiliano Madrid were in demand up and down the country. The factory spewed out money and sucked in young workers. David Pérez left school at sixteen and was soon earning as much as €2500 a month. 'We earned so much money. The only people who didn't have a BMW were the ones who didn't want one,' he told me. 'People bought houses, they bought boats – all with the money from Emiliano Madrid.'

The flow of easy money began to slow in 2008, the year that saw the great Spanish housing boom finally turn to bust. No one was building new houses. No one was buying new windows. Salaries were cut and the factory went through several rounds of lay-offs. In October 2012 Emiliano Madrid finally went into receivership – one more corporate casualty of the worst economic crisis in modern Spanish history. Overnight, the unemployment rate in Cebolla shot up to 40 per cent. Out of a population of 3860, more than 900 men and women found themselves out of a job. For younger workers like Perdones, who was thirty at the time, and Pérez, who was twenty-six, the closure was traumatic. Both lost their jobs in 2012 and soon struggled to make sense of their long, empty days and seemingly aimless lives. Perdones told me he was keen to set up a business but was finding it hard to raise the money. Pérez relied on his unemployment cheque, worth €1200 a month, and spent as much time running and at his local gym as he could. He needed the activity. 'Otherwise, I would go crazy.'

The two young men had every right to feel despondent. I had come to speak to them in early 2013, at the very moment when Spain's labour market was plunging towards its lowest point. A few days after my visit, the country's national statistics institute published a new labour market survey showing that 6.3 million workers were out of a job – 27 per cent of the total workforce.[2] More than half a million Spaniards had lost their jobs over the past twelve months. In one out of ten households in the country, every single working-age member was on the dole. Youth unemployment stood at more than 50 per cent. Hiding behind these figures were fates such as those of the two young men in Cebolla. They knew, as did everyone in the country, that the suffering and humiliation inflicted on millions of unemployed Spaniards would not be over for a very long time to come.

Amid this ocean of economic misery, one group stood out: young, unskilled workers like Pérez and Perdones. At the time of my visit, there were 1.8 million Spaniards below the age of thirty looking for a job. Of those, more than half had left school with only the most basic certificate, the Educación Secundaria Obligatoria (ESO), or with no formal qualification at all. Many of them had made a good living working on construction sites and in factories that produced the bricks, doors and windows for Spain's property miracle. But most of these jobs had now disappeared and were not likely to return. The men and women left behind were rapidly coalescing into a new Spanish underclass that would become more difficult to dissolve with every year that passed. Already, some 640,000 jobless Spaniards below the age of thirty were – despite their age – classified as long-term unemployed. And their ranks were growing larger all the time.

Spain's recession officially came to an end in the autumn of 2013. No economic crisis goes on for ever. Yet even the long-awaited return to growth would do little to help unskilled young workers who had already spent years on the margins of Spain's dysfunctional labour market. 'The question is not whether or not we will come out of this crisis,' Manuel de la Rocha, a Socialist politician and economist, told me. 'The real question is what kind of country we will be living in ten years from now. And there is almost no discussion of this.'

Unemployed workers have less chance of finding a new job with every month that goes by. Their skills erode over time, and prospective employers grow wary of candidates who have spent too much time without paid work. After two years, which happens to be when Spanish unemployment benefits run out, the unemployed are 50 per cent less likely to find work than at the start of their term. 'It is very hard to send these people back to school,' explained Marcel Jansen, a professor of economics at Madrid's Autonomous University. 'Many of them have family obligations or they have bought houses. They have low levels of education, and often their only experience is in the construction sector. Some have been unemployed for years.'

The economic harm was not restricted to the jobless themselves. Spanish tax revenues had collapsed as millions lost their jobs and thousands of companies went out of business. Consumption was contracting sharply, meaning the treasury in Madrid also had fewer sales taxes to collect. At the national level, the impact was plain to see: in 2007, the final year of the boom, the government took in just over €400bn in taxes and social contributions from companies and citizens.[3] Two years and a housing bust later, that figure had fallen to €330bn. At the same time, the sharp rise in unemployment meant the government was now spending billions more on benefits. Public finances, in other words, came under fierce pressure in terms of both revenue and expenditure. But the effects were also visible in small towns such as Cebolla. Over in the town hall, the mayor acknowledged that the crisis had forced him to slash expenditure 'to the bone'. Rubén del Mazo Fernández showed me a table comparing the cost of the most recent local fiesta to the one held three years ago. Among other expenses, Cebolla had once paid €6000 for fireworks, €10,000 for a mobile disco and €40,000 for bulls (who would be put to the sword in the local arena). In the new age of austerity, the cost of fireworks and the disco had been cut by more than half, and the traditional bullfight had been cancelled altogether. 'It was a very unpopular decision but we had to do it,' the mayor sighed.

*

One of the first things the government of Mariano Rajoy did after taking office in December 2011 was to reform the labour market. The leader of the Popular party had won the November general election by a landslide, in part due to his promise to put Spain's moribund economy under new and more competent management. Breathing new life into the labour market, which had shed millions of jobs since the start of the crisis three years before, was among Rajoy's most urgent priorities. Under the leadership of Fatima Bañez, the labour minister, and Luis de Guindos, a former civil servant turned banker turned economy minister, the administration drafted and implemented the kind of employment legislation that had become standard among market-friendly, pro-business governments in Europe. The new law took an axe to the country's historic collective bargaining system, allowing companies to strike more wage deals at factory level rather than wait for a nationwide agreement. The reform also made it easier to hire and fire workers, a move that the government correctly believed would cause more pain in the short term but would also speed up the recovery. The opposition and unions went to the streets to protest the proposal but their efforts were easily ignored. The country's economic condition was too dire and the government majority in parliament too secure to halt the progress of the reform.

Today, most economists believe the overhaul – for all the controversy it still provokes – did deliver lasting benefits. Several studies[4] found that the changes allowed the labour market to create new jobs at rates of economic growth far lower than before. The fact that growth in the number of jobs set in almost immediately after the broader economy started to expand suggests that assessment was right. But the political cost of the reform was high all the same: Rajoy was asking workers to shoulder a substantial – indeed, in many cases, life-changing – economic burden, at the very moment that banks up and down the country were being showered with public funds to keep them from bankruptcy. The need to prevent a wholesale collapse of the banking system was paramount, for sound economic reasons. For millions of ordinary Spaniards, however, it was hard to understand why the government was saving the very institutions that had helped bring about the crisis while imposing austerity on the wider population. It was that impression of deep injustice, along with the poison of political corruption, that did so much to destroy trust in Spain's political class.

For most companies, of course, the labour market reform delivered an undiluted benefit: the cost of labour fell, and they were finally able to manage their staff in a more flexible manner. For many workers, this meant good news and bad: finding a job would become easier, but the job itself would almost certainly be more precarious and less well paid than before the crisis. For unskilled workers with little experience outside construction, there was no benefit at all. Lowering the cost of labour does nothing if no one wants your labour in the first place.

And that, precisely, was the problem facing so many of the young men in Cebolla. At Emiliano Madrid, for example, most workers remained in the same post in the same section of the assembly line for years. 'There were people, all they did was put a piece of rubber inside the window frame,' Perez recalled. 'Now the only thing they know how to do is put a piece of rubber in a window.'

Before leaving the small Castilian town, I headed over to the one place that could – and should – have made all the difference: Cebolla's local high school. Throughout the boom years, teachers had watched in frustration as more and more of their students abandoned their coursework and headed to the factories and building sites, lured by the promise of modest but instant prosperity. 'It was very easy to get a job,' Armando Salgado, the headmaster, told me. 'Now they realise that things are different – but they don't have the suitable skills.'

The causes of Spain's unemployment crisis were complex and plentiful, but few would argue that the country's education system was without blame. For decades, Spanish schools had served as a battlefield in a bitter ideological contest, pitting conservatives against progressives, state schools against those run by the Roman Catholic Church, teachers' unions against ministry officials. The result was – and still is – a system that changes virtually every time the government changes, and that disappoints at every level. International comparative studies, like the one published by the Organisation for Economic Co-operation and Development, showed that Spanish pupils were doing worse not just than their counterparts in Britain, France and Germany but also than students in countries such as Portugal, Poland and the Czech Republic.[5] The most damaging failure of the system showed up not in reading and writing tests, but in the number of so-called early leavers. According to the official definition, early leavers are young people aged eighteen to twenty-four who have completed at most their lower secondary education and have not been involved in further education or training. At the height of the boom, the number of young Spaniards who fell into that category was staggeringly high: Eurostat, the European statistics agency, found that in 2007 more than 30 per cent of Spaniards aged eighteen to twenty-four were early leavers – more than double the EU average.[6] In some ways, however, the data became more shocking the closer you moved towards the present. Leaving school as a teenager in 2007 was a terrible idea but one can see how it might have appeared attractive at the time. There were, after all, plentiful jobs available for any young man willing to stick a piece of rubber into a window frame from morning until night. In 2016 there was no such prospect, and no such excuse. The share of school leavers did fall, but only to 19 per cent.[7] Almost a decade after the end of the housing boom, one in five high school students was still dropping out of education at sixteen – condemned to a life of low-skilled, low-paid work if he or she was lucky, and a life of unemployment if not.

One of the key reasons why young Spaniards were more likely to leave school early was that so many of them were forced to repeat a year. The practice had long dismayed education experts, but it remained far more common in Spain than in other European countries. As the case of the teenage Perdones shows, this often left students so frustrated that they preferred to quit altogether. The second problem was the absence of a German-style vocational training regime that would allow less academically inclined boys and girls to learn a proper craft and other useful skills. Such training courses – known as *formación profesional* – did exist in Spain but they suffered from an exceedingly poor reputation. Spanish parents wanted their children to go to university, no matter how mindless or esoteric the course, a preference that was mirrored among the younger generation as well. The result was, and still is, a labour force that looks a bit like an hourglass: a huge bulge of university graduates at the top, a similar bulge of low-skilled or non-skilled workers at the bottom, and not much in between.

Back at the school in Cebolla, teachers told me that they had done all they could to keep their students in class. But often they were struggling not just against the boredom and frustration of the young, but also the indifference of their parents. 'The parents supported the kids. They said: "I cannot help it if he doesn't want to study,"' Emiliana Suela, the school psychologist and career adviser recalled. Salgado, the headmaster, made a similar complaint. 'They grew up in a culture where everything was easy. When I tell them now that things are very difficult, for them it is hard to understand.'

A little over a year after my visit to Cebolla I travelled to a different corner of Spain, still looking to understand the crisis facing the nation's youth. Andalusia, the vast, populous region in the south, had long been one of my favourite parts of the country. Seville, in particular, I found hard to resist. The city was delightful and opulent – crammed with imposing monuments, crumbling palaces, lush parks, and bars that swooned to the sound of flamenco until late at night. I loved the city's two great feasts, the Easter week with its dramatic candle-lit religious processions, and the Feria de Abril, a bewildering blend of drinking, dancing and horse-riding in a sprawling tent city on the fringes of Seville. I also adored the ubiquitous bitter orange trees that lined even the most humble street and gave off a sweet, intoxicating scent. Having grown up in a cold climate, I could never stop thinking of oranges as exotic. In Seville, I saw them hanging untouched above my head in their thousands – or splattered carelessly on the pavement. Seville, of course, was just a small speck on the map of Andalusia: the region also boasted the glorious Moorish heritage of Granada and Córdoba, the unspoilt, windswept coast between Tarifa and Cádiz, the white villages of the Alpujarras Mountains and the olive groves of Jaén, countless dots of dark green on blood-red soil, stretching as far as the eye could see.

On this occasion, however, the purpose of my trip was to look at the economic reality that lurked behind all that beauty. Andalusia harboured the worst poverty and unemployment in the country. At the time, the region had an unemployment rate of 35 per cent – more than ten points above the national average.

*

I picked up Marta Alba from a hotel opposite the main train station in Seville, Andalusia's regional capital. She had just finished a job interview – yet another job interview – and was still dressed in a smart business suit, her face and hair carefully made up, and wearing a big smile on her face. The job on offer was not the one she had dreamed of as a child, and she did not even know how much it would pay. But she knew it was a job, and a job meant everything to her. She was twenty-six years old, unemployed and living in a region where one in three was out of work.

As we drove to her neighbourhood in the west of the city, she said she felt more confident than she usually did after an interview. Alba was told that she was one of only five candidates invited, and that there were two jobs as sales representatives for a pharmaceutical company on offer. 'I don't even know what the conditions are, but whatever they are I would take the job. It would sort out my life,' she said.[8] Her dreams had never been that big. Alba said that all she wanted was a 'traditional life', to have a flat of her own, if possible in the same Seville *barrio* where her parents lived, and to start a family with Pablo, her long-time boyfriend. Alba had spent five years studying to be a nurse, but no one was hiring nurses now. She lost her part-time job at a dental clinic the previous year and her unemployment benefits would only last so long. She wanted a job – any job – that would help her get a little closer to the life that her parents were able to enjoy, a life that seemed so normal to them and so unattainable to her.

Her interview had gone well, Alba said, but maybe not well enough. Her rivals seemed better prepared, and had previous experience in sales. As she turned to say goodbye to the interviewer, he had told her: 'Whatever happens, don't lose your smile.' It seemed like a message of consolation, a few words to weigh again and again over the coming days, until the final answer arrived.

Unemployment had indeed done little to repress Alba's smile. A boisterous young woman with long brown hair and expressive, dark eyes, she had little time for self-pity. 'I am very lucky,' she told me repeatedly, sipping Diet Coke after her job interview. Alba felt lucky because both her parents still had jobs and could help her out; lucky, because her boyfriend earned some money working with computers; lucky, because she could use her family's holiday flat on the coast, which was almost like going on holiday. But she felt lucky, above all else, because there were so many young people in Spain who were even worse off. Among her class at nursing college, she knew only two out of a hundred who had managed to find a job in the profession. Among her close circle of friends, seven out of ten were without a job. Almost all were still living with their parents. Those who did find work, Alba explained, usually laboured in precarious conditions, on temporary contracts, almost always for little money. Safe, permanent jobs with benefits and decent pay – the kind of job that would allow you to buy a house and start a family – were the stuff of fantasy. 'I don't know anyone who has a permanent contract,' said Alba. 'It's not something I think is feasible. It's not even something I think about.'

We went for a walk through her neighbourhood, and she pointed out the young unemployed we passed along the way, as common as lampposts or parked cars. 'Unemployed,' whispered Alba, spotting a friend and neighbour in her twenties, who was out walking her dog in the middle of a weekday morning. They stopped for a brief conversation. Seconds later, another young woman cycled by. 'She as well,' said Alba.

When the crisis hit in 2008, companies up and down the

country responded by firing the people they could fire – those who were still on temporary contracts. It was a cynical but natural response to Spain's notorious two-tier labour market, in which workers on permanent contracts enjoy better pay and more benefits, and are more difficult to fire, while their colleagues on temporary contracts are paid less and can be sacked without much fuss. The vast majority of workers on temporary contracts, unsurprisingly, were young people fresh out of school or university. The early years of the crisis cut through their ranks brutally and indiscriminately: between 2007 and 2013, the unemployment rate among 16–24-year-olds soared from 18 per cent to 57 per cent.[9] The European average at the time was 24 per cent. In Germany it was less than 8 per cent.[10] Job losses were particularly appalling for those who worked in the construction sector, but young employees in industry and services were also fired en masse.

At the time of my visit to Seville, Spain's youth unemployment rate was the second highest in the European Union behind Greece. One in four young Spaniards aged between eighteen and twenty-nine was in neither education, training or employment, one of the highest rates in the developed world.[11] The Spanish economy was starting to show signs of recovery and unemployment was falling, but those who had the bad fortune to leave a Spanish school or university during the crisis faced a bleak future all the same. With jobs still in desperately short supply, many would be afflicted by what economists call the 'scarring effect'. The term describes a well-known pattern associated with young workers who fail to find a job early on: even if they do eventually join the labour market, their earnings and career prospects will never be what they could have been.

And their loss was not just about money and economic advancement. Shut out of the housing market and forced to live with their parents or relatives, countless young Spaniards

102

were effectively barred from starting their own families. For some, locked in perpetual financial dependence and economic insecurity, that moment would never come. The share of young Spaniards below the age of thirty still living with their parents shot up during the years of the crisis and beyond, and would reach more than 80 per cent.[12] Many were reduced to living off handouts from their parents, much like boys and girls waiting for their pocket money. The very idea of long-term planning, of slowly graduating towards adulthood and independence, had gone out of the window. 'It is as if someone hit the pause button on your life,' a thirty-something friend in Madrid told me at the time. Spain's birth rate, already one of the lowest in the world, fell even further during the crisis years.

That did not bode well for the country's long-term future, and neither did the fact that so many of the country's young would enter middle age not just with meagre economic resources but also with their sense of self-worth diminished. Alessandro Gentile, a sociologist at the University of Zaragoza, was not the only one worried about how Spain's youth would fare in the decades ahead, and what the country that depended on them would look like. 'This crisis is not like the other crises. It is a crisis that will leave scars,' he told me.[13] 'Leaving home doesn't just mean being independent. It also means assuming commitment and responsibility. The danger is that you will end up with a passive generation, and one that is not ready to face risks and challenges.'

It was hard to tell. Some of the youngsters I spoke to seemed like they were indeed close to giving up. They were cautious, pessimistic, trained to assume the worst. Others managed to retain their optimism. Some became entrepreneurial, setting up their own businesses or leaving the country to seek a better life abroad. Others again were burning with righteous anger, more ready than ever to stay and fight for a better system – or, in the case of Catalonia, for a new country. But they all knew one thing for sure: that the aspirations their parents' generation had taken for granted were no longer a given – not the steady job, or the safe pension, or the confidence that comes with drawing your own salary, buying your own home, raising your own family. They had to bid farewell to the notion, deeply ingrained in Spain as it is elsewhere, that every generation will live a better life than the last. And they all had to develop strategies to make it through the long, empty days, hoping that the moment would come when one of their countless job applications would finally translate into work.

Esperanza Roales, a twenty-eight-year-old jobseeker from Seville, told me she had already sent out more than a thousand CVs, and delivered at least a hundred by hand. She had a degree in public relations, and had worked short stints for the regional employers' association, as an event organiser, and even in a local shoe shop. But it had been more than a year since she last had a job, and some days it was hard to keep the hope alive. 'I remember when we were young and still at school we thought that at twenty-five we would be going to work in an office every day, holding a briefcase. That's what I thought my life would be like,' she said, brushing aside the straight dark hair that fell like a curtain across her face. 'And now I live like my mother. I live like a housewife at home. It's painful but it's the way it is.' For Roales, the fact that so many young Spaniards shared her plight was no longer a consolation: 'In the beginning you think: I am not the only one. Everyone is like me. But then it gets to the moment when you say to yourself: Why me? What did I do wrong? Why can't I get a job, not even in a shoe shop?'

Before we sat down to talk, Roales gave me a brief tour of the small, spotless flat she shared with her boyfriend, proudly pointing out the little pieces of furniture she designed and made herself. She was working on a website to publicise her design and textiles ideas, and advertise the handiwork she created in her ample spare time: 'Many people now take initiatives like this because they are tired of waiting. I know I am not going to earn a lot of money with this, but it is about using your time and showing that you are still a useful person.'

It was with much the same thought in mind that Ernesto José Díaz showed up every day at the adult education centre in Seville's Polígono Sur, one of the poorest and most run-down of the city's districts. Surrounded by blocks of flats made from decaying slabs of concrete, the centre was something of an oasis: its backyard had been converted into an orchard where locals came to tend neat rows of tomatoes, carrots and lettuce. Inside, it looked just like any other school, except that its corridors were filled with subdued adults instead of noisy teenagers.

A heavily built twenty-eight-year-old with drooping eyes and thinning hair, Díaz looked too large and too weary to squeeze his bulky frame behind a school desk once again. But he felt he had little choice: much like his compatriots in Cebolla, Díaz had left school during the boom years, when he was just sixteen, to work in a factory producing windows. It was good business as long as the boom lasted. He even had a permanent contract, but eventually lost his job all the same. 'Before the crisis you could find jobs without having A-levels. But now you need them even to register for training courses,' he said. 'I sent thirty CVs since I became unemployed but no one has even called me. There are companies – they don't even bother to pick up your CV.'

About an hour-and-a-half's drive south of Seville is the ancient port city of Cádiz, the ultimate unemployment black spot in Spain. The official jobless rate for the city and surrounding province at the time of my visit stood at more than 40 per cent, but – as everywhere in Spain – younger workers had fared even worse. With such odds in mind, it came as little surprise that many students at the local university looked to their studies not as a path to a career but as temporary shelter from Spain's unforgiving labour market. 'The majority of people who study here do so because there are no jobs,' said Daniel Arana, a twenty-one-year-old student at the University of Cádiz, who was waiting with a friend outside the lecture hall. Daniel told me he had really wanted to become a policeman. Then he realised there would be no jobs in the force, and decided to study labour sciences instead. He said he hoped the economy would improve by the time he graduated, but worried that it would be hard to get a job even then without personal connections. Where, then, did he see himself in five years' time? Daniel shrugged. 'I'm 90 per cent sure I'll be standing in the unemployment line.'

The anger and disillusionment that gripped so many of Spain's young radiated across to their parents, who watched the struggles of their offspring with pity, alarm, frustration and – occasionally – exasperation. The country's baby-boomer generation knew only too well that it was lucky to enter the crisis with its mortgages paid off and its pensions still funded. Indeed, official data showed that the financial hit suffered by younger Spaniards was far greater than the wealth losses of the older generation. The country's pensioners actually grew richer over the course of the crisis.[14] Far from enjoying their good fortune, however, countless Spanish parents and grandparents were forced to provide a roof and financial safety net for their adult offspring. Even those who liked to keep their children close admitted that it was tough watching sons and daughters in their twenties or thirties disappear into the same bedroom they had inhabited a couple of decades earlier.

'Young people today don't have a life. There is no independence,' said Mari Carmen Rosas, fifty-three, whose twenty-three-year-old was unemployed. 'My son, whenever he wants to go somewhere or wants to do something, he has to ask me. He depends on me to give him money.' When she was twenty-three, Rosas was already married, had left her parents' home and was working. She still did, selling sticky cakes and souvenirs in a pastry shop tucked away in the warren of tiny lanes between the town hall of Cádiz and the city's opulent cathedral. Later that day, her son José Luis showed up at the shop, as reticent as his mother was outspoken. He told me he wanted to become a fitness instructor, but needed money for the course. For the moment, he was spending his time going out with friends and doing sport. But he had no time for politics. 'You get nothing out of going to demonstrations,' he said.

As she pondered her son's future, Rosas worried that her generation had been too protective of its offspring, too quick to jump in and fulfil the desires and needs of children who were now struggling to stand on their own feet. 'My son is a good boy. He is a good friend to his friends,' she told me. 'But I do give him hell. I tell him to get on with things. It sometimes feels as if he is a weight that I have to carry around.'

It was, of course, not just the young who suffered during the crisis. In 2017, with Spain in its third year of solid economic growth, I found myself in the back room of a job centre on the Paseo de la Castellana, the vast north–south avenue that cuts Madrid in two. Sitting at the other end of a long table were José Alberto Celdran, a man looking for work, and Lucia Martín, the woman assigned to help him find it. Celdran was a tough case, and he knew it. I watched as he tried to piece together an employment history long in years yet short on detail. He left school with the most basic qualifications, spent a few years in the military, drove a taxi on Tenerife and worked as a security guard on building sites and in shopping malls. He had once caught a thief.

But all that was a long time ago. Celdran had not had a job – or even a job interview – since 2008. He was fifty-one years old, overweight and had a bad knee. For the past eight years, he had nothing to put on his CV except odd jobs and welfare payments. He did not even have a fixed address: Celdran was part of a small collective of homeless people who had made Madrid airport their home. It was, under the circumstances, not the worst place to stay: he had a roof and heating, there were benches to sleep on and – sometimes – sympathetic security staff who would allow the men to use the showers. But his was evidently not the kind of biography that employers were looking for. 'We have to be positive,' Lucia Martín, the case handler, told her new client. 'We have to forget about the word "No".'[15]

It was a message that Spanish ministers – and policymakers across Europe – were trying to get across with growing urgency. Spain's economic recovery was now well entrenched, and un-employment numbers had fallen. Celdran, however, was not likely to benefit from the upswing. He was what all the youngsters I spoke to – in Cebolla, Seville, Cádiz or Madrid – were desperately hoping not to become: long-term unemployed. By definition, the category includes all jobseekers who have been out of work for more than a year. But the great downturn had shut millions of workers in Spain (and other southern European countries) out of the labour market for far longer than that. In Spain alone one in four unemployed had been jobless for more than four years.

The problem, according to Jansen, the labour market expert, was that 'high long-term unemployment will transform into high structural unemployment'. In other words: even if the Spanish economy continued to improve in the years ahead, Madrid would struggle to reduce jobless numbers beyond a certain point unless it found ways to make the long-term unemployed employable again.

After years of neglect, the Spanish government finally decided to pay attention. Madrid had realised that to tackle tough cases like that of Celdran, the authorities had to depart from the one-size-fits-all model of unemployment support. These people needed highly individualised coaching and training to get them even close to the regular labour market. They would now be handed over to so-called tutors, each of whom would deal with no more than 120 cases at the same time. Crucially, the government also decided to farm some of the hardest cases out to the private sector. Employment agencies such as Manpower, which ran the office where I met Celdran, were awarded contracts to take some of the workload off the public employment services. The help they were asked to provide ranged from the most basic (writing a CV, setting up an email account) to the most complex – such as boosting the confidence and self-worth of their disillusioned clients. 'We have to build them up again. Many of them have experienced so much rejection that they have decided to throw in the towel,' Manuel Solis, the chief executive of Manpower in Spain, told me. The key, he argued, was getting the long-term unemployed back into work – any work, no matter how short-term or poorly paid. 'It is very hard to get that first contract. After that, the second and third contracts are not so hard,' Solis added. 'Every insertion [into the job market] is good. But getting a permanent job or even a six-month contract in such a situation is just not realistic.'

For many, the recent shift in policy was likely to come too late, especially for unemployed workers who were close to retirement age. Others simply could not be abandoned. 'There are people who are in long-term unemployment and they are only in their twenties. They will be around looking for work for another forty years, so it would pay hugely if we manage to reconnect them with the labour market,' Jansen said. 'Spain cannot afford to turn its back on them.'

In all my conversations and interviews with young unemployed Spaniards during and after the crisis, one stood out. Ramón Espinar was a spokesman for the campaign group *juventud sin futuro* (youth without future) when I met him for coffee in Madrid, not long after my trip to Andalusia. A graduate in political science who spoke flawless English, Espinar was unemployed and still living with his parents. 'We used to have certain promises about our lives and how they would pan out. They told us that if we study and go to college and learn languages there would be a future for us, that we would be able to find work and live our life. That promise existed until 2008. But now the promise is broken for me and for a whole generation,' he told me. 'Before the crisis, people used to have precarious work before moving on to proper jobs. Now precariousness is a reality for people until they reach thirty or forty or maybe even sixty,' Espinar added. 'Precariousness is your life.'

Like tens of thousands of his compatriots, Espinar had started to apply for jobs and grants outside Spain, fed up with the lack of opportunity offered by his home country. Hard numbers describing the scale of the exodus were difficult to come by. But there was little doubt that Spain was losing some of its best-educated and most talented youngsters, the ones with languages, and with the degrees and drive to build a new life abroad. 'Leaving your country is no longer a matter of choice,'

Espinar told me. 'We have to leave the country because there is nothing left here for us.'

They sounded like parting words and I did not hear from him again until a year later, when I saw him speak – with the same passion and eloquence – in altogether different surroundings. It turned out that Espinar had found a well-paid, prestigious job in his home country after all: as a member of the Spanish senate. He entered the august institution in July 2015 after a string of local and regional elections that resulted in triumph for Podemos, the new political movement that Espinar now belonged to. The anti-establishment party was the most remarkable political phenomenon to emerge from the Spanish crisis. It came out of nowhere to achieve stunning success, fuelled by the charisma of its leader, disgust with the old party regime and – above all else – by the rage and desperation of young Spaniards who were left without shelter in the economic storm.

CHAPTER FIVE

Storming the heavens

The faculty of political and social sciences at the Complutense University of Madrid makes no secret of its ideological leanings. Its long, red-brick corridors are covered with anti-capitalist slogans, strike appeals and stickers bearing the communist hammer and sickle. The atmosphere is cheerfully anarchic: students light up cigarettes despite a university-wide smoking ban. Amid the thick tobacco smoke, the pungent scent of marijuana is unmistakable. The hall outside the faculty library is the scene of regular unlicensed parties.

The academic department itself has a well-deserved reputation as a bastion of left-wing political theory, a place to study neo-Marxist thinkers and analyse the revolutionary movements of Latin America. In recent years, however, the faculty has become famous for an altogether different reason: as the epicentre of a political earthquake that shook Spain's decades-old party system to the core. Podemos, the anti-establishment party that took the country by storm in the years following the crisis, was founded by a tight-knit group of Complutense academics. Pablo Iglesias, the pony-tailed party leader, studied and wrote his thesis here, before taking on a job as an assistant professor. Juan Carlos Monedero, a professor of political sciences and the oldest of the founders, acted as the intellectual father of the group. Carolina Bescansa, a sociologist, honed her skills as a reader of social trends and polls at the faculty. The youngest of the gang, Iñigo Errejon, was another alumnus of the Complutense. Indeed, the preface to his 654-page doctoral thesis – 'The struggle for hegemony during the first MAS government in Bolivia 2006–2009: a discursive analysis' – reads like a Who's Who of the future Podemos leadership: he thanks Monedero and Bescansa for their courses and 'Pablo, who continues to be at war'. Even Ramón Espinar, the soon-to-be senator we met in the previous chapter, is name-checked.

With the exception of Iglesias, whose wit and debating skills had already made him a fixture of late-night political talk shows, none of the Podemos founders was known outside a small circle of far-left activists in Madrid. That, and much else, would change over the course of 2014, as the party shot from obscurity to international fame. Podemos ('We can') was formally unveiled on the stage of a tiny neighbourhood theatre in Madrid's grungy Lavapiés district in January 2014. Its founders, however, had worked towards this moment – whether consciously or not – for a very long time. Monedero, Iglesias and the others were linked not just through their research and academic work at the Complutense, but also through years of political activity in left-wing groups such as Contrapoder ('Counterpower') and Izquierda Anticapitalista ('Anticapitalist Left') and a political televison show called *La Tuerka* ('The Nut') that Iglesias had set up. Iglesias had long been obsessed with television and the mass media. He was convinced that they offered the chance to gain a wider following for his (still) marginal brand of politics. Towards the end of 2013, with unemployment at record levels and the government engulfed in corruption scandals, Iglesias and his colleagues decided that the moment had come for the next step – the launch of a political party. The name Podemos was cooked up by Iglesias and Miguel Urban, the leader of Izquierda

Anticapitalista, while they were driving home from a dinner outside Madrid: 'We had to give a name to this thing we had been thinking about for the past two months. We didn't want an acronym soup,' Urban recalled a year later. 'I said: "Podemos", and everyone liked it.'[1]

Podemos was founded without money, without a programme and without members. Yet it struck a chord almost immediately. Less than two days after Iglesias appealed for support from the theatre stage in Lavapiés, Podemos had collected the 50,000 signatures it said it needed to compete in the European Parliament elections.[2] Podemos made international headlines four months later, when it stunned forecasters by winning 8 per cent of the vote and five seats in the pan-European legislature. The party's first ever election campaign had been a revelation for the upstart politicians: wherever they went, halls and squares were full of supporters and well-wishers. On social media, too, the party was hoovering up fans: a little over four months after Podemos was formally unveiled, it boasted 194,000 followers on Twitter, more than either the governing Popular party (141,000) or the opposition Socialists (140,000).[3] Local Podemos branches, known as circles, appeared up and down the country, sometimes without the knowledge of the Madrid leadership. Pablo Echenique, an early convert who would take on a senior role inside the party almost immediately, asked Iglesias for advice on how to organise during those heady first days of expansion. 'Pablo said it was like sex: you start off doing it badly, but learn with experience,' he recalled.[4]

Towards the end of 2014, less than a year after its creation, polls showed that Podemos had overtaken its establishment rivals and was now the best-supported party in Spain. All of a sudden, the scruffy newcomer had become a serious contender for government. Facing a vast crowd in the Vistalegre arena at the founding party congress in Madrid, Iglesias gave voice to the soaring ambition and boundless confidence of his movement. 'You don't conquer heaven by consensus,' he declared. 'You storm it.'[5]

The emergence of a movement like Podemos should perhaps not have come as a surprise. Political discontent had been boiling in Spain for years, and, unusually, voters seemed to loathe both mainstream parties in equal measure. The Socialists had presided over the nation's slide into recession, and the PP was at the helm when the crisis reached its nadir. Both parties had signed off on tough austerity measures, both had been embroiled in corruption scandals, both were led by old men whose experience, habits and discourse were a world away from the country's disaffected youth. Less than three years before the launch of Podemos, tens of thousands of young protesters had occupied Madrid's Puerta del Sol square for weeks, demanding an end to budget cuts. In conventional terms, the so-called 15M movement (the occupation started on 15 May) was a resounding failure. Neither the government nor the opposition took the protests seriously. Indeed, later that year, voters handed an absolute majority to the conservative PP of Mariano Rajoy, who seemed to embrace the exact 'neo-liberal' policies that the protesters had denounced. But the ideas and impulses that animated the 15M movement refused to die, and would resurface three years later – in the form of a new party that offered a radical alternative to Spain's ossified political establishment.

'Podemos existed before it was created,' Julio Martínez, a Complutense history student and party activist told me when I visited the campus. 'The general sense of indignation was already there. What happened was that it was finally transformed into a political movement.'[6]

I heard much the same explanation when I went to see

Carolina Bescansa, officially the number three in the party hierarchy, in Podemos's makeshift headquarters off the Plaza de España in Madrid. The party grew so quickly that its institutional and administrative capabilities seemed to be permanently lagging behind. In the early days of the party's success, arranging interviews with senior leaders was less than straightforward: assistants and spokespeople were changing jobs all the time, diaries were overflowing, and there were never enough hours in the day. Soft-spoken and serious, Bescansa seemed unaffected by the helter-skelter around her. She was a good debater but appeared on television much less frequently than her male colleagues, who clearly relished their turn on the big stage. 'Podemos is saying at the institutional level and in the media what people have been saying in the streets and on the plazas for years,' Bescansa said.[7] 'We did not invent anything. We have given a voice to the people . . . and that is why our support is so large.'

Podemos was keen to be seen – above all else – as an anti-establishment movement. It railed against the corruption of Spain's political elite, called for an end to austerity and promised to restore dignity to the millions of Spaniards suffering the effects of the recent crisis. The party vowed to roll back the government's labour market reforms, to shield financially troubled homebuyers from eviction and to raise the pressure on banks and businesses. Podemos leaders also enjoyed bashing Angela Merkel, the German chancellor, whom they portrayed as the real power in Spain, imposing austerity by diktat. Beyond such slogans, however, it was hard to trace the outlines of a political manifesto. In its first three years, the party went through a remarkable series of policies, programmes and ideas. It called for parliamentary control of the European Central Bank, then quietly dropped the idea. It questioned whether Spain and other southern European countries should honour their debts, then called for an 'audit' of such debts, and then stopped talking about the issue altogether. Some of these shifts reflected the unavoidable birth pangs of a new movement as it brought together different strands of left-wing and radical thinking. Yet the ambiguity was at least in part deliberate. Iglesias, Errejon and the other founders were keen students of the works of Ernesto Laclau and Chantal Mouffe, a husband-and-wife team of post-Marxist academics whose 1985 book *Hegemony and Socialist Strategy* served as something of an intellectual playbook for Podemos.[8] Laclau and Mouffe urged the left to embrace a new kind of populist struggle that centred on charismatic leadership, social antagonism and building a broad, transversal alliance between different marginalised groups. For such an alliance to flourish, however, the demands and positions of a new radical movement had to be kept both simple and vague. As Laclau wrote in his 2005 work *On Populist Reason*, 'in some situations, vagueness is a precondition to constructing relevant political meanings'.[9] All over Europe, the political right was using populist techniques and populist rhetoric to gain ground. It was time for the left to strike back. As Mouffe told Iglesias in an episode of his *La Tuerka* show: 'The choice today is between rightwing or leftwing populism.'[10]

Iglesias himself made clear from the outset that he did not want Podemos to be defined as a party of the left. Spain's political divide, he argued, did not run between left and right, but between above and below. Podemos wanted to be the party of those below, no matter what their previous ideological home.

Bescansa told me that Spanish voters, whether on the left or right, tended to share a small number of political impulses and convictions: disgust with political corruption, for example, or the belief that Spain's economic problems could only be ended by

118

new leaders untainted by the crisis. According to her, they also shared the idea that Spain needed to restore its 'sovereignty' (a word that came to resonate strongly with populist movements on both the left and the right in the years to come). None of these themes fitted easily into the established agendas of Spain's political parties, but they would come to dominate the Podemos discourse, especially in the early years. What is more, Iglesias showed time and again that he was ready and willing to appropriate political language that had traditionally been anathema to the Spanish and European left. He referred repeatedly to the *patria*, or fatherland, and spoke of his pride in Spain. Criticism of the Catholic Church and the monarchy, the two traditional targets of the Spanish far left, was muted.

Iglesias explained this approach in a detailed interview with Britain's *New Left Review*, citing the recent visit by King Felipe of Spain to the European Parliament (of which Iglesias was a member at the time).

A concrete example of this is the complex scenario we've had today [15 April 2015] with the visit of the King of Spain to the European Parliament. This confronts us with a difficult issue: the monarchy. Why difficult? Because it immediately takes us out of the centrality of the field. Basically there are two options. The first, traditionally taken by the left... is to say: 'We are republicans. We do not accept the monarchy, so we will not go to the reception for the King of Spain; we do not recognize this space of legitimacy for the head of state.' That – even if it's an ethically and morally virtuous position, which we can recognize and acknowledge – immediately puts one in the space of the radical left, in a very traditional framework... The monarchy is one of the most highly valued institutions in Spain, so that immediately antagonizes social sectors that are fundamental for political change. So, two options: one, we don't go to the reception and stay trapped within the traditional framework of the far left, in which there is very little possibility for political action. Or, two, we go, and then Podemos appears surrounded by the parties of 'the caste', respecting the institutional framework – as traitors, or monarchists, or whatever. So what did we do, in this uncomfortable, contradictory scenario? We went, with our usual aesthetic – casual dress and so forth, disregarding their protocol; it's a small thing, but it's symbolically representative of the kind of things Podemos does. And I gave the King a present of the DVDs of *Game of Thrones*, proposing it as an interpretive tool for understanding what is going on in Spain.[11]

I wanted to quote this passage in full because it shines a revealing light on the party's obsession with pragmatism and appearance. Iglesias evidently shared the classic republican critique of the Spanish monarchy, but in his quest to keep the appeal of Podemos as broad as possible, he was willing to sacrifice – or conceal – his beliefs for the sake of appearance. The fact that he acknowledged this approach so openly made it all the more stunning. Iglesias was telling his core audience on the left: Forget your long-held aversions and well-rehearsed talking points. This is what you have to do to get power. This is what I will do to get power.

For Iglesias, as for many of his allies, the original sin of the Spanish left was that it had put principle above power, and ultimately failed to deliver on both. In his own book, *Politics in a Time of Crisis*, Iglesias ridiculed this approach as 'leftism' and – borrowing a phrase from Lenin – denounced it as an 'infantile disorder'. He went on to say that 'radicalism in politics is not a question of principles or exalted language; what matters is the radical nature of the results'. He pleaded for 'tactical flexibility as opposed to dogmatism and sectarianism,' and concluded:

[Leftism] has never stopped being one of the left's most dangerous afflictions. The kind of leftists Lenin depicts have always been with us: white knights of the purity of principle, defenders to the hilt of the symbols and phraseologies most liable to turn theory into catechism, and almost always dreadfully outnumbered, isolated and misunderstood, incapable of confronting their principles with praxis.[12]

Podemos, he made clear, was a party that would not be hamstrung by the need for ideological purity. Neither was it the kind of movement that was going to build its presence slowly and carefully, starting with small concrete projects in local communities before growing into a national party. 'They are not interested in the long path to power,' José Ignacio Torreblanca, a political scientist and columnist, told me. 'They don't want to show that they can be trusted with rubbish collection. They want to go straight to the top. They see a small window of opportunity.'[13]

In late 2015, a few weeks before Podemos would contest its first general election, I sat down for lunch with Iglesias at a bookshop café in Madrid that specialised in all things cinematic. He was delighted with the venue. A film buff and self-confessed addict of television series such as *The Wire* and *House of Cards*, Iglesias took evident pleasure in the fact that all the dishes on the menu were named after European and American art house directors and classic movies. 'Ah, all the salads are Italian neo-realist,' he remarked, as he studied the lunch options. Iglesias went for the Amarcord salad, a goat's cheese and rucola combination that paid homage to Federico Fellini's film about adolescence in Mussolini-era Italy. I opted for the day's special, partridge with rice, which came without the benefit of an obscure Werner Herzog or Ingmar Bergman title.

I asked him about the future of the European left, and about the fate of the continent's grand old Social Democrat and Socialist parties in particular. From France and Germany to Italy and Spain, centre-left parties were going through a torrid time, squeezed by the anti-establishment far left on one side and the centre right on the other. Iglesias told me the shift was 'unstoppable', and that parties such as Spain's centre-left Socialist Workers' Party (PSOE) and Greece's Pasok only had themselves to blame. 'The politics of austerity have been shown to be a huge failure. The principal victims of that failure are the citizens but another victim is Social Democracy, which has lost its traditional space.'[14] In Iglesias's view, the centre left had betrayed its working-class voters when it signed up for the austerity measures and free-market policies that were implemented across Europe at the height of the crisis. There would be a special place in progressive hell for Germany's Social Democratic party, which he described as a 'crutch' to the government of Angela Merkel, the arch villain in the Podemos narrative of the crisis.

Iglesias admitted, however, that his own party had recently moderated its position once again. With the election drawing closer by the day, that famous pragmatic streak was shining through more than ever. 'Of course we have become more moderate,' he said. 'We have realized over the past 18 months that it is not the same to stand in a European Parliament election with the aim of taking a kick at the political system and to stand in an election with the aim of winning it, to become prime minister and to change the country... This means we have to say, "OK, there are some things we would like to do that we now have to do more slowly."'

I was curious to hear how Iglesias was dealing with his sudden fame – and the intense scrutiny and hostility he and his comrades were receiving from the press. In some instances, the criticism seemed more than justified: Iglesias and other Podemos leaders were facing pressure, among other things, for their close personal and professional ties to the regime in Venezuela, which was becoming increasingly authoritarian and repressive. Reports that Juan Carlos Monedero had received €425,000 from Caracas and like-minded Latin American governments to draw up a plan for a 'Bolivarian' monetary union (a theme that hardly fell within his field of expertise) presented the party with its first serious scandal.[15] Monedero defended his actions, but ultimately announced he was stepping back from frontline politics to concentrate on his academic career. Iglesias, meanwhile, had recently split up with his girlfriend, the kind of event that – only a few years ago – would have been of interest to no one except the couple and their friends. Now it was all over the news. For the time being, he was suffering the intrusions of political fame (he arrived with two bodyguards in tow) without any of the perks of political power. 'There is one thing I can still do. I can escape on my motorbike. I put on my helmet, and I am an anonymous citizen once again, honking at cars like everyone else. It is marvellous.' Iglesias sounded almost wistful, but he quickly checked himself, insisting that he was not complaining about his fate: 'We are trying to change the history of our country, so you can't really moan about not being able to drink a beer in peace.'

The desire to change history was plain, but the question was whether Spanish voters would let him. Podemos was still doing impressively well in the polls for a party that had been founded only two years earlier. But the surveys also showed that support for the new movement had peaked, and was gradually declining. Iglesias seemed untroubled. As a good student of Antonio Gramsci, the Italian Marxist and cultural theorist, he was determined to look beyond the fleeting noise of opinion polls. Gramsci famously argued that revolutionary movements were often thwarted by the bourgeoisie's iron grip on values, language, culture and social norms. For communism to triumph on the battlefield of politics, it would first have to obtain cultural hegemony. 'Gramsci didn't write so that university professors could study his work. He wanted to understand reality and he was aiming for [political] action,' Iglesias said. The Podemos leader claimed that he and his party had already scored considerable successes in their Gramscian campaign to wrest cultural hegemony from enemy hands. The party had introduced new words into Spain's political lexicon, and laid claim to others. Anyone speaking about 'change' or 'regeneration' or 'caste' in the country was now doing so on Podemos's terms. The party had shifted the axis of political debate – from left versus right to old versus new, establishment versus insurgence. 'Reality is defined by words. So whoever owns the words has the power to shape reality,' Iglesias told me.

In the four-week campaign leading up to the December 2015 election, Podemos sought to project a message that was both disruptive and inclusive. Its official campaign slogan was *Un país contigo* ('A country with you') but in speeches and interviews its leaders spoke of the need to 'reconstruct' Spain, and a new beginning for the nation. Polls predicted that Podemos would come a distant fourth but the party managed to beat the predictions handsomely, winning 21 per cent of the vote and 69 seats in the 350-seat parliament. Rajoy and the PP were still the largest party in the legislature but the conservative share of the vote had plunged from 45 per cent in 2011 to 29 per cent in

2015. The Socialists, too, had lost support, beating Podemos into third place by only a few hundred thousand votes. The battle for supremacy on the Spanish left had been won by the PSOE, but only by a hair's breadth. Iglesias was jubilant. The convoluted result gave him and the other Podemos leaders confidence that the next electoral contest would come soon – and that this time the Socialists could and would be beaten.

The rise of Podemos caused fear and loathing in many quarters, but nowhere more so than inside the headquarters of Spain's Socialist party on Calle Ferraz. Long before the 2015 election, PSOE strategists had realised the danger that the new party posed to the erstwhile standard bearer of the Spanish left. Podemos drew much of its support from young or disengaged voters who had never backed the Socialists anyway. But it also drew millions of voters away from the PSOE, especially in urban areas. At every Podemos rally, no matter where in Spain, one could find people like Juan María Hernández, a life-long Socialist who was now carrying a purple Podemos flag, and was determined to back the new anti-establishment left. 'We need a change in this country – and with the big two parties nothing has changed,' he said. 'Podemos will at least try.' I met him on a bitingly cold January day in 2015, on the fringes of the biggest Podemos rally ever. The party had called its faithful to Madrid's Puerta del Sol – the very square that saw the birth of the 15M movement back in 2011. They responded in vast numbers, with estimates ranging from 100,000 to 300,000 participants, many of whom had arrived from distant corners of the country. Whatever the precise number, the images were spectacular: the square and the streets leading towards it were overflowing with people. It was hard to think of another movement, except perhaps the Roman Catholic Church, that could fill the hexagonal expanse of the Puerta del Sol on a winter's day. Certainly, no other political party could. But Podemos could, and did.

Not only was Podemos offering a politically viable, genuinely left-wing alternative to the Socialist party, it also placed the PSOE in a strategic bind. In the wake of the 2015 elections, that bind became painfully clear: with parliament more fragmented than ever, parties would now be defined by their readiness – or not – to strike deals with their rivals. Without such coalitions and alliances, the path to power seemed barred to any one of the four major political parties in parliament: the Popular party of prime minister Mariano Rajoy on the right, the Socialists on the left, Podemos on the far left and Ciudadanos, a new centrist party that burst onto Spain's political scene not long after Podemos. Founded by a group of anti-independence activists and intellectuals in Catalonia, Ciudadanos was initially intended purely as a regional party. Led by Albert Rivera, a pugnacious young lawyer who once posed naked for a Ciudadanos campaign poster, the party eventually decided to capitalise on the weakness of the corruption-tainted PP and expand into the rest of the country. The general election in 2015 was the first nationwide contest fought by Ciudadanos, and the upstart party emerged with a credible 14 per cent of the vote.

The two political newcomers were in many ways polar opposites: Ciudadanos was a free-market pro-business party, and fiercely opposed to any concession towards Catalonia's separatists. Podemos campaigned against corporate power, vowed to tax the rich and was open to holding an independence referendum in the unruly northern region. In other ways, they competed head-on. Both Ciudadanos and Podemos presented themselves as crusaders against political corruption, and both offered Spain's weary voters a clean break with the country's discredited party duopoly. Those looking for a new start in Madrid now had two flavours to chose from.

To the PSOE, meanwhile, this new tableau looked deeply menacing. If the Socialists went into an alliance with Podemos, it faced two risks: one, it might alienate older, centrist Socialist voters – precisely the group that had not defected to Podemos – and drive them into the arms of Ciudadanos. Two, the PSOE risked advertising its own obsolescence. If the Socialists turned left, into an embrace with Podemos, would voters not prefer the original version? Turning right, however, posed risks on much the same scale. Should the Socialists decide to back a Rajoy government, they would be confirming the central argument of the Podemos narrative, which held that the PP and PSOE were indistinguishable, two sides of the same establishment coin. Pedro Sánchez, the relatively untested new leader of the Socialist party, tried to escape this dilemma with a bold manoeuvre: he struck a coalition deal with Ciudadanos, in the knowledge that, even together, the two parties did not have sufficient numbers in parliament to get him elected prime minister. Sánchez was in essence trying a political ju-jitsu move – turning the thrust of the Podemos attack on the PSOE against Podemos itself. He was hoping to present Iglesias with a dilemma of his own: he could either back Sánchez and his centrist coalition, and implicitly accept the Socialists' role as the dominant party of the Spanish left. Or he could join the conservative PP in voting against Sánchez, thereby ensuring the continuation of the Rajoy government, and very likely forcing a repeat election. Either way, Podemos would have to side with one of the two establishment parties. It seemed like a difficult choice but in truth the outcome was never seriously in doubt. Iglesias refused to support the Socialists, Sánchez lost his bid for power, and Spain called a repeat election for June 2016 – just six months after the previous vote.

PSOE leaders cried betrayal, and accused Iglesias of a cynical gambit that placed narrow party interest above the need to oust Rajoy and shift Spanish politics at least a fraction to the left. That charge, however, was not only naive, it missed the essential point about Iglesias and Podemos. This was a party that wanted power – real power. When faced with a choice between two strategies, it would always opt for the one that provided the path to power. And for Podemos, there was only one such path available: it had to overtake the PSOE as the largest party on the left, and then build a coalition of left-wing and regional parties comprising Podemos, the Socialists and lawmakers from the Basque country and Catalonia. That, in realistic terms, was the only way Iglesias would ever make it to Moncloa, the government compound outside Madrid. And, as so often, the Podemos leader had made no secret of his position. Writing in May 2015, Iglesias argued:

> Our vital goal this year is to overtake [the] PSOE – an essential pre-condition for political change in Spain, even if we don't manage to outstrip the PP. The hypothesis of the Socialists undertaking an 180-degree turn and rejecting austerity policies, so that we could reach an understanding with them, will only come into play if we effectively outdo them. At that stage, [the] PSOE will either accept the leadership of Podemos or commit political suicide by submitting to that of the PP.[16]

The December 2015 elections had brought Podemos close to parity with the Socialists but nothing more. The key, as Iglesias wrote, was to overtake the PSOE; until that happened there would be no deal, no accommodation, and no coalition. It was exactly the sort of uncompromising approach to politics that the party prided itself on. Indeed, it was no coincidence that Iglesias had chosen the DVD box set of *Game of Thrones* as a gift for the new Spanish king. The violent fantasy series about scheming princes and warlords battling for the Iron Throne of Westeros had long been an inspiration to the Podemos leader. He even edited a tongue-in-cheek book about the series and its relevance for the political sciences. The title: *Win or Die – Political lessons from the Game of Thrones*.

When Spain went to the polls again in June 2016, Podemos felt certain that the great prize – political hegemony on the Spanish left – was within reach. The polls showed Podemos was likely to emerge as the second-biggest party, vindicating two bold decisions taken by Iglesias ahead of the campaign. The first was a deal to run on a joint electoral platform with Izquierda Unida (IU), an amalgamation of left-wing and far-left groups that included the Spanish Communist party. IU had won close to one million votes in the December ballot, but due to the quirks of the Spanish electoral system, it had emerged with only two seats. Podemos had won five times more votes, but earned thirty times more seats than IU. By joining forces with Podemos, far more of those traditional far-left votes would translate into seats, making it more likely that the combined list would overtake the Socialists. The second bold move was related to the campaign strategy itself. In a bid to remain as inclusive and transversal as possible, Podemos decided to run on a warm, optimistic – and slightly fuzzy – message that centred on a decidedly a-political word: Podemos promised to make Spain 'smile' again. The theme was repeated endlessly on posters, television and on social media. No speech was complete without a reference to 'the smile of a nation', the official campaign motto. It could have been an advert for toothpaste.

At precisely 8 p.m. on Sunday, 26 June 2015, this softly-softly strategy looked to have delivered a historic triumph. Exit polls predicted that Podemos had indeed overtaken the Socialist party, both in the share of the vote and in parliamentary seats. Better still, Podemos and PSOE looked likely to win an overall majority in the legislature. For a brief, intoxicating moment, Iglesias was not just a plausible candidate to become the next Spanish prime minister – he was the frontrunner.

Then the counting started, quickly crushing Podemos's hopes. It turned out that the exit polls were badly wrong, and so were all the upbeat forecasts published before election day.[17] Podemos – or Unidos Podemos, as the combined list called itself – captured one million fewer votes than the parties had won individually just six months before. Not only had Unidos Podemos failed to overtake the Socialists, the gap between the two parties had widened further. By any conventional reckoning, of course, Podemos was still a success story: the party had again taken more than 20 per cent of the vote, and its allies were still in control of town halls in Madrid, Barcelona, Zaragoza, Cádiz and countless other cities. Podemos was too big to be ignored. But the June result felt like a blow all the same. Both inside and outside Podemos, many sensed that this had been the party's great chance – perhaps the best chance it would ever have – to become the pivotal player in Spanish politics. As much as they liked to denounce Spain's economic recovery as a chimera, Iglesias and his comrades knew that the worst of the crisis was over. Unemployment was falling, and society at large was beginning to breathe a little more easily. After more than two years in the limelight, Podemos had also lost some of its novelty value. Iglesias himself was far less popular than he used to be. Some found his style grating, and women voters in particular seemed to dislike his persona. Maybe he had simply become over-exposed? I thought back to something Pablo Simón, a professor of politics at Madrid's Carlos III University, had told me the year before. 'Podemos has only one bullet,' he said. 'And they have to fire it in 2015.'[18]

Simón did not mean that Podemos would simply disappear if they failed to win power in that year. He meant that there was a rare – and possibly unrepeatable – combination of factors in place at that time that made the Podemos bid for power credible. These included the economic crisis, the political crisis facing the mainstream parties, the accumulation of corruption scandals, and the general feeling of discontent swirling around Spanish society. Those factors had not all disappeared over-night, nor would they in the years ahead. But it was unlikely that the precise political, economic and social constellation of the post-crisis years, which had been so favourable to a new party, would return any time soon. Iglesias put on a brave face in the wake of the second ballot defeat. 'Sooner or later, Unidos Podemos will govern this country. It is a question of time,' he told a television interviewer.[19] Others were not so sure. 'The party has to face the reality that with its current discourse it has reached a ceiling,' José Fernández-Albertos, a political scientist at Spain's CSIC research centre, told me after the election.[20] Podemos, he argued, had raised hopes among frustrated voters that political change was both possible and imminent. When that change failed to materialise – or failed to materialise as rapidly as they had hoped – these voters drifted away. 'One of the reasons for the recent success of Podemos was that the party managed to mobilise non-voters who were otherwise little engaged in politics,' Fernández-Albertos said. 'But that support seems to have been lost, and it will be very hard to regain. An important part of its support turned out to be ephemeral.'

It did not take long for the internal recriminations to start. In the years since it was founded, Podemos had taken great care to project the image of a band of brothers (and, to a lesser degree, sisters) that stood united against the corrupt establishment. Iglesias, Errejón, Monedero and the other leaders were not just party colleagues – they were friends. But in the wake of the June disappointment, fissures widened into cracks and cracks widened into rifts. The man at the centre of the controversy was Errejón, the architect of the 'smile' election campaign and the Podemos founder who seemed the most – for want of a better word – centrist of the leadership team. His view was that Podemos needed to remain open and attractive for mainstream voters, and had to avoid being pushed into the far-left corner. That notion had been central to Podemos from the outset, and had enjoyed the enthusiastic backing of Iglesias himself. Now, however, the party leader felt that Podemos was at risk of blurring its profile too much. The two men sparred via Twitter but otherwise maintained a cordial relationship. Further down the hierarchy, though, the party was splitting into two opposing camps – Pablistas and Errejonistas – who fought each other fiercely and openly.

I wondered what Monedero, the father figure of Podemos, made of the fratricidal strife, and called him a few months after the June disappointment. 'I think the party has a great ideological debate ahead of it,' he told me. 'We have come through two years with seven elections, with a lot of focus on tactics and little on strategy. We paid too much attention to the how, and very little to the what.' It was clear that he, like Iglesias, was keen to sharpen the party's ideological profile – in a way that ran counter to Errejón's plan for a softer, more inclusive line.

To Monedero, there was no doubt that the 'smile' campaign had played a crucial role in the party's recent electoral setback. 'People were tired of elections, turnout fell, and some people thought we had not done enough to form a government [with the Socialists]. But the main reason why voters left us is because we moderated our discourse. Our campaign was too social democratic in tone.' Monedero voiced confidence that Podemos would govern Spain one day, but his thinly veiled attack on the number two in the party hierarchy boded ill for the immediate future.[21]

To outsiders, including me, the debate raging inside Podemos was hard to follow. It seemed like both sides were wrong for different reasons. Errejón wanted to keep the party attractive for centre-left voters, but without losing its far-left base. Iglesias wanted to shore up the far-left base but without giving up on the original Podemos aspiration to become a broad party that could draw support from the centre. To become a party of government, it needed to win votes across the political spectrum. But when it tried softening its message, Podemos lost support on the left. In essence, the debate between Pablistas and Errejonistas was a debate over how to draw warmth from a blanket that was simply too short. Cover the feet and you leave the shoulders exposed. Draw the blanket over the shoulders, and the feet stick out. As Alberto Penadés, a politics professor at the University of Salamanca, told me, 'there are just not enough votes for them to grow and be radical at the same time'.[22]

The simmering party tensions finally erupted at Podemos's party conference in February 2017. Errejón and Iglesias presented opposing political progammes and opposing lists of candidates for the key decision-making bodies. Iglesias made it clear that he would accept nothing but total victory. Should

Errejón's programme win out, he would no longer be ready to lead the party no matter how much support he gained for his personal candidacy. In the end, Iglesias got what he wanted: his policy platform won 51 per cent of support from the party base (compared to 34 per cent for the Errejón platform), and Iglesias was reappointed to the post of secretary-general with the support of 90 per cent of the vote. Errejón admitted defeat, and accepted his demotion to the second rank of the party leadership. His new status was consecrated a few weeks later, when he took his parliamentary seat in the second row of Podemos deputies. His old seat, the one right next to that of the party leader, would now be taken by Irene Montero, the new Podemos spokeswoman in parliament, and Iglesias's new girlfriend.

The party moved on, but it paid a high price for the turbulence and strife within its ranks. In relegating Errejón, Podemos had relegated one of its brightest minds and most popular leaders. Nor was he the only casualty. In the weeks before the 2017 party congress, Carolina Bescansa decided to step back from the party leadership, as did Podemos's economics expert, Nacho Álvarez. Bescansa made no secret of her frustration with the internal squabbles. 'Podemos was born to change our country, not to split into Pablistas and Errejonistas,' she said.[23] Yet another Podemos founder, Luis Alegre, went one step further, accusing Iglesias of leading the party to 'destruction'.[24]

The losses were not just personal but also political. Most importantly, Podemos was unable to capitalise on the weakness of the Socialist party, which was going through a crisis of its own in the second half of 2016. After suffering a series of regional election defeats, Socialist leader Pedro Sánchez was ousted in an internal party coup that was as dramatic as it was damaging. Sánchez had fallen out with the party's powerful regional leaders, in part over poor election results but also over his refusal to allow the formation of a new Rajoy government. His party rivals felt that stance was highly irresponsible, and would ultimately force Spain to hold a third general election in the space of just twelve months. None of Sánchez's Socialist critics was keen to see the conservative prime minister return to power, but many felt that the political uncertainty hanging over the country simply could not go on. Sánchez disagreed. The clash came to a head on 1 October, a Saturday, at a meeting of the party's federal committee. All through the day, Sánchez supporters had gathered on the street outside the PSOE headquarters in Madrid. When news of his defeat and resignation filtered through, their apprehension turned to despondency. 'Well, adiós to the PSOE,' I heard the man next to me mutter. A cartoon in the newspaper *El Mundo* captured the prevailing mood perfectly: it showed Rajoy and Iglesias standing over a coffin marked PSOE, exchanging a smile and a handshake. The implication was clear: the Socialist party was dead and buried, leaving Podemos and the PP to divide up the corpse's belongings.

The cartoon, of course, turned out to be spectacularly wrong. As we will see in the next chapter, Sánchez managed to stage one of the great political comebacks in recent Spanish history: six months after being kicked out by his rivals, PSOE members voted him back in as party leader. Another twelve months on, Sánchez was sworn in as prime minister of Spain, having finally succeeded in ousting his old nemesis, prime minister Rajoy. He did so with the help of none other than Podemos. In a move that had seemed unthinkable only a year earlier, Iglesias finally decided to give up the party's long-running reluctance to vote a Socialist candidate into government.

On the face of it, the Podemos U-turn in May 2018 looked surprising. The party had finally become what it had never wanted to be: a stepping stone on the Socialist path to power. In other ways, however, the decision to support Sánchez highlighted a tendency that had been part of the Podemos mindset from the very beginning: it was simply the most pragmatic thing to do. The only alternative to putting Sánchez in government would have been forcing a new election. And if polls were to be believed, such a snap poll would have resulted in a triumph for Ciudadanos, the only party apart from Podemos that stood for political regeneration and renewal. Under the circumstances, a minority Socialist government seemed like a more appealing option.

Podemos's support for Sánchez allowed the Spanish left to return to power – but at the price of weakening some of the core arguments that had underpinned the party's rise since 2014. Despite all his previous protestations, Iglesias finally agreed to make common cause with the hated political establishment. Despite the party's high-flying ambitions, it now served in a role that essentially made it the junior partner to the PSOE. Adding to Podemos's woes was a renewed outbreak of internal divisions, which saw Errejón join a breakaway left-wing party led by Manuela Carmena, the mayor of Madrid. The split – coupled with Spain's increasingly formidable economic recovery and the evident resurgence of the Socialist party – left Iglesias with an unenviable task when Spain did eventually return to the polls. He made the best of a bad hand in the run-up to the April 2019 election, showing humility on the campaign trail, and winning plaudits for his calm tone at a time when other party leaders were trading harsh insults and bitter recriminations. Polls made clear from the outset, however, that Podemos was auditioning for a supporting role only: the great battle for leadership of the Spanish left had been decided, at least for now.

The story of Podemos has been so turbulent, so unpredictable and so improbable that it would be foolish to make any forecast about the party's future. Its impact on Spain, however, is indisputable. The arrival of Podemos led to a historic schism of the Spanish left that shows no signs of healing. Podemos took a huge bite out of the PSOE's historic voter base, especially in the cities, among the young, in the north of Spain and among the well educated. Some of those voters did return to the Socialist party at the general election in April 2019, but more than 3.7 million – or 14 per cent of the total vote – stuck with Podemos.

At the same time, the emergence of Ciudadanos cut deeply into the PP's traditional electorate, especially in Catalonia, while Vox captured voters on the right-wing flank of Spain's conservative party. The arrival of three newcomers on Spain's political scene – Podemos on the left, Ciudadanos in the centre and, later on, Vox on the far right – turned the country's decades-old party duopoly into a messy and seemingly unwinnable struggle for fleeting majorities. Barring a dramatic shift in the years ahead, no single party can hope to govern with the kind of absolute majority that used to be taken for granted. Over a period of more than three decades, Spanish governments had been well equipped to implement their policies and programmes, even against a furious and highly organised opposition. Today, Spain's government struggles to do anything at all. That, too, is the legacy of Podemos.

When I spoke to Monedero, shortly after the June 2016 election, he insisted that the analysts and pollsters had Podemos wrong. This was not a movement that needed to win fast or wither away. 'I never shared this thesis [that Podemos could succeed only in the midst of a crisis],' he told me. 'It never seemed realistic to me. There is no case in the world where a political movement emerges out of nowhere and governs the country two years later. This needs time.' Monedero wanted the party to go back to first principles. He felt Podemos needed to develop a sharper ideological profile, and devote more time to the so-called *circulos*, or circles. This was the name given to the Podemos grassroots branches, set up to represent either a specific region or district or a certain profession or social group. There was a Podemos *circulo* for the Madrid district of Chamberi, for example, and one for journalists, nurses, artists, pensioners and the lesbian, gay, bisexual and transgender community. The students of the Complutense, needless to say, also had a *circulo* of their own.

In early 2017, three years after the party was founded, I set out to visit some of these *circulos*, to find out what the Podemos base made of the recent tensions at the helm, and what they thought about the party's future. Most of the members I spoke to seemed to share Monedero's serene assessment. 'We have grown. We have matured. People have had to adapt to the institutions,' Carlos Caballo, a thirty-six-year-old Podemos activist, told me. He had joined the party's *circulo* in Villaverde, a working-class neighbourhood in southern Madrid, two years before. Caballo said he was as committed as ever, but had come to accept that political work was a long, hard slog. 'You start with the illusion that you can change a lot of things but then you realise that the mechanisms move more slowly.' Listening to Iglesias during the 2019 election campaign, it seemed like he had come to similar conclusions. In speeches and interviews, he no longer promised a great rupture, instead setting his sights on more modest goals. In a televised debate with other party leaders six days before election day, Iglesias came across as perhaps the mildest of the lot. The one political promise he kept on returning to during the debate also seemed remarkably down-to-earth: a reduction in value-added tax on feminine hygiene products.

All over Spain, Podemos leaders and members had discovered that power and political change would not come in one sudden rush, but slowly, over time, as a result of patient work. 'It is impossible to build this without a strong base,' Caballo said. That base, however, was now there, as evidenced by the thousands of activists who would show up at the *circulos* every week. More than 150,000 members and sympathisers had cast their vote in the Podemos leadership contest in February that year – more than the venerable Socialist party would muster in their party primary three months later. Podemos had found its space in Spain's political landscape, and had put down roots. The metaphors and words used to describe the party after 2016 – all that talk of base and roots and back to basics – could not have been more different from the imagery evoked during the 2014–15 surge. But the achievement was no less impressive. Podemos had yet to conquer political heaven. But neither had it crashed down to earth. Whether the establishment liked it or not, the upstarts were here to stay.

CHAPTER SIX

The quiet Galician

Mariano Rajoy knows the battle is lost. His rival has the support he needs to oust him. The one ally he cannot afford to lose is gone. Tomorrow, Spain's parliament will hold a historic vote, and the result is a foregone conclusion. For the first time in the country's modern history, a majority of deputies will declare that the prime minister no longer has the confidence of the legislature. Tomorrow, the great survivor of Spanish politics will meet his end.

How does a man who has held the highest office in the land for seven years spend his final day in power? Does he fight on, no matter how hopeless the struggle seems? Does he howl and rage about the injustice of it all? Does he stay in parliament, and listen to the speeches – some full of glee, others full of regret – that pave the way for the final vote?

Rajoy does none of those things. He finishes his speech, waits for the end of the morning session, goes for lunch – and does not come back. For eight solid hours, he sits with friends and colleagues around a table at Arahy, a discreet but elegant restaurant near the Retiro park that is famed for its fish and sea-food. The hours run by, and the pavement outside the restaurant fills up with journalists and camera teams, all wondering – much like the viewers back home – what on earth is going on inside. Finally, at five minutes past ten, Rajoy emerges into the Madrid night, flanked by his bodyguards. There are isolated chants of support from passers-by, and some insults as well. The prime minister – dressed in his habitual dark-grey suit, white shirt and green tie – smiles and waves briefly into the camera lights, then heads for his waiting car. He has not said a word.

Mariano Rajoy's decision to skip the afternoon debate was met with incredulity and condemnation. How dare the prime minister show such a lack of courtesy and deference to the nation's seat of power? Words such as 'disgrace' and 'shame' were flung around with abandon. Yet others pointed out that spending eight hours enjoying food, wine and loyal company in the middle of a government crisis was quintessential Rajoy. Throughout his long career in Spanish politics, Rajoy had cultivated an air of detachment. As prime minister and party leader, Rajoy kept his distance from both people and events. His face, his expression, his tone – they never seemed to change, no matter whether he was celebrating a historic election victory or responding to humiliating defeat.

The next day, 1 June 2018, Rajoy waited for the votes to be counted, then walked across stony-faced to shake the hand of his rival, the new prime minister. Pedro Sánchez, the leader of the Socialists, had beaten him at last.

Rajoy's political career was over, but he looked like a man who did not mind all that much. Had he not made clear all along that he didn't need politics? That he would be happy to go back to Galicia, his beloved home region, and return to his career as a property notary? He had said it a hundred times. As Rajoy left the parliament building that day, it would have been tempting to believe him. 'It has been an honour,' he said. 'Best of luck to all.'

*

The two men who traded places that day offered a study in contrasts. Sánchez, the seventh prime minister of Spain in the modern era, was more than two decades Rajoy's junior. He had worked and lived abroad, spoke English and French, and understood how to use social media. He was also strikingly handsome: tall and athletic, with jet-black hair, dark-brown eyes and the chiselled looks of a television broadcaster. They called him *el guapo*, the handsome one, and more often than not they didn't mean it as a compliment. Critics dismissed him as a lightweight. Others were scandalised that he had dared to make common cause with the Catalan nationalists and the far-left Podemos party to oust Rajoy. And some noted – with surprise and a dose of admiration – that there was quite a bit of steel behind those velvety looks. Sánchez, in fact, had pulled off a remarkable political feat: Rajoy and his conservative Popular party controlled the biggest bloc of votes in parliament. Ciudadanos, the centrist party leading in the polls ahead of the political showdown, was also opposed to the Socialist motion. Sánchez needed the support of the PNV, a conservative regional party from the Basque country that had helped Rajoy pass his latest budget just a few weeks earlier. Without the five PNV lawmakers, the numbers didn't add up. But Sánchez persevered – and got the votes he needed.

For all their obvious differences, there were some things that the two men had in common. Both Rajoy and Sánchez were victims of the extreme political fragmentation that had befallen Spain, and much of the rest of Europe. Neither Rajoy's Popular party nor Sánchez and his Socialists had a majority in parliament. Sánchez, like Rajoy before him, had managed to assemble a fleeting alliance for a day that allowed him to enter office. Yet neither came close to building a long-term coalition that would provide stable government. Rajoy at least had the comfort of controlling 137 out of 350 seats in parliament.

Sánchez commanded less than a quarter of the legislature. With no reliable ally in sight, he had to test the viability of a minority government to the absolute limit. Indeed, after a brief political honeymoon, the strain started to show. He suffered his first defection from the cabinet just a week after taking office. Much like Rajoy over the course of his second tenure, Sánchez at times seemed to be in office, but not in power.

The second similarity between the two was that both were political survivors. Sánchez had been ousted from the leadership of the Socialist party in dramatic fashion less than two years before. He had spent the following months on a road trip through Spain, visiting local branches of the PSOE and talking to anyone who would listen. In Madrid, they had been quick to forget him and his talents. Out in the country, however, among the rank-and-file members of the party, Sánchez's grit and determination had won admiration. He said his voyage was part of an effort 'to listen to those who have not been listened to'.[1] In truth, he was quietly, patiently assembling a grassroots army that would carry him straight back into the office he had lost in the leadership coup in October 2016. When the time came to elect a new party chairman, in May of the following year, the PSOE base decided to punish the plotters and restore Sánchez to his former post. Almost exactly one year later, he moved on Rajoy, bringing down the man who – for all his aura of quiet detachment – sat right at the heart of the story of Spain in the years following the great crash.

The first official portrait of Mariano Rajoy hangs in a gloomy meeting room on the first floor of the provincial government building in Pontevedra. It dates from 1986 and shows the future Spanish prime minister with a thick, black beard and king-sized spectacles. There is no hint of pride on Rajoy's face, not even the faintest of smiles; he stares into the distance with the same inscrutable look he would wear so often as prime minister, three decades later.

Judging by the coarse brushwork and mangled contours, the artist did not take the commission too seriously. Why should he? The man he was painting was the outgoing president of the provincial government in Pontevedra. Most of the presidents who came before and after Rajoy were swiftly forgotten, even by the residents of this remote city in Galicia, the region in north-western Spain. There was, by all accounts, no reason to believe that the trajectory of this thirty-one-year-old conservative would be any different.

Spain's provinces form the administrative layer between the municipality and the region. Most Spaniards struggle to explain what they are actually for. Many who do know want to see them abolished, arguing that there is no need for a fourth level of state bureaucracy in a country the size of Spain. Whatever the merits of that argument, few consider the provincial government to be a springboard to political greatness. Certainly not the local leaders who knew Rajoy all those years ago. 'Rajoy was not especially popular. He had a great memory but he was shy and tried to stay away from confrontations and difficult decisions,' said José Rivas Fontán, who was mayor of Pontevedra at the time. 'Did people think he could be prime minister one day? No one.'[2]

Rajoy was underestimated, belittled and ridiculed for most of his political career. For Spain's former prime minister, being held in low regard turned out to be both a curse and a blessing. Above all, it was simply a fact of life, an essential part of his political persona. Different people had different reasons to dislike him, but they were united in disbelief that this grey man from the provinces had managed to make it so far. Right-wingers inside his own party dismissed him as a milquetoast-conservative, too bland and too fearful to press for the hardline demands – on abortion, gay marriage, taxes and Catalan independence – that they hungered for. And for the left, Rajoy would always be the man who imposed austerity at the peak of the crisis, the leader who found billions to bail out Spain's banks but slashed spending on health, education and welfare. In secession-minded regions such as Catalonia and the Basque country, Rajoy was loathed as the cold, hard face of Spanish intransigence, refusing to cede even an inch on their demands for greater autonomy and self-determination. Intellectuals in Madrid and Barcelona cringed at the prime minister's lack of worldliness. They bemoaned his inability to speak English (or any other foreign language), and sniggered at his unconcealed lack of interest in books, arts and ideas. Rajoy was a knowledgeable sports enthusiast – football and cycling in particular – but he rarely mingled with the fans. He shared the common passions, but lacked the common touch. Encounters with Rajoy were almost always marked by a certain awkwardness radiating from the man at the top.

His personal poll ratings were devastating for so long that pundits and politicians – apparently including Rajoy himself – stopped paying attention to the surveys. He was unpopular both as opposition leader, and as head of government. According to a typical poll taken just before the 2015 election, only one in four Spanish voters said they approved of their prime minister.[3] Only one in ten picked him as the best available leader for Spain. Yet he still won the election. And that was the other side of the Rajoy phenomenon. For such an unpopular man, he proved remarkably adept at staying on top. Spain's prime minister was in office for more than seven years, allowing him to outlive not just the legions of rivals and pretenders at home, but also many of his peers abroad. Whether at EU summits or G20 meetings, towards the end of his tenure, Rajoy would sit down at the table as one of the longest-serving leaders. The fact that he kept his post even after presiding over the worst economic crisis in Spain's modern history – as well as a batch of damaging corruption scandals – made his longevity even more remarkable.

Some of his critics came to see Rajoy's political career as evidence of deeper flaws within Spanish politics and society. Pedro J. Ramírez, the founder of the right-leaning *El Mundo* newspaper and one of the country's most famous journalists and editors, put it to me like this: 'The one who prospers in Spanish politics is not the most brilliant, or the best speaker, or the most intelligent, or the one with the greatest vision, or the most handsome. The one who prospers is the most docile.'[4]

Others have argued that Rajoy's success was based on a relatively uncommon combination of talents and strengths, few of which were apparent at first sight. 'Rajoy never plays the short game. He always plays the long game, and he has the discipline to see it through,' Antón Losada explained to me when the prime minister was still in office.[5] A professor of politics at the University of Santiago de Compostela and author of a book about his fellow Galician, Losada was deeply critical of Rajoy's record. But I also sensed a sneaking admiration for the skills that had got him to where he was. 'The second thing is that Rajoy is a man who knows how to manage time. He doesn't mind uncertainty and he doesn't get nervous. He resists pressure very well. And his third strength is that he has allowed others to build up a caricature of him, as this guy who only reads the sports pages, who doesn't like taking decisions and so on. Everyone is busy fighting this caricature, and not the real Rajoy. The real Rajoy is a political killer.'

When he was picked to lead the centre-right Popular party in late 2003, he was not the most imposing, or the most popular, or the most charismatic candidate. José María Aznar, the then prime minister and party leader, alighted on Rajoy because he seemed like a safe pair of hands, with the experience of four cabinet posts under his belt and a particular focus on domestic politics. Rajoy was the most affable candidate, and perhaps also the most malleable of the dauphins clamouring for the succession. After announcing his choice, Aznar praised Rajoy as 'a secure option, calm, moderate, someone you can trust'.[6] The decision was seemingly accepted by the party without reservation, though the reaction and comments from senior PP officials at the time are telling. One party leader said that even among those who didn't support him, Rajoy was always the 'second choice'. Another said: 'Rajoy doesn't have a large team of people behind him who give him unconditional support but neither does he have people who are against him.'[7]

After eight years of conservative government, the 2004 general election was supposed to be a coronation. Spain's economy was strong, and Rajoy was facing an inexperienced and gaffe-prone Socialist opponent. The final opinion polls showed the PP to have a commanding lead. Only the size of Rajoy's majority was in question. Then, three days before the election, al-Qaeda operatives blew up four commuter trains as they were pulling into Madrid's Atocha station, killing 192 people. It was the deadliest terror attack on European soil since the 1988 Lockerbie bombing. In his final days as prime minister, Aznar badly botched the aftermath of the bombings. Despite clear and growing evidence to the contrary, his government insisted that the perpetrators were members of Eta, the violent Basque separatist group. As allegations mounted that Madrid was hiding the truth for electoral reasons, voters turned their backs on the PP in droves, and Rajoy lost his first nationwide election.

Four years later, with the country enjoying the last days of tranquillity before the great crisis, he lost again. Rajoy's rivals in the PP thought their moment had come, and tried to oust him at a party conference in Valencia in June 2008. He survived, but at the price of breaking with his erstwhile mentor Aznar, who made no secret of his disappointment with his chosen successor. Rajoy knew that few leaders are allowed to lose two general elections in a row. If he lost again, he would go down in Spanish political history as a spectacular failure.

Fortunately for the PP leader, the next election really was unloseable. It took place in November 2011, in the midst of a devastating economic crisis, with one in five Spaniards out of work and markets fretting about the stability of the nation's banking system. José Luis Rodríguez Zapatero, the Socialist prime minister and the man who had beaten him back in 2004, was drained of credibility and popular support. He made way for his interior minister, but the Socialists never stood a chance. The PP won by a landslide, taking 45 per cent of the vote and an absolute majority of seats in the Spanish parliament. Not for the first time, and not for the last, Rajoy's patience and perseverance had been rewarded.

For a brief moment, the quiet Galician was riding high. His calm, unhurried nature and unflashy image, his reputation for solidity and his tendency to play things safe, seemed exactly what Spain needed in the midst of the crisis. Just as it had done in 2003, Rajoy's low-key personality looked like an asset, not a liability. To call it a honeymoon period would be wrong – he was never exactly the kind of leader who inspired love – but the period of initial bliss was quickly over all the same.

The state of the Spanish economy, it turned out, was even worse than imagined. In the years since then, Rajoy's response to the crisis would come to be seen – especially outside Spain – as his greatest achievement. The Rajoy government passed a landmark labour market reform, pushed through an aggressive plan to stabilise the banking system, and cut the deficit from 10 per cent to 4 per cent in the space of three years. After a harsh recession in 2012 and 2013, Spain returned to growth in 2014 and the economy has been expanding ever since. This turnaround tale looks impressive, but it ignores the fact that Rajoy and his cabinet were flailing around for much of the first half of 2012. They had severely underestimated the gravity of the banking crisis, wasting precious time before finally being pushed into a massive bailout which was funded by the EU. Rajoy and his ministers insisted at the time that Spain had avoided the humiliation of a sovereign bailout, because the rescue money was strictly speaking for the banking sector only, but the blow was still a severe one. Barely six months into his tenure, Rajoy was already facing questions over whether his government could survive.

Over the course of the crisis, Rajoy would come to rely heavily on a small group of advisers. The most important among them was Álvaro Nadal, a Harvard-educated economist who served as Rajoy's main economic adviser for big international meetings and summits. Supremely confident, he was prone to turn interviews into lectures, and there were rumours that he took the same approach with senior European officials and even government ministers. His admiration for Rajoy, however, struck me as generous and genuine. 'He is firm about his decisions. He has taken some of the hardest decisions of any prime minister in Spanish democracy. Once he is convinced of a decision, he sticks to it,' he told me.[8]

Like other officials in the inner Rajoy circle, Nadal painted the picture of a calm, unflappable leader who was equipped with a phenomenal memory and capacity for hard work. Rajoy, they said, never lost his nerve or raised his voice. He was loyal and expected loyalty. And – on economic matters at least – he always had his eye on the main objective. The 2012 labour market reform, for example, was certain to hasten job losses in the short term. But Rajoy – along with cabinet members such as Luis de Guindos and advisers like Nadal – was convinced that the reform would deliver benefits over time. With more than three years to go until the next general election, Rajoy felt he could trade short-term pain for long-term gain. And so he did. By the time the 2015 election came around, Spanish employers were creating half a million jobs a year.

In 2011, the year he was finally elected prime minister, Rajoy published a short book about himself and his 'project for Spain'. Written from start to finish in simple, declarative sentences, it makes no attempt to pass the author off as more sophisticated or profound than he is. He speaks of his privileged but provincial childhood in northern Spain, first in León then in Pontevedra; about his schooling, his family, the cooking of his mother and the life lessons taught by his beloved father. His youthful adventures sound, to modern ears, so mild they hardly merit mention. On page 1 of the book, he tells the story of how he travelled to the Mediterranean island of Ibiza with his cousin and three friends when he was sixteen. He asked his father for permission; his father thought it was a bad idea, yet allowed young Mariano to go on the trip regardless, and even gave him some money for the journey. It was, he concludes, 'a great adventure'. Later, during his military service, he spent six months on cleaning duty, before being put in charge of acquiring the barracks' cleaning materials. He studied law, then became the youngest ever graduate to pass the exacting test to become a property notary. His political career ebbed and flowed until he was finally called to Madrid by Aznar for a senior party job, and then to the cabinet. He married late in life, at forty-one, to Viri, whom he had met four years earlier. The couple had two sons, but any information about his family or emotional life is sparse. For the most part – especially when Rajoy sets out his political ideas – the book makes for deeply dull reading. Occasionally, however, there are flashes of that bone-dry humour that is said to be typical of Galicia. In one passage where Rajoy lavishes praise on his 'perfectionist father', he continues:

> My father, for example, did not like speaking of things he did not know about, an approach I share and which I think should be a national virtue in a country where oftentimes the opposite occurs. Sometimes the frivolity with which people speak and write of things they do not know sufficiently well is astonishing. As [Manuel] Azaña [president of the Spanish Republic 1936–9] already said, if in Spain people would only speak of things they know about, the silence would be deafening.[9]

Readers searching the book – or any of Rajoy's speeches and interviews – for signs of an overarching political ideology, for anything approaching Rajoyism, would be disappointed. He was radical only in his moderation. His brand of conservatism had nothing to do with the free-market conservatism of the centre-right in the US and the UK. If anything, Rajoy held fast to the traditional tenets of Christian Democracy as practised on the European continent: he favoured a market-based economy but with a strong social component and a pivotal role for government and the state. At the height of the crisis, and in the years since, critics on the left have sought to portray Rajoy as a slash-and-burn reformer and austerian, who dismantled the pillars of the Spanish welfare state. That charge failed to hit the mark. Rajoy did not push for structural reforms and budget cuts in 2012 as part of a broader plan to slim down the state and unshackle the markets. He did it because he and his advisers felt the steps were necessary to address grave economic imbalances. As one Madrid business leader with close ties to the PP told me at the time: 'He is a true conservative – he only does what is needed to keep the equilibrium.'

Manuel Arias Maldonado, a political scientist at the University of Málaga, put it slightly differently: 'Rajoy seems almost like a liquid leader. He must have a political core but we don't really know what it is. He doesn't have an ideological agenda that he is determined to impose. Rajoy is a reactionary in the true sense of the word – he reacts to events.'

Spain's prime minister knew when to react, but – perhaps more importantly – he also knew when to remain still. Indeed, his ability to let a situation play out, to wait for his opponents to commit mistakes, to find exactly the right moment to strike, was legendary. Perhaps the best example of this trait came in 2016, after his party emerged with the largest number of seats in the general election but failed to secure an outright majority. In a move that was widely criticised at the time, he declined the offer of King Felipe to form a new government, instead putting his Socialist rival Pedro Sánchez on the spot. Sánchez tried to form a government but failed to secure a majority in parliament, paving the way for a new election. Throughout this fraught period, Rajoy waited patiently for his moment to arrive. The repeat elections in June 2016 saw the PP expand its lead, cementing Rajoy's claim that he alone was in a position to lead a government. He fell short in his first attempt to secure a mandate from parliament, then waited some more. Eventually, after more than ten months of stalemate, the Socialists caved in, allowing the formation of a minority government under Rajoy's leadership. Half-despondent and half-admiring, former Socialist prime minister Felipe González remarked: 'Rajoy is the only creature that advances without moving.'[10]

It is a technique that the veteran leader perfected like few other modern politicians. In the hothouse world of American or British politics, advisers talk of winning the twenty-four-hour news cycle. Rajoy, in contrast, preferred to think in cycles of months, if not years. The only thing that counted for him was to win the next election – what the polls and pundits said in the intervening four years was of no relevance. Rajoy secured victory through patience, and through the lack of patience of his opponents. His long career path was lined with the bodies of rivals who were handed rope and enough time to hang themselves – and duly did so. One of Rajoy's preferred techniques was to entrust ambitious rivals with a high-profile but inherently risky task. On one occasion, it was abortion reform, a perennial source of tension in Spain. Rajoy's justice minister – a potential rival – promised to deliver on the campaign pledge to tighten the regulations put in place by his Socialist predecessor. In the face of fierce protests from women and progressives, the plan was dropped with the tacit support of the prime minister. Humiliated, the justice minister resigned from his post. On another occasion, it was the candidacy to become mayor of Madrid. Esperanza Aguirre, one of Rajoy's fiercest internal critics, was desperate to run. She did, lost, and never menaced the prime minister again.

A few weeks after my arrival in Madrid, the editor of the *Financial Times* and I went to interview Rajoy. It was a strange experience. We were ushered into a large conference room, and sat at a table the size of a boat. There was no attempt to charm us with intimacy, but a clear determination to dispel some of the well-worn perceptions about his personality. 'It is the old cliché that Rajoy never takes decisions,' he told us. 'They say about the Gallegos [Galicians] that they like to wait and see – and they say the same thing about me. But in the years since I took over the government I reduced the public deficit in a situation where we were in recession. I pushed through structural reforms and a reform of the banking sector. I would like to know: How many non-Gallegos would have taken those decisions?'[11]

When asked to describe Rajoy, Spaniards would often say that he was a typical Galician. According to a popular stereotype, the Gallego is reserved, cautious, sarcastic, reluctant to give a clear answer, always keen to keep his options open. A Spanish saying claims that if you meet a Gallego on the staircase you never know whether he is going up or down. Whether or not such clichés fit the population in general, they certainly capture something of Rajoy, who told us he was 'proud and happy' to be from Galicia.

The timing of the interview was no coincidence. Rajoy and his advisers clearly felt that the worst was over for the Spanish economy (the banking bailout had taken place six months earlier), and that Madrid finally had some good news to report. He predicted – correctly as it turned out – that the recession would end in the second half of 2013, and that the recovery would start to gain traction the following year. Beyond steering the country back from crisis, however, it was hard to make out what Rajoy wanted to be remembered for. When we asked, his response was predictably bland. He wanted to 'lay the foundation for a strong economy', he said, and 'help European integration'. Lionel Barber, my editor, was not satisfied. Where, he asked, was the poetry in his political ambition? 'Poetry?' Rajoy queried, momentarily taken aback. 'My thing is prose.'

We left the Moncloa compound thinking that Spain's prime minister had probably put the worst behind him. The economy was still in decline but bankers and business leaders were increasingly confident that Rajoy's recent reforms – and the flood of cheap money released by the European Central Bank – would soon make a difference. They were right about the economy, but in political terms, Rajoy was about to hit one of the lowest points of his career.

A few days after our interview appeared, *El Mundo* published a front-page story about alleged off-the-books cash payments made to senior Popular party leaders by the PP treasurer, Luis Bárcenas.[12] A couple of weeks later, *El País* released copies of the handwritten ledgers kept by Bárcenas himself, carefully detailing hundreds of individual cash payments he had made over the years.[13] Spain's ruling party – Rajoy's party – had apparently operated a secret slush fund for more than twenty years. The prime minister himself had, according to the ledger, received thirty-five cash payments worth a total of €322,231 between 1997 and 2008. Bárcenas, meanwhile, appeared to have used his position to amass a fortune of €48m, which was stashed away in bank accounts in Switzerland and other countries. This was, without doubt, one of the gravest political scandals to rock Spain since the country had returned to democracy in the late 1970s. Rajoy denied all wrongdoing, and in fact was never charged or even declared a formal suspect by the magistrate investigating the scandal. But there was no doubt that, whatever his direct involvement in the scandal, he did bear a heavy political responsibility. He had been the party leader for much of the time that the slush fund was in operation. He had worked closely with Bárcenas for years. Their offices were in the same building, the PP headquarters on Madrid's Calle Genova. Was it really credible that Rajoy had no idea what was going on? And if it was, should he not take responsibility all the same? This was his party. These were his people. The money had been used to further the interests of the PP – his interests. Rajoy was unrepentant. Appearing in parliament later that year, he could bring himself to admit only that he had been wrong to trust the treasurer. 'I was wrong to maintain confidence in someone who clearly did not deserve it. I was cheated,' the prime minister said in his speech to the legislature.[14] Alfredo Pérez Rubalcaba, the leader of the opposition Socialists, told Rajoy it was time to go. 'I ask you today to leave. I ask you for an act of generosity towards a country that can no longer take having a prime minister like you.' Polls showed that Pérez Rubalcaba was echoing a senti-ment felt by many Spaniards. Just as the economic crisis was drawing to a close, Rajoy found himself embroiled in a fight for his political life.

The scandal would fester for the remainder of his tenure. It would also metastasise: the Bárcenas slush fund, it turned out, was no isolated case, but part of an intricate and interlocking web of scandals that drew in more and more politicians from the Popular party. Most Spaniards soon lost track of the details of these sprawling cases, and of the roll call of names that were dragged into court to face charges of money laundering, embezzlement and fraud. What was striking was the impression – overwhelming at times – that Spanish politics, and the PP in particular, was riddled with corruption. It was this impression, more than anything else, that caused voters to turn their backs on Rajoy and his party in the following years. Asked to name their three greatest worries in November 2012, just 10 per cent of Spaniards mentioned corruption.[15] Three months and the first batch of Bárcenas revelations later, that number had increased more than four-fold. Two years later, it would reach an all-time high of 60 per cent.

It was the outrage over corruption that, eventually, caused the downfall of Rajoy. The audacious parliamentary move that led to his ousting in May 2018 did not come out of nowhere. It was a direct response to a landmark court ruling in the Bárcenas case that was handed down by the national criminal court just one week earlier.[16] The judges imposed prison sentences ranging from five months to fifty-one years on twenty-nine defendants; Bárcenas was jailed for thirty-three years and four months, and ordered to pay a fine of more than €44m. The real blow for Rajoy came elsewhere in the verdict. First, the court found that even the PP had enriched itself illegally, and ordered the party to pay a fine of €245,000. Secondly, and more damaging still, the court said it doubted the 'credibility' of the testimony provided by Rajoy himself. That was the opening that Sánchez and the other opposition leaders had been waiting for. Never before had the prime minister looked so weak: the political quagmire in Catalonia had already raised questions over his leadership, polls showed the PP to be in freefall, and the party's grip on parliament was precarious at best. The only thing missing was an excuse to pull the trigger – and that excuse came in the form of the 24 May court ruling. The Socialists filed their no-confidence motion the following day. Rajoy dismissed the move as a stunt, but he was clearly rattled – so rattled, in fact, that he hastily cancelled a trip to see an important football match (his beloved Real Madrid were due to play Liverpool FC in the final of the Champions League the following day). By the end of the next week, he was packing his bags for good.

The end of Rajoy came so suddenly and so dramatically that it was easy to overlook perhaps the most remarkable aspect of the entire business: how long it took for the corruption scandals finally to bring him down. Rajoy remained prime minister for more than five years after news of the Bárcenas scandal first broke – far longer than even the most optimistic pundit had predicted at the time. How he survived, why he survived, was a question that tormented the prime minister's many critics on a daily basis. Pedro J. Ramírez, the editor whose paper broke some of the most damaging stories, thought that Rajoy should have stepped down after *El Mundo* published text messages sent by the prime minister to Bárcenas. 'Luis, be strong,' one of them said.[17] It was written after the scandal surfaced. The text messages, and the *El Mundo* front page revealing them, would be flung in the face of Rajoy during parliamentary debates, television shows and in the media again and again. But even that barrage failed to sink the prime minister.

In my own view, Rajoy was able to ride out the affair for so long due to three key factors. Most importantly, for much of the time, he enjoyed an absolute majority in parliament, and could count on a party determined to close ranks. There were no obvious challengers to the prime minister inside the PP – or at least none who were untainted by the scandals themselves. No less important was the fact that prosecutors and investigating magistrates never accused Rajoy personally of any wrongdoing. Until the May 2018 verdict and the passage about his credibility, he was able to brush aside all accusations against him as mere speculation. The ruling shattered that pretension. The final reason for his survival was less obvious, and was related to the peculiarities of Rajoy's character, and the public perception of the prime minister.

I was alerted to this factor in a conversation with Jorge Galindo, a political analyst and columnist, who explained one of Rajoy's secret strengths with a simple sentence: 'Just look at the cartoons.' He was right. Looking at the cartoons in papers such as *El País* and *El Mundo* had long been a favourite part of my morning ritual. Biting, sharp, funny and – quite often – profound, they offered some of the most trenchant commentary on political affairs in Spain. All had their own peculiar way of portraying Rajoy: Peridis in *El País*, for example, usually depicted Rajoy lying down – sometimes half-asleep – on a plush chaise longue, a leader forever in repose. Ricardo, the brilliant cartoonist in *El Mundo*, liked to draw Rajoy on one of those armchairs with a pop-up footrest, or talking to his wife in bed. They, and other satirists, were poking fun at Rajoy's perceived slowness, his provincialism, his desire to be left in peace, his tendency to sit and wait until a problem disappeared. They never showed him driving flashy cars, or counting banknotes. They never showed him being greedy. The cartoonists – and the country at large – sensed that the prime minister, whatever his failings, was not likely to have acted out of a rapacious desire for personal financial gain. The man's tastes were simply too ordinary for that. Some of his party colleagues had clearly developed a fondness for the high life – for yachts, hunting trips, nice cars and elegant seaside villas. Rajoy, in contrast, unfailingly spent his summers in rainy Galicia, close to Pontevedra, walking around the countryside in ill-fitting leisurewear. He seemed, perhaps even to his critics, to be simply too boring to be corrupt.

If Rajoy's strengths remained somewhat hidden, his weaknesses were always plain to see: his lack of charisma, his difficulty in connecting with people, the absence of an idea or ambition that went beyond being a competent manager of the state. There were moments when his determination to govern in prose not poetry turned into a severe handicap. At the height of the crisis, for example, I was struck by the fact that Rajoy never showed up at an unemployment centre to meet desperate jobseekers, or invited young unemployed people to talk to him at Moncloa. He never found the words to rally, inspire and comfort a nation roiled by insecurity and economic misery. He lacked empathy – or the words to give voice to his empathy – at a moment when millions of Spaniards were left without hope. Some of his advisers and party colleagues were clearly aware of this failing, but when I asked them about it, all they could do was shrug. This was just the way he was: defensive, averse to risk, but also averse to the human element in politics. Rajoy gave countless speeches setting out his reform plans, and promising a better future, but he could never bring himself to say: I feel your pain.

Rajoy's political and personal traits seemed well suited to steer the country through the crisis. He took his decisions rationally, without fretting about the short-term damage he was doing to his electoral standing. Yet other aspects of Rajoy's personality – his caution and passivity, his reluctance to move boldly and swiftly, and his inability to channel the public's fears – also meant that he stayed on the sidelines at critical moments that demanded leadership of the kind he was unable to provide. Catalonia was the paramount example. Looking back at the years leading up to the October 2017 clash, I could not help but wonder: Was there really no point at which Rajoy and his government could have taken steps to defuse the conflict? Was there no proposal he was willing to put on the table to persuade moderate nationalists to keep faith in the union? Had there really been no better way to deal with the illegal October referendum than to send in the riot police?

Here was the gravest political challenge facing Spain since the transition to democracy, yet Rajoy was reluctant to take the initiative. Caught between his own preference for reaction over action, and the fierce hostility towards the Catalan independence movement among his own party, Rajoy retreated into empty phrases and legal arguments: The law had to be upheld. The constitution had to be defended. There would be no referendum.

There was nothing wrong per se with any of those statements. Of course the democratically elected head of the Spanish government had to uphold the law. Of course Madrid could not permit flagrant violations of the country's constitution. But in a time of crisis, a prime minister should have done more than that. It was incumbent on Rajoy to show a way out of the Catalan labyrinth, to make a proposal, to entice and to cajole, to persuade and seduce. Catalans felt the hard arm of the state, barring their path towards independence. They rarely heard the calm voice of Madrid making the case why secession was wrong in the first place, why Spain and Catalonia were – to echo the campaign against Scottish independence – better together. And if Rajoy was the wrong man to make that case, why did he not find men and women to make the case for him? Why were there no Catalans in his government? And why was no effort made to give Catalonia a larger stake in Spain and its institutions? There was no shortage of proposals, changes and gestures that could have been made – from expanding the teaching of Catalan in Spanish schools to moving institutions such as the Senate to Barcelona. None was ever debated by the Rajoy government.

Today, the prime minister may have changed, but the challenges facing the government in Madrid have not. Spaniards went to the polls again in April 2019, the third electoral contest in less than four years, and once again the result failed to deliver a clear majority. As the results came in on the night of 29 April, it became clear that Sánchez had led the PSOE to its best result in years, taking 28.7 per cent of the vote. Fragmentation – for so long an ailment of the left – had gripped the right on this occasion. Led by Pablo Casado, the young conservative who replaced Rajoy as leader of the PP, the centre-right party lost more than half its seats in parliament. Even in combination with the far-right Vox party and the centrist Ciudadanos movement, Casado came nowhere near the number of votes he needed to become prime minister. The Socialist triumph, however, was tinged with regret. Even with the support of Podemos and the backing of smaller regional parties, Sánchez fell just shy of a working majority in parliament. For the third time in a row, Spain's electorate had delivered a legislature so fragmented that decisive government action seemed unlikely.

Given what lies ahead, the country's drift towards ungovernability is lamentable. Sánchez – and whoever comes after him – must keep the recovery alive, ensure that unemployment continues to fall, and make certain that the economic scars left by the great crisis can heal at last. No less important, he or she must find a way to prevent a fresh surge in tensions with Catalonia, and lay the groundwork for a new political process aimed at resolving the region's grievances. Sánchez's approach to Catalonia is – at least in theory – different from the stonewalling tactics employed by his predecessor. As the Socialist leader has made clear repeatedly, he believes that only a reform of Spain's constitution can solve the Catalan crisis. His vision is that of a federal state, in which the responsibilities of regional and central government would be much more clearly defined. Beyond that, a revised constitution would have to recognise the 'singularities' of certain regions such as Catalonia. As Sánchez told me in an interview more than three years before taking office: 'It is perfectly possible to resolve the crisis in Catalonia by way of constitutional reform. But for that we need political will. We have it. Sadly, Rajoy doesn't.'[18] In the first few months after taking office, there were occasional flashes of that will, but little in the way of concrete action. A reform of the constitution requires a two-thirds majority in parliament, a level of support that Sánchez was never likely to obtain. Much like his predecessor, the new prime minister learnt quickly that minority government and bold politics rarely go hand-in-hand.

As for Rajoy, his legacy is likely to be a mixed one. Corruption, and the resulting loss of trust in politics, is certain to loom large in any assessment of his tenure. Beyond that, I would not be surprised if Rajoy will come to be seen as the leader who boldly led Spain out of its worst economic crisis in modern history – only to stand by and watch as the nation succumbed to a political crisis unlike any it has faced since the death of Franco.

CHAPTER SEVEN

A history of violence

It's in the eyes, Carlos Totorika said.

If you want to understand what is happening in the Basque country, you have to look into people's eyes. 'You notice it in the eyes if someone hates you or not. You see it in an instant, even if they don't say a word,' he told me. 'And the eyes look different now. People are leaving the hate behind. You notice it in the bars. You notice it in meetings. You see it in their eyes.'[1]

Totorika was a young man when he was first elected mayor of Ermua, a small town in the Spanish Basque country, back in 1991. He has been mayor ever since. Now a silver-haired man in his sixties, he has learnt everything there is to know about hate, and what it does to people. He buried comrades killed by an assassin's bullet, and saw his own name, address and car licence plate on a terrorist target list. He spent fifteen years walking in the shadow of armed bodyguards. The men were there to protect his life, yet they reminded Totorika that he, too, was a prisoner of the murderous political climate in his homeland. Then, suddenly, everything changed.

After five decades of terror the Basque separatist group Eta[2] decided to abandon what it called its 'armed activity'. The news broke on 20 October 2011, sparking joy and relief right across Spain. In the years leading up to Eta's announcement, the group's operational capacity – its ability to kill and maim – had been severely weakened by the increasingly close co-operation between police in Spain and France, which led to a string of high-profile arrests. The French Basque country, for decades both a hiding place and command centre, was no longer a safe haven for the gunmen of Eta. But the group also seemed exhausted by the growing hostility towards its senseless deeds coming from within its own camp of sympathisers. As observers were quick to point out, Northern Ireland had been freed from the scourge of political violence more than a decade before. That left Eta as the last home-grown terror group in Western Europe. With every year that passed, its actions seemed not just brutally amoral, but also anachronistic.

The 2011 announcement brought an end to a bloody campaign that had started in 1968, when Eta killed its first victim, a police officer. Founded a decade earlier, the group initially set out to fight against the dictatorship of Francisco Franco, and to campaign for the independence of the greater Basque country, a region straddling both sides of the Franco-Spanish border. Much like the people of Catalonia, the two million Basques living in Spain had long prided themselves on their distinct culture, history and – perhaps more than anything else – their language. Basque is a unique linguistic phenomenon, entirely unrelated to Spanish, and is the only surviving language that predates the arrival of Indo-European languages in Western Europe. Many Basques saw – and still see – themselves as a nation apart, with norms, customs and values that differ from those of the rest of Spain. That notion, however, was twisted into a murderous perversion by Eta over its decades-long campaign of violence. The group went on to assassinate Franco's chosen successor in 1973, a killing that had profound political repercussions. In the years that followed, Eta's attacks grew increasingly indiscriminate, with the vast majority of murders committed long after Spain returned to democracy. Estimates vary but the most detailed study to date puts the number of Eta victims at 845.[3] Most died in the small sliver of land the group claimed to be fighting for.

Now, finally, the killing was over, and so was the fear of being killed. Politicians, prosecutors, judges and journalists stopped looking over their shoulders and under their cars. Hundreds were relieved of their bodyguards. 'I am a free man,' Totorika said. 'I live without fear. I can walk home without people walking by my side. I can go out with my wife. I can go to the cinema.' We were sitting in his office, on the first floor of Ermua's imposing Baroque town hall. It was a gloomy, rain-lashed day, not untypical for the Basque country. But the mayor's eyes lit up as he reflected on his new life. 'It is wonderful. There is no other word for it. To live freely and without fear is wonderful.'

The sense of wonder was evident across the Basque country, from the villages in Gipuzkoa that were once a bastion of Eta support to the boulevards of Bilbao and San Sebastián. There was talk of a return to normality, and an effort to bolster what Spaniards call *convivencia* – living together. Many saw a bright new future for the Basque country, already one of the richest regions in Spain, an industrial powerhouse and a magnet for tourists and foreign investors alike. The leaden atmosphere of terror had finally given way to a lighter mood: Basques today are counting Michelin stars, not bodies.

In the years since the Eta announcement, regional politics – once murderously divisive – had become almost ordinary. A few months before my conversation with the mayor of Ermua, I watched Iñigo Urkullu at a campaign event in Basauri, an industrial town just outside Bilbao. I was there to cover the September 2016 regional election, the first to be held without the threat of Eta violence hanging over the country. Urkullu, the regional president, seemed the perfect candidate for this tranquil new era: he spoke calmly and slowly, more family doctor than political firebrand, switching from Basque to Spanish and Spanish to Basque after every paragraph in his speech. He promised new water treatment plants, more jobs and better care for the elderly. Though he and his party defined themselves as Basque national-ists, Urkullu avoided all talk of an independent Basque state. And he kept firmly to the campaign motto that was displayed in giant letters behind the stage: Look to the future.

Bland as it may have sounded, the slogan of the governing Basque National party (PNV) would ultimately propel Urkullu to yet another comfortable election victory. It also captured the broader spirit of the moment. The Basque country went to the polls in 2016 determined not to dwell on the past. After decades of bloodshed, terror and fear, voters were revelling in a new kind of politics. Many here spoke of a return to normality, or whatever counted as normality in a territory scarred by political violence like few others in Europe. 'The issue of terrorism and of Eta used to hang over Basque politics like a toxic cloud,' Andoni Ortuzar, the head of the PNV and a close ally of Urkullu's told me.[4] A small, rotund man with a shiny bald head and an easy smile, Ortuzar was visibly delighted by the new political reality. 'The fact that Eta has disappeared from our lives means we can now have the kind of political debate that all other modern societies have,' he said. 'We talk about jobs, and social policies, and about self-government and our relationship with Madrid. We also talk about peace and reconciliation, but in a way that is no longer contaminated by Eta violence.'

At a time when Catalonia was pressing for secession with more urgency than ever, the issue of Basque independence had been pushed firmly to the margins. 'For more than thirty years, the independence movement was stronger in the Basque country than in Catalonia. Now it is the other way round,' said Alfredo Retortillo, a professor of politics at the University of the Basque Country.[5] A week before the 2016 elections, a poll found that only 18 per cent of Basques supported an independent state – an exceedingly low number by historical standards, and far below the level in Catalonia.[6] The apparent decline in separatist sentiment, Retortillo argued, was at least partly explained by the region's strong economic performance. Spain's recent crisis had hit the Basque region, too, but its strong industrial base and export-driven corporate sector meant the region was less brutally affected than other parts of the country. 'In the Basque country it is much harder than in Catalonia to convince people that they should support independence on pragmatic grounds,' he told me over coffee in a bar next to Bilbao's famous San Mamés football stadium. 'It is hard to tell them they will be better off in a separate country. People here already think they are doing better than the rest of Spain.'

For most people living there, an independent Basque country seemed neither viable nor desirable. Unlike Catalonia, the region already enjoyed sweeping financial autonomy. It raised its own taxes and spent its own money, allowing the government in the regional capital of Vitoria far more leeway to determine its own political course. Crucially, that deprived Basque secessionists of perhaps the most potent argument for independence; for good and for bad, the political and economic fate of the Basque country was already largely in Basque hands. 'Spain robs us' – that great Catalan battle cry – was not a phrase anyone could seriously utter in Bilbao or San Sebastián. For the governing PNV, that meant there was little incentive to ratchet up the secessionist pressure. Instead, it adopted a distinctly pragmatic stance. It would defend the Basque country's special status and tax privileges to the hilt – but it was also ready to help out the Spanish government of the day on difficult votes (Rajoy's minority government would come to rely heavily on PNV support in Madrid, though the Basques would eventually play a key role in his downfall as well).

The recent story of the Basque country offered an instructive counterpoint to the territorial tensions that gripped Spain in the wake of the crisis: it showed how a region with a strong historic claim to nationhood could find its place within Spain. Some of this clearly had to do with fiscal arrangements and economic performance. But it was also striking how easily Basque politicians found their role inside Spain's leading political parties, whether on the right or on the left. There were Basque ministers in the government of Rajoy, and Basque lawmakers competing for the post of Socialist leader. More interesting still, I thought, was that their presence struck everyone involved as normal. Their Basqueness was not an issue (and neither had it been an issue in previous years, when Eta was still active). In the case of Catalonia, this was different. A Socialist leader from Catalonia would have been probed endlessly on his or her views on secession and self-determination. Most likely, he or she would have been treated with a degree of suspicion. Being Catalan and Spanish was awkward – not for everyone, but for many. Being Basque and Spanish, in contrast, seemed much less fraught. What that meant for the conflict in Catalonia was not easy to tell. But I thought the Basque experience offered a powerful reminder that greater autonomy and closer allegiance could indeed go hand-in-hand. In the Basque country, region and state had found a settlement – legally and emotionally – that appeared to be working, at least for the moment.

'Here, in the heart, we will continue to want independence,' Ortuzar told me, thumping his chest. His head, however, had pushed him and other PNV leaders towards a different proposition: constitutional recognition as a separate nation within Spain, new guarantees for Basque autonomy, and a new relation of equality between Madrid and the territory in the north. Independence, Ortuzar said, was an 'unviable project in the Europe of today'. Mindful of the deep divisions that remained in Basque society, he added: 'It is not worth tearing apart the country for the sake of independence.'

He was right to be cautious. For amid the new-found political tranquillity, it was hard not to detect an undercurrent of tension. There was too much unfinished business. On one side of the political divide, there was bitterness that Eta's announcement had not prompted conciliatory steps from the Spanish govern-ment, for example with regard to the treatment of Eta prisoners, many hundreds of whom continued to languish in Spanish jails. On the other side, there was exasperation that Eta took another seven years formally to disband, and that it refused to hand over its weapons to the Spanish authorities. Eta continued to make news, albeit sporadically, whenever one of its dwindling band of members was arrested by the French or Spanish police, or when it released another weapons cache to international observers. In April 2018 Eta broke new ground by issuing an apology to its victims, or at least to those 'who did not take part directly in the conflict'. The statement still fell short of Madrid's demands for a complete cessation, but was widely interpreted as a step towards formal disbandment.

One month later, finally, Eta did. In a short letter released on 2 May 2018, the group announced that the 'journey has ended'.[7] Eta had 'dismantled all its structures' and 'put an end to all its political activity'. The letter removed whatever doubts had lingered in Basque and Spanish minds since 2011: Eta was gone and it would not be coming back. At the same time, the group's final communiqué made clear that the broader struggle – for an independent Basque state and a break with Spain – was far from over. 'The conflict did not start with Eta and it does not end with the end of Eta's journey,' it said.[8]

There was another source of tension in the years since the guns had fallen silent, one that was easy to detect yet hard to define. It showed up in the words that people used to describe the recent past, in the way they counted the victims, and the starting point they chose to tell their tale. It had to do with the struggle to fit a million memories of fear and loss into a broader narrative, and find a version of history that was generous enough to unite a people torn by trauma, yet true enough to sort victims from perpetrators. It was about who got to tell the Basque history of violence, and how.

This was no academic dispute between rival historians, although historians played an important role. This was the struggle that breaks out every time a cruel regime falls, a campaign of terror ends or a civil war draws to a close. Who was right and who was wrong? What must we do so the killing does not happen again? And what was the reason we started shooting in the first place? The questions that were being asked in the Basque country were the same ones that haunted South Africa and Bosnia a generation ago, and that have surfaced more recently in places such as Northern Ireland and Colombia. Then as now, many prefer not to ask. But those who do are well aware that defining the past means shaping the future. And, according to some of the leading combatants in the Basque struggle over memory and history, it was a contest that neither side dared to lose.

The Basque country is tiny – just a quarter of the size of Belgium, and a bit larger than the US state of Delaware. But it packs an awful lot of geography into that small area, from the rough Atlantic coast to the peaks of the Basque Mountains and a patchwork of steep, narrow valleys in between. Building land is so scarce – and so much is taken up by industry – that even small towns have been forced to build high-rise buildings. This is no quiet countryside: wherever one looks, one sees bridges, railway lines, factories, apartment blocks and ancient churches jostling for space.

The drive from Ermua to Lasarte, a small town just outside San Sebastián, took less than an hour. There was no one to talk to here, just a place to find. I wanted to see the scene of a notorious crime that had been committed two decades ago – the murder of Miguel Angel Blanco.

I was told that locals were normally reluctant to speak about the killing, but this new era seemed to have made people more relaxed. Within minutes of my ordering a few *pintxos* – the typical Basque snacks – in a local bar, the waiter had tracked down one of the ambulance drivers who had recovered the body. We set off in his ancient Volvo, along the river and past the old railway bridge, until the car came to an abrupt halt at a bend in the single-lane track. 'It was here,' my guide said. There was nothing to see except trees and undergrowth glistening in the rain. The ground rose steeply on both sides of the river but there was a flat section by the fast-flowing stream that would have been just big enough to stage an execution. As unremarkable as the scenery appeared, what happened here changed the course of Basque history.

A twenty-nine-year-old local councillor from Ermua, Blanco had served on the same council as Carlos Totorika. He was a member of the conservative Popular party, and Totorika a life-long Socialist. But the mayor liked the young councillor, and admired his courage. He remembered Blanco telling the mother of an Eta prisoner in a public meeting that her son was a criminal not a hero. Such plain speaking was rare and dangerous in the Basque country at the time. Still, Blanco thought he had no reason to be afraid. He always told his family and friends that he was not important enough to be an Eta target.

He was wrong. Blanco was abducted by an Eta commando unit in July 1997, held for forty-eight hours, and finally taken to this forest outside Lasarte. His killers forced him to kneel on the ground, before firing two bullets into his head. He was still breathing and had a pulse when the ambulance arrived. Blanco's family, which had been wrongly informed that he had suffered only light injuries, raced to the hospital in San Sebastián full of hope. But he never stood a chance. Blanco died from his wounds at 4.30 a.m. on 13 July 1997.[9]

Eta had killed hundreds of people before, and would kill dozens more afterwards. But this time was different. Perhaps it was the person of Blanco himself, a small-time local politician with a soft face and dreamy look who appeared even younger than his years. Or it was the psychological torture inflicted on his family and friends, who knew that Madrid had a firm policy of never acceding to any demand handed down by Eta. The group had told the government to move all Eta prisoners to jails in the Basque country within forty-eight hours, but the deadline had served no purpose other than to keep Blanco's family, and the nation, in cruel suspense.

This time, however, Spaniards refused to wait meekly for the inevitable. In the two days between Blanco's abduction and his killing, an estimated six million people took part in rallies and vigils across the country to demand his release. In the Basque country, ordinary citizens also decided it was time to stand up to Eta and its sympathisers. The revulsion was universal, and would follow the group all the way to 2011; Eta had killed a man, but it dug a grave for its own ambitions along the way.

In Ermua, where locals had waited, hoped and prayed outside the town hall for two days and two nights, it fell to Totorika to break the news. Television cameras captured the moment, and the collective howl of anguish and rage that drowned out the mayor's words. Fearing that the angry crowd might be goaded into attacking known Eta sympathisers in Ermua, Totorika decided to lead a spontaneous demonstration. 'We marched for three hours in the brutal sun,' he recalled. It was a desperate attempt to channel the raw emotion into activity, and prevent the town from descending into a spiral of violence and retribution. All the local politicians and activists with affiliations to Eta had already left town or had shut themselves away in their homes. The street was no longer theirs. It was – perhaps for the first time ever – their turn to fear the wrath of the people.

'When they killed my brother, no one came up with the slightest justification. It took people until 1997 to realise that the victim of terrorism is innocent,' Mari Mar Blanco told me.[10] She was twenty-three years old when her older brother was abducted and killed. The sense of loss was still raw when I spoke to her in her Madrid office two decades later. But, looking back, she also saw the murder as a rare moment of moral clarity for Basque society. 'People realised that the victims are always the innocent ones, and the perpetrators are always the guilty ones.'

The image of Blanco's grief-stricken face as she watched her brother's coffin being carried down the streets of Ermua is still etched into the minds of many Spaniards. The country took the death of Miguel Angel Blanco personally, in a way it had never done before. 'I remember people telling me: "He is only twenty-nine,"' she said. 'Not that the killing would have been any more justified if he had been forty but somehow people looked at him and saw a son, a brother, a boyfriend. People would tell me: "I have a picture of your brother in my living room, next to the photo of my family." Everyone in that moment saw him as part of their family.'

Today, Mari Mar Blanco is a member of parliament for the ruling Popular party, and a prominent advocate for Spanish victims of terror. She appears regularly on the pages of the conservative media, but has a much lower profile in her native Basque country. The PP is a mere splinter party in the region, where the main conservative force is the moderately nationalist PNV of Urkullu and Ortuzar. Indeed, many Basques view Spain's centre-right party much like Blanco regards the region's radical secessionists: as hardliners, extreme and divisive. 'They know that they lost,' Blanco told me. 'They will never admit it in public but they know they were defeated. And they know they cannot afford to lose the other battle – the battle for the historical narrative.' She added: '*We* cannot afford to lose this battle.'

One prominent combatant in this particular struggle is Florencio Domínguez, a soft-spoken former journalist who now presides over the Foundation for the Memory of Victims of Terror. His office in the Basque capital of Vitoria was as bare as a monk's cell when I visited him in late 2016, but it offered a view of the building site across the road that will one day house a museum dedicated to the history of terror in the Basque country. One of Domínguez's tasks was to fill the building with objects, pictures, words – and a coherent narrative. He also oversaw a well-funded research programme that involved many of the Basque country's most prominent historians.

'We are in a paradoxical situation. Younger people who are now in their twenties have little direct experience of terrorism. They are not well informed, and this all seems like a distant thing to them. And then we have the grown-up generation that knows from experience what terrorism is. But they often just want to turn the page,' Domínguez said. 'We want to reach as many people as possible, make them aware of what terrorism is and make clear that there is no justification for terrorism.'[11] That educational impulse, he admitted, had run into two serious obstacles. One was the desire, shared by many Basques, to move on and simply forget about the past. The other was a powerful counter-narrative that viewed the recent history of the Basque country differently: as a conflict between two sides, in which both Eta and the Spanish government had committed their own share of abuses, and in which both sides had suffered trauma, death and injustice.

'They are trying to win one battle because they lost the other,' said José Antonio Pérez, a professor of history at the University of the Basque Country, who was in charge of the terrorism research group.[12] A thin, ascetic-looking man with a grey goatee and dark eyes, Pérez was one of the foremost experts on Eta and the group's impact on Basque society. He was also one of the researchers behind the most authoritative study to date on the victims of terrorism in the region, a grim 190-page document whose sober prose and dry tables sought to counter some of the historical mythology that surrounded Eta.[13] 'They lost the military battle. But there is still the battle for the historical narrative. If you convince, you win,' Pérez said.

He went on: 'The story they are trying to establish is that there was a political conflict that is both origin and justification for the violence [of Eta]. They are putting in place a whole sprawling apparatus of pseudo-history that tries to place the actions of Eta within a sea of different violations and sufferings. As Hannah Arendt once said, where everyone is guilty, no one is.

*

'They' are the members of the so-called Izquierda Abertzale, the pro-independence radical left in the Basque country. This was the movement that provided the political element in Eta's 'politico-military strategy'. Over the years, the Izquierda Abertzale gave birth to a variety of political parties, some of which – like Herri Batasuna – were banned by Spanish courts for their close ties to Eta. As time went by, more and more members of the movement turned against Eta's violence. But in the battle for narrative raging today, they insist that the recent history of the Basque country is no simple tale of darkness and light.

'We need to construct a history that is inclusive – a history of histories. What we don't need is a history of victors and vanquished.' That was the central argument of Arnaldo Otegui, the leader of EH Bildu, a Basque political party that is the latest – and likely most permanent – incarnation of the Izquierda Abertzale. A former member of Eta, Otegui spent long years in jail, most recently for his role in trying to re-establish the banned Herri Batasuna party. He was released in 2016, just in time for the Basque regional elections, though a Spanish court subsequently banned him from running as a candidate.

In the rest of Spain, he was – and is – loathed as an apologist for terror by all but a small minority. In the Basque country, things are different. EH Bildu won 21 per cent of the vote in the 2016 ballot, making it the second-largest bloc in the regional parliament. Otegui himself won praise, even from some of his political opponents, for helping to push Eta towards its 2011 declaration. Unsurprisingly, that was also the view of Otegui. 'Eta is no longer engaged in armed struggle because the Izquierda Abertzale took the political decision. If the Izquierda Abertzale had not taken that decision – to say we have to end this phase, we have to pursue political and democratic paths – then Eta would still be active today. I have no doubt at all about this.'[14]

Otegui insisted that the era of violence was over. But he also warned against a version of history that presented Eta's deeds in isolation. 'If you look at the history of this [Basque] country, you will see that in the last three or four centuries there is not one generation that hasn't known armed conflict,' he told me, sitting in a messy back room of the Basque parliament in Vitoria. 'Evidently, there is a political reason why this is happening. That is not to justify what happened. But to hide it is absurd.'

To understand the abyss in perception that threatens any discussion of Basque history and politics, I headed to Hernani, just a short drive inland from San Sebastián. A prosperous town with an unemployment rate far below the national average and an old town brimming with bars and shops, Hernani did not look like an obvious breeding ground for political violence. Yet this was the very heart of Abertzale territory. For many decades, Hernani and the towns and villages around it served as a crucial source of manpower, funding and political support for Eta. No fewer than 23 of the four hundred or so Eta prisoners still in jail at the time of my visit were from tiny Hernani. Walking around town, I was reminded of something Pérez, the historian, had told me a few days before: 'The Basque country has the highest quality of life [in Spain]. What we saw here was terrorism of the rich. The areas where Eta enjoyed the strongest support were the areas with the highest income per capita not just in the Basque country but in all of Spain.'

Here, too, it used to be hard for journalists to find people who would talk.[15] But the recent political thaw had opened both minds and doors. One led me to the small, tidy apartment of Ricardo Mendiola, a life-long Abertzale who served as mayor of Hernani from 1983 to 1987. It was a period that brought a horrific wave of violence and death to the Basque country. 'There was fear and there was hatred. Visceral hatred,' he recalled.[16] For Mendiola and his voters, the fear and the hate were not directed at Eta but at the Spanish police and the security forces – and at mercenary far-right death squads such as the notorious Grupos Antiterroristas de Liberación (GAL). Financed and supported by senior members of the Socialist government, the GAL alone had killed twenty-seven Eta operatives and suspects between 1983 and 1987, often burying them in anonymous quicklime graves. In total, far-right and paramilitary groups murdered sixty-two people, mostly members or sympathisers of Eta.[17]

The so-called *guerra sucia* (dirty war) waged during that era forms one of the darkest chapters in the history of modern Spain. The interior minister at the time of the GAL killings was one of several top officials who would later be convicted in court for their links to the group. But it was also the security apparatus itself that stretched the limits of state authority to breaking point. A study released by the Basque regional government in 2016 found that more than 4000 detainees were tortured by Spanish security officers between 1960 and 2013.[18] Reports by the UN detailed cases of torture as recently as 2004[19] (prompting strong denials from Madrid, where officials argued that Eta had invented torture claims to blacken the government's name abroad). Mendiola told me that for many years he and his neighbours lived in constant fear of the Guardia Civil. Police torture – including beatings, asphyxiation, sleep deprivation and stress positions – was so widespread, he claimed, that 'it could happen to anyone'.

Torture, the GAL, quicklime graves – these were the memories that resonated in towns such as Hernani. They also loomed large in the thick set of ring-binders containing the official town history that sat waiting for me on a table when I entered the mayor's office. Luis Intxauspe, who hailed from the same party as Otegui, insisted from the outset that the local history project had nothing to do with the version being written by the professors in Vitoria. 'When we talk about historical memory our view goes back to 1936 and the start of Francoism. That is where we begin the historical narrative,' the mayor said. Eta, he added, could not be understood in isolation. 'The problem and the conflict did not start when Eta was founded and didn't stop with the end of Eta... Memory has to be integral, and has to capture all the sufferings in this village. So we start in 1936 and we finish [today], because the consequences of the conflict are still very notable. This village, for example, still has 23 [Eta] prisoners that are dispersed across Spain.'[20]

His argument went to the heart of the Abertzale intellectual defence: yes, Eta had committed atrocities. But these came, at least initially, in response to Francoist atrocities. And they in turn provoked atrocities committed by the Spanish state, or at least sanctioned by leading members of the Spanish state. What is more, the injustices committed by the government were never seriously punished, while Eta's gunmen continued to languish in jail. That, in essence, was the narrative put forward by Abertzale leaders and their supporters. Where the likes of Mari Mar Blanco saw killers and victims, they saw a complicated web of crimes and responsibilities in which everyone was guilty – and no one was guilty. In their worldview, not even Spain's transition from dictatorship to democracy made a difference. Mendiola, the former mayor, summed up the typical Abertzale opinion of the transition when he told me that 'the old [Francoist] regime continued, they just changed the name'.

To me, the argument seemed absurd. Spain's transition to democracy was far from perfect, but to argue that there was no difference between dictatorship and democracy struck me as wilful blindness. In the quest to explain why the terror had lasted so long, however, this belief was a factor that could not be ignored. Eta kept on killing not least because it retained the support of a small but significant part of Basque society that regarded modern Spain as a legitimate target, and because tens of thousands of Basques had been hardened by the experience of state repression and violence.

Historians like Pérez did not question the crimes of the Franco dictatorship, nor the violations committed during the dirty war in the name of Spanish democracy. But he remained deeply wary of the broader reasoning. There was, he argued, no straight, simple line that linked the Franco dictatorship to the killings of Eta to the murders of the GAL and to the situation of Eta prisoners today. 'For them, context means justification,' he said. Whatever the crimes of the Franco regime, they could not be taken as an excuse for a wave of killings that ended thirty-six years after the death of the dictator. Indeed, more than 90 per cent of Eta victims were killed after Spain's transition from dictatorship to democracy. The GAL, meanwhile, killed its last victim in 1987 – a decade before the murder of Miguel Angel Blanco. It took Eta another fourteen years before the group finally decided to end the 'armed struggle'.

The issue of Eta prisoners, meanwhile, remained acute – and intensely controversial. In places like Hernani, they were awarded a status approaching martyrdom. The narrow lanes of the old town were plastered with banners showing their faces and names. There was a black-and-white mural near the town hall with portraits of all the Eta prisoners from Hernani (among them Mendiola's nephew). Every time a prisoner was released, his or her portrait was struck off. Abertzale leaders insisted that all the prisoners be freed, as would happen in any normal post-conflict agreement. At the very least, they said, the Spanish government should end the policy of dispersal, and allow the prisoners to complete their sentence in a Basque jail. Many had been put in prisons in faraway Andalucia and other distant regions – part of an effort by the Spanish authorities to prevent communication and curb the group's operational capability.

In Madrid such pleas cut little ice. As long as Eta refused to hand over its remaining weapons and formally disband, the Rajoy government declined to contemplate any alteration in its prison policy. The 2018 change of government in Madrid brought tentative signs of change, but little more: three months after taking office, the new Socialist-led administration announced that it was moving two Eta prisoners from nearby Asturias to detention facilities in the Basque country.[21] But the government insisted that the transfers were based on existing rules, and should not be read as a broader gesture. As for the notion of a normal post-conflict settlement, the view in Madrid never wavered: there was no conflict. Eta killers were murderers plain and simple, and would be treated as such.

The real outrage, said Mari Mar Blanco, was the hero's welcome that released Eta prisoners continued to receive, and the acts of public homage that were still common in places like Hernani. Like many Spanish politicians who had experienced the sharp end of terror, she insisted that there could be no compromise, no concession and no negotiation with the group and its sympathisers. 'The younger generation needs to know that to kill, as Eta did, achieves nothing. Eta achieved nothing in any of the causes that it claimed to kill for: it didn't achieve the independence of the Basque country, and it did not bring home the prisoners. They achieved nothing, except to cause terrible pain.'[22]

While in Vitoria, I met another prominent sister, and heard another story of grief and loss. Pili Zabala entered politics only in 2016, when she emerged as the leader of the anti-establishment

Podemos party in the Basque country. Before that, her surname was known to Basques and Spaniards alike mainly in connection with one of the most notorious crimes of the GAL: the abduction, torture and killing of José Ignacio Zabala in 1983. Her older brother disappeared when she was fourteen, together with another Eta suspect from the same village. Year after year, the families pleaded with the Spanish authorities to confirm the deaths and reveal the whereabouts of the two men's remains. But it was only in 1995 that a forensic examination was able to confirm that two bodies discovered a decade earlier in a quicklime grave near Alicante were those of Zabala and his friend, José Antonio Lasa.[23]

'Eleven years, five months and five days,' Zabala said. 'You always cheat yourself. I always dreamt that my brother was alive. It was a dream but it was also a defence mechanism, a survival mechanism.' A slight woman of forty-eight, her voice was reduced to a whisper as she recalled the time following her brother's disappearance. 'You are lost in the world. You no longer have any references. I used to have moral and ethical references, religious references. They all broke. Justice doesn't exist. Because of my own experience, I can say: there is no justice in the Spanish state.'

For more than a decade, the family had no grave to visit, and received no help from the authorities. Worse, they were convinced that the very authorities they should have been able to turn to were actually behind the crime: 'We were aware that the very enemy that took my brother was governing us ... We felt a terrible impotence.' Even today, Zabala said, she could not bear the sight of Felipe González, the prime minister at the time ('I have to turn the television off.'). Her view of Spain, and of the country's much-vaunted transition to democracy, was tinged by bitterness and doubt. The murder of her brother – and the lack of punishment meted out to his murderers – suggested to her that Spain still had a long way to go before it could call itself a true democracy. Looking back at the decades of bloodshed and violence, what struck Zabala was the sheer absence of empathy with the other side. 'Here, everyone managed the violence in their own way. People felt the pain of the victims on their side, but not on the other. There was no compassion, and no solidarity.'

I had heard much the same thing from Mendiola, the former mayor of Hernani, when I asked him about how Abertzale towns like his had lived through the days of Blanco's abduction and murder. 'There was indifference,' he said. 'Some thought: we suffer. Now you suffer.'

It is difficult to convey today how hard it was to escape from the terror that stalked the Basque country – how all-engulfing it was. So many deaths, so much fear, in such a small space. Victims and perpetrators, running into each other in those narrow village lanes over and over again. I remembered something that Iñaki Soto, the editor of *Gara*, an Abertzale newspaper based in San Sebastián, told me: 'This was an untypical conflict in the sense that there was no social segregation. We lived in the same buildings. We took our kids to the same schools.'[24] During the years of terror, Basques simply had nowhere to hide – no safe streets or neighbourhoods, not even safe houses. The murders, the betrayals and violations were committed – sometimes quite literally – by one neighbour against the other.

There were years in which the deaths came at a rate of one every three days. And while Eta initially targeted policemen and state representatives, the circle of death would widen further as time went by, until the targets appeared almost random. Run your finger down the list of victims and you will find taxi drivers, housewives, bakers, barmen, and a couple of migrants from Ecuador, caught in the wrong place at the wrong time. In 1987 an Eta bomb exploded in a Barcelona supermarket, killing twenty-one men, women and children who never had the slightest reason to fear the group's wrath. It was the deadliest attack ever committed by Eta.

The suffering of the victims and their families went on long after the debris was removed and the dead were buried. In a cruel inversion of normal human behaviour, it was often Eta's victims and their relatives who were isolated and stigmatised, while the perpetrators received shelter and solidarity from their community. Neighbours would avoid talking to the widow. Children would be ostracised in school. Txema Urkijo, a Basque activist and lawyer who worked on human rights and victims' affairs for the regional government between 2002 and 2013, explained to me the typical response to an Eta killing, especially during the hate-filled 'years of lead' in the late 1970s and early 1980s. 'There was no commiseration for the families of the murdered. They suffered not just the trauma of the murder, but also the silence afterwards. They were basically made to feel ashamed for being victims.' In his own village of Llodio, just south of Bilbao, Eta murdered two people, in 1979 and in 1980. What happened afterwards, I asked. 'Nothing,' Urkijo said. 'Absolutely nothing happened. Not one flower, not one act, not one reaction.' He went on: 'The killer did not just kill the victim, he also marked his family. People said they must have killed him for a reason. And that reason left a stain on the family that stayed. The widow and the children, they carried around a stain of guilt.'[25]

The sense of helplessness and isolation is captured with haunting accuracy by the Basque writer Fernando Aramburu in his 2016 novel *Patria*. The book tells the story of two families from the same Basque village that are bound together – first by friendship, then by murder and betrayal. A publishing sensation in Spain, the novel brings home the hurt, the cowardice, the fear and the remorse haunting the Basque country. Here is the brother of an Eta murderer, tormented by the deed done, and by his own inability to show decency towards the victim's family in the aftermath. He is asked:

'Will you write to the widow?'

'Of course not. And if there is no way around it, I will lie to my father and tell him I did it anyway. He cannot find out. Why am I behaving like this?'

'Out of cowardice.'

'Exactly. Because I am just as cowardly as he is, and as all the others in my village who are even now telling one another in hushed tones: this is a disgrace, a pointless spilling of blood, this is not how you build a homeland. But no one will lift a finger. They will already have hosed down the street to remove any stain of the crime. And tomorrow there will be whispers in the air, but on the ground everything will stay the same. The people will still attend the next demonstration in support of Eta, because they know it is better to be seen as part of the pack. That is the price that has to be paid to have a quiet life in this land of the silent.'[26]

According to historians such as Pérez, this twisted social dynamic was one major reason why Eta was able to go on killing for so long. 'What happened here for decades was this: when Eta killed someone, people would say that the victim must have done something. The burden of proof fell on the victim. Eta was given the benefit of the belief that if they killed someone it must have been for a reason. The killer was given solidarity when he was arrested. The day after an Eta commando was arrested there would be a demonstration, and so on. But it took until the

187

late eighties and early nineties for there to be demonstrations in solidarity with the victims.'

The balance finally tipped in those fraught July days of 1997, as Spain waited for news about the fate of Miguel Angel Blanco. Ermua, the village he came from, became a symbol of this new mood of defiance. 'Terrorism needs social paralysis, it needs to create a spiral where every killing creates more fear. That spiral was broken in Ermua,' recalled Totorika, the mayor. Looking back, he felt pride in the rallies and protests that started in his village, then spread across the whole nation. But that was a long time ago. Today, Totorika told me, 'We are tired of Eta and tired of talking about Eta. Even the victims are tired. They want to close this chapter. But we can't close it just like that.' History matters, he said. It always does. 'What is history today becomes social reality a generation from now. And, what is more, the victims have a right to the truth.'

The history of violence in the Basque country is a traumatic, absorbing and – ultimately – a hopeful one. It suggests that murderous hatred can be overcome, that old fears and suspicions can and do dissolve over time. For all the divisions that remain, everyone I spoke to seemed convinced that Basque society would not allow the killing to return. Yet as I drove from village to village, talking, listening and looking, trying to understand what had happened and what could happen still, I realised that the Basque story contained a lesson that went far beyond current politics and nationalism. It was a deeply human lesson about courage and cowardice, and about the small acts and simple words that separate civilisation from barbarity.

Courage comes in many forms, as does cowardice, but I have long thought that we pay too much attention to physical cour-age – the kind of courage displayed by soldiers, police officers, and the men and women who rush to the scene of battle or disaster. In my time as a journalist, I have had the opportunity to study some of these people in close proximity. They are certainly worthy of admiration, but I also sensed that courage came easily to many of them: they were part of a team, a battalion, a tribe, with clear moral codes. They were sure of their place and their task, and of the support of their peers.

There is another type of courage, however – moral courage – that forces you to stand alone, to say yes when everyone else says no, and to say no when everyone else says yes. It is the kind of courage that leads you into conflict with your community, and that is punished with ostracism, ridicule and isolation. It has no place on the battlefield but it is needed in the schoolyard, in the workplace, in ministries and government cabinets – and it was needed desperately in the villages and towns of the Basque country, as Eta covered the region with a shroud of fear. I found myself profoundly touched by tales of the small acts of humanity and grace that cut through that fear: the businessman in Ermua who closed his shop out of respect for a murdered Basque politician, despite the threats from Eta's local henchmen; the handful of activists who stood silently in village squares to protest the latest abduction, surrounded by a fearsome mob of fanatics, unflinching amid the curses and death threats; the unsung local councillors from the Socialist party in Hernani who went into politics knowing full well the cost that entailed: a life that would never be normal again, a life with bodyguards, with streets and bars that could never be visited, with menacing graffiti painted on the walls of their homes, and the nagging fear that a terrible fate awaited them or their families.

This was truly courage of the few, small shards of light that shone all the brighter for the cowardice and fear that surrounded them. 'Eta was not the gunmen,' Totorika told me. 'If it had only been the gunmen they would have been nothing.' Eta survived for so long, he explained, because of the enablers and the sympathisers, the people who shouted in the streets, and those who simply turned a blind eye.

The mayor himself had chosen a different path. He had not remained silent, not even when locals enraged by the murder of Miguel Angel Blanco threw a firebomb at the Ermua headquarters of Herri Batasuna. He had rushed to the scene to help put out the flames, but also to send a message: 'I am a democrat. I am not like them. And I won't let this happen in my village. In my village, we don't attack each other in the street. We don't burn down party headquarters. You cannot fight hatred with hatred. I am not like that, and I don't want to be like that.'

It was still raining outside. I had spent several hours talking to the mayor, revisiting the dark days and also the days of hope. I had one more question. What made him carry on, I asked, through all those years, knowing that at any moment the assassin's bullet might come his way? Totorika paused. 'I lived through Francoism,' he explained. 'I spent my eighteenth birthday behind bars. They caught me at a demonstration and threw me in prison. Freedom is a very precious thing, especially when you don't have it. When you have it, you don't notice it, just like money or health or family. But when you don't have it... Well, some of us thought it was worth fighting for.'

CHAPTER EIGHT

Spain's cross to bear

Fifty kilometres north of Madrid, in the granite mountains of the Sierra de Guadarrama, stands the tallest stone cross built anywhere in the world. At more than 150 metres high, it looms over a vast basilica that is hewn into the rock below. The sprawling architectural ensemble, coldly symmetrical and entirely grey, is home to a Benedictine abbey, along with a religious boarding school and a hospice. There is a decent restaurant that specialises in traditional Spanish fare, and a mud-covered football pitch that comes to life whenever the pupils of the school emerge to play a match.

Mostly, however, this is a place of death. Known as the Valle de los Caídos, or Valley of the Fallen, it is the final resting place for more than 33,000 bodies. With one notable exception, all of them were killed during the Spanish Civil War, which lasted from 1936 to 1939. The odd one out is the man who started the bloody slaughter, and emerged from it victorious. His grave can be found right behind the high altar, at the very end of the imposing, windowless basilica: a modest granite slab, perpetually adorned with a bouquet of fresh flowers and the simplest of inscriptions: Francisco Franco.

The Spanish dictator died more than four decades ago but his resting place, much like his legacy, is far from settled. Franco's grave had been an issue of fierce – and somewhat ritualised

– controversy for many years, and it burst back onto the political agenda as soon as the Socialists returned to power in May 2018. Prime minister Pedro Sánchez announced shortly after taking office that he would push for the removal of Franco's remains 'immediately', adding, 'I believe that a mature European democracy like ours cannot have symbols that divide Spaniards.'[1] His announcement was followed by a vote in parliament that backed the removal of the dictator's tomb, but – at least at the time of writing – that decision had yet to be implemented. What was striking, however, was just how divisive the plan to remove Franco's grave remained, even forty years after his death. The motion to dig up his body won the support of just 176 out of 350 members of parliament, with 165 deputies abstaining.[2] Out on the streets, Spaniards seemed equally split: one poll found just 41 per cent in favour of exhuming Franco, while 39 per cent were opposed.[3] Curiously, a majority of Spaniards – more than 54 per cent – thought that now was not 'a good moment to deal with this issue'.

Outside Spain, Franco is often placed alongside Hitler and Mussolini as one of the continent's most reviled twentieth-century leaders, a brutal dictator who plunged his country into war and went on to preside over the death, incarceration, torture and exile of hundreds of thousands of his opponents. In Spain, however, the government pays for the upkeep of the Valle de los Caídos, tombstone and all. It forms part of the state's *Patrimonio Nacional*, or National Heritage – the same status awarded to royal palaces and landmark monasteries. Hundreds of thousands come to visit the site every year. Spain's Roman Catholic Church jealously guards its role as the custodian of the Valley, and provides the monks and priests who sanctify the vast granite complex with their daily songs and prayers.

*

Even after four decades, there is still no national consensus on what the Civil War and Franco's dictatorship meant. Only a tiny minority of Spaniards voice genuine nostalgia for the old regime but the number of those clamouring for a frank reassessment of the past is not large either. The former dictator and his deeds are widely shunned as a topic of conversation, whether in school, in parliament or around the family table. Polls are few and far between but when they do surface they often show a lingering sense of ambivalence, perhaps linked to the extraordinary economic boom that occurred during the later years of the Franco regime. One typical survey found that six out of ten Spaniards believe that Francoism had 'both good sides and bad sides'.[4]

But it is not just in the Valley that Franco continues to have his place. Despite a purge in recent years, many Spanish cities still boast streets and squares that honour his memory and celebrate his victories and those of his generals. According to one official count conducted in 2018, there were no fewer than 1143 streets across the country dedicated to Franco and other figures associated with the regime.[5] There were entire villages that took the name of Caudillo – the title Franco claimed for himself. Visitors to Salamanca, the ancient university town in northern Castile, could still find the portrait of Franco attached to one of the eighty-eight arches that showed profiles of Spanish rulers through the ages (it was finally removed in June 2017). In the Spanish enclave of Melilla, on the Moroccan coast, a small statue of the dictator looks out over the sea towards Spain. There is also a popular motorway restaurant halfway between Madrid and the southern coast that is filled with mementoes and pictures of Franco, along with placards disparaging democracy and recent Spanish leaders. In Madrid itself, there is a prominent foundation that is dedicated to celebrating the dictator's life and work. Once a year, its members and other Franco sympathisers come to the Valle de los Caídos for a special mass, and to pray for his eternal soul.

To some Spaniards, the site and the annual ritual are an abomination, a stain on the country's democratic record. They argue that Spain, perhaps uniquely in Western Europe, has never truly made an effort to confront its past. Far from allowing old wounds to heal, this failure has, they argue, kept old divisions alive, the original sin of Spanish democracy, still unatoned for after all these years.

One man who believes this more strongly than most is Emilio Silva, a political scientist and journalist who rose to prominence as the co-founder of Spain's historical memory movement. 'Can you imagine a church in Germany where the priest prays for the soul of Hitler? Can you imagine a square in Italy that is named after Mussolini?' Silva asked me, over coffee in a noisy bar in Madrid.[6] The movement he started almost two decades ago is best known for locating and digging up the graves of Spanish Republicans killed by Franco's Nationalists before and after the war. More than 1300 bodies have been recovered from roadside ditches and secluded forests, and accorded a proper burial. For the relatives, this process has often been momentous – allowing them finally to come to terms with six decades of pain. The broader aim of Silva and his allies is to shatter Spain's so-called pact of forgetting – the unspoken agreement between left and right in the wake of Franco's death to look to the future, not the past. In legal terms, that pact is cemented in the 1977 amnesty law, which shields former Franco officials – including the regime's most notorious torturers – from criminal prosecution. Yet it is also reflected in Spain's schools, where the history of the Civil War and Franco's dictatorship remain marginal subjects. And it finds an echo in the singular absence of any national museum or monument – aside from the Valley – to commemorate the war.

'We are a country full of ignorance,' remarked Silva. 'If there wasn't so much ignorance, Franco would no longer be there [in the basilica]. For a society with even a little bit of understanding, it would simply be intolerable.'

Francisco Franco Bahamonde was born in 1892, in the Galician coastal town of El Ferrol. He was supposed to follow the family tradition and join the Spanish navy, but the Spanish-American war of 1898 and the resulting loss of Cuba, Puerto Rico and the Philippines had sharply reduced the need for new cadets.[7] Franco joined the army instead, where he rose swiftly through the ranks. He became the youngest captain in the Spanish armed forces, then the youngest major, the youngest colonel and finally the youngest general.[8] He made his mark as a commander in Spain's Foreign Legion in Morocco, which was engaged in a savage, decades-long campaign to quell anti-colonial uprisings. A dedicated soldier who neither drank nor womanised, he was known as a cruel disciplinarian who had no qualms about his troops mutilating the bodies of the enemy.[9] His physical appearance was less than imposing – he was short, and even as a young man he had a pot belly and a high-pitched voice[10] – but Franco quickly gained the respect of his men as a fearless commander, often riding into battle on a white horse that made him an easy target. As a young man he showed little interest in politics or religion, though he did develop an intense hatred of both communism and freemasonry. Like many of his fellow soldiers, he had little regard for democracy, blaming the humiliating loss of Spain's colonies on the weakness of the Republican leadership. Throughout his life, contemporaries would describe him as aloof, controlled, impassionate and utterly cold. As the British historian Hugh Thomas recounts:

The failure of humane democracy in Spain had given way to one of the coldest-hearted men, a man intolerant of human foibles, humourless but able, calm and determined. One day in winter, Bernhardt [Johannes Bernhardt, a German SS general based in Madrid] was lunching with Franco (whom he admired). The question came up as to what to do with four militiawomen, captured, armed with rifles. Franco believed that all women captured in arms should be shot. 'There is nothing else to be done', he said, 'shoot them', without changing the tone that he would use for a discussion of the weather.[11]

Franco biographies are packed with similar tales. In the immediate aftermath of the war, determined to 'cleanse' Spain of all traces of Republican resistance, the dictator signed thousands of death sentences – casually, over coffee, often in the presence of his personal priest.[12] Paul Preston, another British historian writing on Spain, has used the word holocaust to describe the mass slaughter ordered by Franco both during and after the war (though he also insists that the scale does not compare to the systematic murder of the Jews by Nazi Germany). By his estimate, Franco was responsible for the murder of more than 200,000 people during and after the war, on top of the 200,000 soldiers who had died in battle and an unknown number of civilian victims of the fighting.[13] The historical parallels with Hitler and Mussolini are hard to ignore, not least because German and Italian support proved instrumental during the war itself. But Franco did two things that neither of the other two dictators managed: he knew when to stop, and he knew how to survive. The first point is crucial. Despite pressure from Germany, Franco kept Spain neutral during the Second World War. Had he joined the Axis powers, his rule would undoubtedly have ended in 1945, if not earlier. Instead, he held on to power until his death in 1975 – long enough to regain the favour of Western allies such as the US, and to preside over an economic recovery that went at least some way towards changing Spanish perceptions of the dictator. The *dictadura* became a *dictablanda* – a soft dictatorship. Spain in the 1960s and 1970s was a repressive, authoritarian regime, a grey backwater cut off from the European mainstream, a country where a woman needed her husband's permission to conduct even the simplest legal or commercial transaction, and where opposition activists were persecuted and jailed without mercy. But as long as you played by the rules of the Franco regime, you had little to fear from the government. Over time, the space allowed for artistic expression and economic activity grew. Directors such as Luis Buñuel, Carlos Saura and Luis García Berlanga made some superb, even subversive, films under Franco.[14] And bankers and businessmen with the right connections made plenty of money. Here lies one of the roots of today's ambivalence towards Franco: if he had died in 1939 or 1940, Spain might have remembered him only as a monster. But large parts of Spanish society came to acquire a more complex memory of the man and his deeds in the decades thereafter. I had to think of a line from *Sonnenallee*, a 1999 film about growing up in communist East Germany. 'There once was a country and I lived in it,' the narrator says at the end. 'And if you ask me what it was like I will say: it was the best time of my life. Because I was young and I was in love.'

Normal people, in other words, don't think, judge and remember like historians.

For many Spaniards of the post-war era, Franco was a brooding presence in the background, as they went about their daily lives, getting married, having children, buying cars and going to the seaside. The revulsion felt by Silva and others was widespread, but it was far from universal.

*

To its defenders, the Valle de los Caídos is, above all, a site of mourning and reconciliation. They point out that the mass tombs that line those heavy granite walls hold the dead of both sides. What they fail to mention is that many of the Republican dead were brought to the mausoleum without consulting their families – or, in some cases, against the express wishes of relatives. Neither do they question why any Republican would wish to be buried in a tomb built with the help of Republican slave labour, and laden with Francoist and fascist imagery.

At least once a year, the notion of reconciliation becomes impossible to maintain. Every 20 November, the anniversary of Franco's death, his supporters arrive from all over the country, and beyond, for a special mass. I have rarely had cause to attend Catholic mass during my life but even regular worshippers are likely to leave this particular ceremony in a state of dazed wonderment. Part of this has to do with the sheer sense of drama. At the precise moment of the transubstantiation, when the bread and wine are ritually converted into the body and blood of Christ, the vast underground basilica is plunged into sudden darkness. An invisible helper turns off all lights, save for a single spot that is directed at the body of Christ on the cross, along with the hands of the priest holding aloft the wafer. The priest, who is also the abbot of the Valley's Benedictine monastery, then starts his homily with a prayer for the soul of Francisco Franco and José Antonio Primo de Rivera, the founder of Spain's fascist Falange movement. Both men died on 20 November but were separated by a political eternity: Franco passed away in his bed, peacefully, after thirty-six years of unopposed rule. Primo de Rivera was killed by a Republican firing squad in 1936, just months after the start of Spain's Civil War. The two bodies occupy pride of place in the gloomy basilica, buried in front of and behind the altar. Standing at the lectern just above, the priest praised the two fascist leaders for their decision to 'forgive their enemies and seek their forgiveness for themselves'.

When I visited, I was told that some worshippers might offer a fascist salute, but I had not expected arms to be raised quite so brazenly. Some made a discreet, hasty salute on their way to receive Holy Communion, but all inhibitions melted away once the priests, monks and choirboys had left the church. Franco's grave was quickly surrounded by dozens of admirers. They laid down red flowers and knelt to touch the rough, grey stone. Some said a personal prayer. Dozens straightened their backs and offered the raised-arm salute, while friends and wives snapped pictures. Shouts of 'Viva Franco!' and 'Viva España!' echoed through the vast basilica. Neither the guards from Spain's National Heritage nor the remaining monk tried to intervene.

Standing quietly among the crowd was a tall, middle-aged man called Jaime Alonso, the vice-president and spokesman of the Francisco Franco Foundation and the public face of hardcore Francoism in Spain today. I saw him whisper a prayer and cross himself but he quickly turned away from the more raucous crowd surrounding the dictator's grave. Impeccably dressed and softly spoken, Alonso is a lawyer by profession and Francoist by passion. Armed with a wealth of numbers, dates and facts, he made a resolute case in Franco's defence when I caught up with him back in Madrid. He told me he had grown up with a vision of Franco as the 'father of the nation', and still viewed him as 'the man of providence who came to save Spain'. Selfless, upright, a brilliant military commander and great political strategist, Franco was hailed as a towering figure in Spanish history, comparable only to the medieval rulers who drove the Moors from Spain in 1492, or the great kings who held sway over an empire stretching from Peru to the Philippines.

Alonso vigorously defended Franco's military putsch against the country's elected government in 1936, which marked the start of the Civil War, insisting it was a necessary step to put an end to the chaos and violence of the period. 'There was no other option. They could either fight or let themselves be killed,' he said. Franco's post-war achievements were no less significant, Alonso argued. 'In Franco's Spain, at least towards the later years, no one was hungry. Everyone had a car, a home, a television set. There was social security, paid holidays and health insurance... He created a middle class.'

The Franco Foundation was located in a third-floor apartment just up the road from Real Madrid's imposing Bernabéu stadium. It was a large space but slightly dusty, and seemed to be in need of renovation. The offices were packed with memorabilia, signed photos, oil paintings, thousands of books and an archive. Aside from myself, the only visitors to the foundation all looked old enough to remember the days of the Caudillo from personal experience. There was even a small souvenir shop, where visitors could pick up a Franco ashtray for €4.50.

For all his enthusiasm, Alonso admitted that there were few genuine Francoists left in Spain today. Since the return of parliamentary democracy, there had only been one openly Francoist member of parliament. Even during the recent economic crisis, with millions of Spaniards desperately searching for work, there had been no sign of revival in Francoist sentiment. In late 2018, as we shall see later, a new far-right party called Vox did emerge as a genuine contender in Spanish politics. But it also seemed clear that its success had more to do with the Catalan crisis and migration worries than with any desire to turn back the clock to the Franco era. Alonso himself, however, remained convinced that Franco lived on. Why else, he asked, would the country's political mainstream be so silent about his rule? 'They are afraid of him. They know very well that Franco is more than just a reference, that he is something embedded in the culture of the Spanish people as a solution. Today, even if everything falls apart, we have a national ideal that stays with us and that is passed on in our genes. How can Francoism revive today? As bad as the situation is, the idea is there.'

What was striking was not so much the historical narrative put forward by the Franco Foundation but the absence of any official challenge to it. I asked countless Spaniards what they were taught about the Civil War in school. The answer was, almost invariably, nothing. Spain's parties have never been able to agree on a joint condemnation of the Franco dictatorship, or given an official apology to its victims. There has been no official commission, no national museum offering a unified narrative. Historians such as Paul Preston argue that this silence – coupled with the effort by Franco loyalists to preserve the dictator's reputation – has helped create an image that is far more benign than the man deserved.

> To this day, General Franco and his regime enjoy a relatively good press. This derives from a series of persistent myths about the benefits of his rule. Along with a carefully constructed idea that he masterminded Spain's economic 'miracle' in the 1960s and heroically kept his country out of the Second World War, there are numerous falsifications about the origins of his regime. These derive from the initial lie that the Spanish Civil War was a necessary war fought to save the country from Communist take-over. The success of this fabrication influences much writing on the Spanish Civil War to depict it as a conflict between two more or less equal sides. The issue of innocent civilian casualties is subsumed into that concept and thereby 'normalized'.[15]

Among mainstream historians this benign view of Franco is now indeed widely discredited. But it lives on, consciously or not, in some sectors of Spanish society. The idea that Franco did what he had to in 1936, that the Red Terror (the atrocities committed by the Republican side) were as bad or even worse than those committed by Franco's Nationalists, or that post-war Francoist Spain was a country of law, order, justice and progress – all these notions can be, and are, expressed openly in Spain today. Not by many, to be sure, but one does not have to look too hard to come across them.

One place where Francoist sentiment and aesthetics survive in a particularly unabashed form is inside Casa Pepe, a popular motorway restaurant on the A-4, about 250 kilometres south of the Spanish capital. Located conveniently on the halfway mark between Madrid and the Andalusian coast, the restaurant has been a stop for travellers for many years. With the outside painted in the colours of the Spanish flag, there is nothing subtle about Casa Pepe. Entering the bar, I came face to face with hundreds of photos, pictures and old newspaper cuttings of and about Franco. There were 'pre-constitutional' flags showing the Francoist eagle, and banners of the Falange. Hanging above the bar were caricatures of left-wing politicians and a sign that read: 'With Franco: 40 years of peace, justice and liberty. And with democracy: Shit, shit, shit, shit, shit, shit!!!' The adjoining shop offered a bewildering selection of Francoist souvenirs and memorabilia: wine bottles with the face of Franco on the label, bars of chocolate emblazoned with the Franco-era slogan *Arriba España!* ('Up Spain!'), Franco T-shirts, Falangist pottery and baseball caps bearing the emblem of the División Azul, the Spanish division that fought alongside Nazi Germany on the Eastern Front.

It was macabre, strange, repulsive – but also slightly trivial. The bar looked and felt like a fairground attraction, a house of horrors that happened also to serve ham sandwiches and cold beer. Some guests seemed to delight in the surroundings but most looked as if they had been drawn to the restaurant, like myself, largely out of curiosity. Still, it seemed remarkable that a place like Casa Pepe could survive, and indeed commercially thrive, so many years after the death of Franco – and after so many thousands of books and articles had detailed the crimes of his regime. I had grown up in Germany, where *Vergangenheitsbewältigung* (the process of coming to terms with the past) was seen as a collective national duty. With that example in mind, the existence of a place like Casa Pepe spoke to me of a lax – even careless – approach to history. But perhaps I was wrong. In some ways, the survival of this roadside inn represented the opposite of carelessness: it was still here because Spain's transition to democracy was based on a truce that had been successful – and that few dared to question. Casa Pepe was here for the same reason that Franco's body was still in the Valle de los Caídos: because Spain's present – for all its economic and political difficulties – seemed too precious to contaminate with arguments about the past.

I didn't want the government to shut down Casa Pepe either, but I wanted its owners and customers to realise that it was offensive, insensitive and wrong to keep it as it is. I left without ordering anything. Not that it made any difference. When I drove off, the parking area was even fuller than when I had arrived.

For the Spanish writer Javier Cercas, the interplay of memory and history, and the stories people tell themselves about the past, have long been a subject of fascination. His 2001 book *Soldiers of Salamis* is widely hailed as one of the great novels about the Civil War. I called him up in late 2015, a few weeks after the release of another book, *The Impostor*, which dealt once again with history, war, terror – and the lies they bring forth. The book contained an entire chapter about Spain's own struggle – and ultimate failure – to come to terms with its history.

'A country must have a basic accord about the past,' Cercas told me. 'Britain has it. Germany has it. All the strong democracies have this basic accord. But Spain hasn't.' The reason for this, he argued, was obvious: 'There was no rupture in Spain after Francoism. There was a transition, there was peaceful and progressive change from dictatorship to democracy. This means that the Spanish right did not break completely with Francoism. It would be wrong and absurd to say that the Spanish right is Francoist. It obviously isn't. But it has never been able to bring itself to condemn Francoism.'

Not everyone I spoke to was convinced that this mattered. José María de Areilza, a professor of law at Esade business school and former government adviser, spoke for many when he argued that Spain was right to look to the future and 'leave the past to the historians'. 'There is no one way to deal with the past,' he told me. 'Franco died in his bed. But everything that has happened in Spain since has condemned him. He is being condemned every day by the normal functioning of our democracy, by our constitution. Spain has moved on by doing, by acting.'

This also rang true. I found it hard to make up my mind. Part of me was scandalised by Spain's lack of historical rigour, and the nation's willingness to tolerate the overt celebration of Franco and his legacy. But it was also clear that Spain's decision to look to the future, not the past, had been broadly vindicated. The dwindling band of genuine Franco supporters in modern Spain posed no threat to democracy (as Alonso had explained to me, 'we do nothing to subvert the system, the system will subvert itself'). The armed forces were no longer plotting a return to the old days. Why devote political capital and energy to an issue that the majority of Spaniards showed little interest in? Why reopen a tacit accord that had paved the way for four decades of peace, stability, liberty and prosperity?

For Cercas, however, the country's failure openly to confront the past left Spain in a state of heightened fragility. 'If there is no accord over the past, then the past can always be used, can always be manipulated,' he said. 'There is no accord over our past, and that means that finding an accord over our present and our future is much more difficult. Can we live with this? Yes, we can live with this. But would we live better if we had a common narrative? We would live much better.'

The most ambitious attempt to challenge the pact of forgetting came under the Socialist government of José Luis Rodríguez Zapatero, the prime minister from 2004 to 2011. The Zapatero government provided public funding to unearth Republican war graves, and passed a law calling for the removal of Francoist statues and street names. It faced bitter opposition from the centre-right Popular party, and from Spain's Roman Catholic Church (which had served as a pillar of the Franco regime). At the height of the controversy, the country's conference of bishops published a searing attack on the government, saying it was 'opening old wounds' and 'threatening the tranquil co-existence'.[16] The archbishop of Madrid put it even more bluntly. Sometimes, he remarked, 'one has to know how to forget'.[17]

Towards the end of its tenure, the Zapatero government decided to tackle the biggest totem of them all: the Valley of the Fallen. It appointed a commission of experts and asked it to draw up proposals for an overhaul of the site. The commission was formally established in May 2011 – just six months before a general election that Zapatero knew he would lose. Whatever conclusions its members would reach, they were almost certain to be filed away the very instant the new centre-right government took over.

Francisco Ferrándiz knew he was part of an exercise in futility but he decided to accept the invitation to join the commission all the same. A social anthropologist at Spain's National Research Council, he had closely followed the work of the historical memory movement. Here was a chance to shape the debate over one of the most contentious monuments in the world. 'We didn't want to impose a narrative. We wanted to create the conditions for a debate in society that could come up with some kind of consensus about the monument,' Ferrándiz told me. 'I think you have to confront these things at some point. Some countries have done this through truth and reconciliation commissions but in Spain it was just glossed over.'

In the end, after much internal wrangling, the commission called for a radical overhaul. It suggested removing Franco's grave from the basilica and burying him elsewhere, and transferring the body of Primo de Rivera from its privileged site to one of the mass graves that lined the church. Just as importantly, they wanted to convert the sections of the site that housed the dead into a national cemetery – and so remove the graves from the care of the monks.

As expected, the document was shelved immediately by the new government. Asked about the future of the Valle de los Caídos in 2013, the deputy prime minister fell back on the Popular party's standard line that any change required the 'consensus' of all parties. That consensus, of course, remained elusive for as long as the PP was in power. For much of its first term in office, the government of Mariano Rajoy was consumed by the economic crisis, and by the never-ending corruption revelations.

Whenever I asked a government official about the Valle de los Caídos, or about revisiting Spain's approach to the Franco dictatorship, they would stare at me in disbelief. For them, this chapter had been closed long ago.

But the plan drawn up by Ferrándiz and his colleagues was not forgotten. In early 2017, the Socialists and Podemos joined forces in parliament to push through a non-binding resolution calling for the removal of Franco's grave. The following year, Spain's moribund left suddenly found itself back in power. Shortly after taking over the job of prime minister, Pedro Sánchez revived the 2017 motion, and the original plan to remake the Valle de los Caídos – and finally remove the body of Franco. Sánchez seemed genuine in his belief that the monument in its current form was an outrage, but the plan also made sense politically. As the leader of a minority government, the new prime minister lacked the strength in parliament to push through ambitious economic or social reforms. Exhuming Franco was a proposal that a majority of deputies – from his own party, from Podemos, and from regional parties in Catalonia and the Basque country – could rally behind. It also placed the Popular party and Ciudadanos in an uncomfortable position. Neither wanted to be seen as defending Franco, but nor were they keen to hand an easy victory to Sánchez. In the end, both parties abstained. Pablo Casado, the man who replaced Mariano Rajoy as leader of the PP, denounced the move as a 'smokescreen' to hide the government's weakness.[18]

Much as Spaniards wanted to move on from Franco's legacy, it had a habit of popping up, sometimes in the most unexpected of places. In September 2016 I interviewed a researcher at the University of Glasgow who had made a curious discovery while analysing the Spanish edition of Ian Fleming's spy thriller *Dr. No*. As he compared the translation with the original, Jordi

Cornella realised that there were striking differences. 'The last chapter of *Dr. No* was totally distorted because they took out a couple of pages with sexual references. I thought this must be a mistake but then I started researching and found other examples.'[19] Cornella had stumbled across the work of Franco's censors, a joyless caste of editors tasked with removing any content from novels, plays and movies that ran counter to the dictator's ideology. Criticism of Franco himself, passages about the Civil War, sentences that were deemed too sexually explicit or hostile to the Church were removed or rewritten. The problem was that – in some instances at least – these changes were never rectified. To this day, key works by Ernest Hemingway, George Orwell, James Baldwin, Dashiell Hammett and John Dos Passos – to name but a few – are available in Spain only in the version approved by Franco's censors. 'The problem now is that these versions appear even in ebooks, so you can say that censorship is still alive and well in Spain,' Cornella explained. 'This is a legacy of the Franco regime that is somehow invisible. It is there, but readers don't know about it.'

James Bond, the womanising spy at the heart of Fleming's fictional series, suffered particularly gravely at the hands of Franco's censors. Many of his graphic sexual exploits were missing from the Spanish versions of the books decades after the end of the dictatorship. In the case of Hemingway's *Across the River*, even recent Spanish editions included a string of changes made by the censors. A reference to 'lesbians' in the original text is still translated as 'good friends' in the current Spanish hardback edition. A reference to 'General Fat Ass Franco' in the English text appeared as the unspecific 'General Asno Gordo' (or fat donkey) in a 2001 paperback. Coarse language and Hemingwayesque insults such as 'son of a bitch' have been toned down throughout the text.

Here was a small but telling example of the enduring legacy of the dictatorship. Over the course of Franco's long rule, Spanish publishers released close to 500,000 books, all of which had to pass the censors. No one knows how many of these titles were amended or cut, and how many censored editions are still in print. But it is clear that Spanish readers may have to live with the censor's changes for many years to come. Books, as Cornella remarked, 'have a very long life'.

The task of purging Franco and his regime from public spaces has proved no less difficult. As mentioned above, despite the efforts of the Zapatero government, city maps across the country have continued to show streets and squares named after the dictator, or honouring his generals and supporters. Locals had lived with these, and other reminders of Franco, for so long they no longer seemed to offend.

But they did offend a new wave of politicians who won control of Spanish cities in the aftermath of the crisis. The 2015 local elections marked a triumph for Podemos, even if the party itself did not stand in the elections. Instead, Podemos joined forces with other grassroots activists to set up local offshoots – such as Ahora Madrid (Now Madrid) – that in turn fielded a string of charismatic and popular candidates. The results were spectacular: Podemos allies won the city halls of Madrid, Barcelona, Zaragoza, Cádiz, La Coruña and a long list of smaller towns and municipalities. Equipped with slender majorities and little experience, many of the new mayors made symbolist politics an early priority. Among them was Manuela Carmena, the mayor of Madrid, whose administration announced, a few months after taking office, that it would rename thirty streets and squares in the capital (the list would later rise to fifty-two). Only one of the names referred to Franco himself: the Plaza de Caudillo. Most of the remaining sites honoured generals who had taken part in the 1936 military uprising against the Spanish Republic, and who served in the bloody civil war that followed. They included the generals Yagüe, Mola, Varela and Fanjul as well as General Millán Astray, founder of the Spanish legion and an early propagandist for Franco. The plan also called for a renaming of Plaza Arriba España, as well as the Calle de los Caídos de la División Azul. In their place, the Madrid government wanted to honour men and women who had set a different kind of example. Among the proposed new names was Julián Besteiro, a Socialist politician who had died in a Francoist prison in 1940, Robert Capa, the celebrated war photographer, and Max Aub, a writer and diplomat who had helped secure Picasso's anti-war painting *Guernica* for the Spanish pavilion at the 1937 international exposition in Paris. The plan met fierce resistance from the Popular party, with one local leader denouncing the renaming exercise as an 'attempt to promote division and confrontation based on the Civil War, 80 years after the fact'.[20]

As expected, the effort created plenty of controversy, and headlines both in the Spanish and the international press. What it did not do was make much difference on the ground. More than two years after Carmena took office, not one street name had been changed in the capital. Swamped by a series of law suits from right-wing groups, including the Franco Foundation, the municipality announced in July 2017 that it was freezing the plan.[21] The battle for memory had turned into trench warfare; progress, if there was any at all, would have to be measured in inches.

For all his frustration with the failure to overhaul the Valle de los Caídos, Ferrándiz, the anthropologist, had not lost hope that a new generation of Spaniards would eventually demand a less circumspect approach towards the country's past. He pointed out that Spain's political order had come under scrutiny as never before in the years after the crisis. The transition itself had become almost a dirty word for a new generation of political activists who were desperate to sweep away what they saw as a deeply corrupt system. 'We had the prestigious transition that is being taught all over the world as an example of how to move cleanly from a dictatorship to democracy. Now we find that this transition is under fire because it glossed over some of the thorniest issues of the dictatorship – and let the perpetrators die in bed without ever facing their responsibility. Now we have a new generation saying: "We have to face this."'

The younger generation of Spaniards has indeed freed itself of the old fears and reflexes regarding Franco, but most prefer to focus on other issues – issues that seem more burning and relevant than the legacy of dictatorship. 'Franco represents everything I don't like about Spain and about Spanish history – the ultra-right, the relationship between church and state and the whole communion-and-daily-mass way of life,' Sagrario Monedero, a political activist in her early thirties who works for a non-governmental organisation in Madrid, told me. 'But he is also a bit of a comical figure – this small man with a pot belly and a high-pitched voice,' she added. Like a growing number of young Spaniards, Monedero has never visited the Valley of the Fallen. She regards the monument as an outrage but also suggests that her generation sees no urgent need to tackle the Franco legacy. 'History has already given its verdict.'

It is an argument that goes a long way towards explaining the indifference about Franco in Spain today. But if history has indeed given its verdict, why has it not been executed? Why has it been so hard for Spanish democracy to touch that brooding mausoleum in the mountains? 'Let's take this terrible monument as an opportunity,' said Ferrándiz. 'It is the biggest Francoist monument of them all, and it is where all the complexities come together. If the debate has to happen somewhere, if we are to find a consensus about our history, it has to be around the Valley.'

Sooner or later, Franco's remains may be exhumed, and reburied in a different, less exalted place. But even if the grave is finally broken open, the removal of the dead dictator's bones will be nothing more than a political gesture as long as there is no broader debate – and no wider consensus – regarding his position in Spanish history. The reluctance to have that debate remains palpable, despite the apparent flurry of activity by the Sánchez government. Yet eight decades after the end of the civil war, is it not time for Spain to build a new memorial to the victims? Eight decades later, should there not be a national museum to tell the story of what happened, and why? More than four decades after Franco's death, is it not time to shift perceptions as well as tombstones?

Reaching a national consensus remains elusive, however, and those monuments and memorials remain unbuilt. All we have is that vast granite mausoleum in the mountains above Madrid, that will be Franco's for years to come, no matter where his body lies.

CHAPTER NINE

The new Spaniards

From his first-floor office in an industrial estate south of Madrid, Chen Maodong was following the steady flow of bright-orange delivery trucks passing through the gates of his sprawling warehouse complex. Laden with beer, alcohol, soft drinks and snacks, the trucks were on their way to restock thousands of Chinese-run corner shops and convenience stores dotted around the Spanish capital. Business was good. It always had been, even in the worst moments of Spain's economic crisis. In the years since 2008, the country had been through a housing bust, a banking crisis and a deep recession, but Don Pin, the wholesale company founded by Chen, had managed to triple its sales. And with economic success came a change in status – for Chen, and for the Chinese community at large.

'The Spaniards used to look at us like they looked at the other migrants, like people who do the dirty work,' Chen told me.[1] 'Now, when you go to a department store they have signs in Chinese, and staff who speak Chinese. They know: "Here are people who have money."'

The bonfire of bankruptcies that burnt its way through corporate Spain during the downturn left the Chinese largely untouched – a result of hard work, thriftiness, luck and a business culture that valued long-term survival above quick profit. 'In China, we believe that the key issue is not whether you

213

lose money or not, but whether you manage to hold on. So the Chinese have developed a great ability to withstand a crisis. You have to endure,' said Marco Wang, a businessman in Madrid whose assets include Spain's leading Chinese newspapers.

The resilience of these Castilian Chinese was remarkable, but just as remarkable was the story of how they, and millions more migrants from all around the world, got to Spain in the first place. Wang and Chen formed part of one of the most striking demographic shifts experienced by any country in Europe since the end of the Second World War: the transformation of Spain from an ethnically and religiously homogeneous country to a multiracial nation of immigrants. Between 1999 and 2010, Spain's population jumped from 40 million to 47 million, a surge that was almost entirely explained by immigration. The number of non-Spaniards living in the country increased almost eightfold over the same period – from 750,000 to 5.75m.[2] Migrants arrived in unprecedented numbers, and they came from everywhere: the Ecuadorian population, for example, surged from 7155 in 1999 to an all-time high of almost 500,000 in 2005; the Romanian from 3174 in 1999 to almost 900,000 by 2012; the Moroccan community grew from 133,002 in 1999 to more than 790,000 in 2013; and the Chinese from 14,184 in 1999 to almost 210,000 in 2017.[3] Different migrant groups peaked at different times during the boom–bust cycle, suggesting that the crisis did not hit all of them with the same intensity, or at the same moment. But the overall surge in numbers, whatever their provenance, was astounding. The increase in the migrant population was equivalent in size to that of Spain's three largest cities combined – Madrid, Barcelona and Valencia – and the shift took place within just a decade.

More often than not, the arrivals were made to feel welcome. There was little sign of a broad xenophobic backlash, not even at the height of the crisis. That is not to say that migrants were spared casual racism and everyday discrimination, or that Spain was particularly active in combating either. Indeed, Madrid found itself chastised by the Council of Europe as late as February 2018 for being one of only two countries in the forty-seven-nation organisation without an independent anti-racism body (San Marino was the other culprit).[4] At the anecdotal level, there was no shortage of complaints about racist behaviour, along with outrage about the still-widespread practice of 'blacking up' for parades and local festivals.[5] Spain's migrant population also had reason to feel unsettled by political developments in 2018, when a far-right party called Vox started to achieve some electoral success. But given the scale and speed of the population shift, not to mention the massive anti-immigrant backlash in other European countries, Spanish attitudes seemed remarkably positive. That was also the conclusion of several large-scale sociological surveys conducted in the years after the great migration surge. One exhaustive study examining the experience of young immigrants concluded that 'perceptions of discrimination among the children of immigrants are very low. At the average age of 18, only 5 per cent of the sample said that they had experienced discrimination "sometime or many times".'[6]

The wave of arrivals during these years changed the face of Spain, and changed it for good. The newcomers brought with them their food and music, their festivals and traditions, adding dabs of colour to a country that had resisted the blending of cultures and nations for longer than most. Spain had expelled its Jews in 1492, and forced the Moors to convert or flee in the decades that followed. The notorious Inquisition made sure that none of their descendants went back to their old ways. It would take until 1968 for the Alhambra Decree – the 1492 order that had expelled the Jews – to be formally revoked. Both Protestants and Jews had suffered severe discrimination under Franco's dictatorship. Long after the return of democracy, Spain remained overwhelmingly white and overwhelmingly Catholic. Until the very end of the twentieth century, moreover, the country was simply too poor to attract large inflows of migrant workers.

And then the boom happened.

Within little more than a decade, the number of foreigners living in Spain soared from less than 2 per cent of the population in 1999 to more than 12 per cent in 2009. The Socialist government of José Rodríguez Zapatero made it relatively easy for the new arrivals to acquire Spanish citizenship, and pushed through successive 'legalisations' that allowed even undocumented immigrants to stay and work.[7] Wherever they came from, and what little resources they had, all migrants enjoyed free access to Spain's excellent health care system and its state schools. Spanish businesses and wealthy families, meanwhile, delighted in the abundance of cheap labour. Romanian and Ecuadorian men poured concrete and laid bricks on building sites across the country, while their female counterparts cleaned houses, picked up children from school and took care of the old. Suddenly, even middle-class families could afford to keep a uniformed *chica* in domestic employment. The fact that so many of the new arrivals already spoke Spanish or, like the Romanians, were able to learn the language quickly, made their integration – both into society and into the labour force – fairly easy.

For the migrant workers themselves, of course, everyday life was often anything but easy. I often wondered whether Spanish families were aware of the emotional price their *chicas* – typically from Latin America – were paying. Many had left behind their own families, even their own children, to care for the families and children of strangers in a faraway land. Often they had swapped their homes in Ecuador or Paraguay for a tiny servant's room at the back of a luxurious flat or villa in Madrid, and their regular clothes for one of those faintly ridiculous maid's uniforms that well-off Spaniards seemed to regard as the only appropriate outfit for a domestic employee. Those who did not live with their employers usually had to make a long commute from the more affordable outskirts of the capital. In the mornings, I would see them walking the dogs of their bosses, a little plastic bag in hand to scoop up stray excrement. In the afternoons, I would see them at the playground, keeping a watchful eye on the offspring of their employers. Their endurance and discipline were formidable, their exhaustion often plain to see.

Their inner lives, however, remained a mystery, even – or especially – to the Spanish families they were paid to serve. One of the few people who showed a deep interest in their plight was a French documentary film-maker named Vanessa Rousselet, who spent four years trying to win the confidence of Latina domestic employees, and chronicling their lives.[8] The result is a quiet, intense and profoundly moving documentary called *En otra casa* (In another house), about a group of women who leave behind their own children, grandchildren, husbands and parents in order to cook, clean and tidy in Madrid; to brush the hair of other people's offspring, take them swimming and hug them tight. The contrast between the close emotional bond they form with their new charges, and the halting, awkward late-night phone conversations with their own families back home, is jarring. There is one heart-stopping scene during Sunday mass at a Paraguayan congregation in Madrid, when the priest starts repeating back to the worshippers – nearly all of them women – the complaints and laments he has heard from them recently: about the humiliations inflicted by the *señoras* in Madrid, about unfaithful husbands and ungrateful brothers back home, and teenage daughters who have fallen pregnant, without their own mothers around to help. The camera cuts backs to the faces of the women, streaked with tears.

One of the *chicas* portrayed in the documentary says she has grown so accustomed to her new family that she regards her *jefa* (boss) as if she were her own mother, and her employer's children as if they were her own. Another draws a bitter résumé of her life in Spain, and the lack of understanding and gratitude for her sacrifice back home. 'You give up a lot of yourself when you come here [to Spain]. And when you go back home you realise that this sacrifice often has not been worth it,' she says. 'They don't value it. Sometimes your own family does not even value it.'

The case of the Chinese was different. They had arrived not to work in Spanish homes or Spanish building sites, but to set up businesses of their own. According to official data, there were more than 180,000 Chinese living in Spain in 2015, the year I spoke to Chen and Wang, three times more than in 2003. That put them far behind the South Americans, Romanians and even the British in terms of numbers. But they were, in many ways, more visible – and more successful – than any other migrant group. Wherever you went in Spain, from the Balearic Islands to the remotest village in Extremadura, you would find *el chino*, a convenience store with long opening hours. Some sold only food and drink; others sold cheap hardware goods, toys, kitchenware and clothing; and some sold everything at once. More often than not, the *chinos* were marvels of responsive retail management. You always seemed to be able to find exactly what you needed in their cramped, tightly packed aisles. Even without recourse to the sophisticated tracking and stock management technologies employed by big retailers, the owners knew what their customers wanted, and adapted their offerings accordingly. Chinese shops close to playgrounds would offer a huge array of sweets and soft drinks. Stores based in downtown Madrid, especially if they abutted parks and squares, would stock vast quantities of beer, spirits and crushed ice for young revellers who liked to party outside. I lost count of the number of times I rushed out late at night in search of a birthday candle, a bottle of wine, a pack of batteries or an extension lead – only to find the desired goods at one of the many *chinos* in my neighbourhood.

Supplying these stores was the business of Chen, and it was a business that had made him a rich man. Still only thirty-four years old when I met him, Chen had emerged as one of the most recognisable faces of the Chinese community in Spain. His story found parallels across the crisis-scarred countries of Southern Europe, which also saw an increase in Chinese migrant arrivals – and in Chinese economic activity – despite the brutal post-2008 recession. Chinese migration to Spain continued to rise even after the start of the crisis, highlighting how well the community was able to weather the economic storm. In a country where – at the worst moment of the crisis – one in four workers was out of a job, unemployment was virtually unknown among the Chinese. Furthermore, they accounted for a vastly disproportionate share of business start-ups: there were more than 40,000 self-employed Chinese on Spain's commercial register, twice as many as before the crisis. At the same time, there were growing signs that the Chinese were starting to work their way up the economic ladder. Gone were the days when Chinese economic activity in Spain was confined to serving up *rollitos de primavera* (spring rolls) or selling trinkets in dusty 100-peseta shops. There were Chinese-owned fashion chains, import-export businesses, media groups and law firms.

219

According to one estimate, the annual turnover of Chinese-run convenience stores alone amounted to €785m.

The community's success did come, at least to European eyes, at a significant personal cost. Chinese shops stay open from morning until night, seven days a week, and are usually staffed by members of the same family. Chen told me he had never taken a holiday. He returned to China for the first time twelve years after his arrival in Madrid, but he was quick to stress that the trip was mainly for business. For most of his time in Spain, he had spent money only on goods that he needed to make it through the day: 'The moment you arrive in Spain as a migrant, you know that your mission is to earn money, not to enjoy life. You need a bed to sleep in and clothes to wear – nothing more. Later, when you have a business and things are going well, you can allow yourself to buy something, but not before.' He knew that such single-minded dedication to work was viewed by most Spaniards – and much of the rest of the world – as an incomprehensible sacrifice. But Chen had no doubt that it lay at the heart of his nation's extraordinary economic rise. 'It is with this sacrifice that China is conquering the world,' he said proudly.

Dressed in a smartly cut black suit, white shirt and black tie, Chen looked every inch the successful businessman. His replies were short and to the point, but he broke into a wistful smile when I asked him how it had all begun. A native of Qingtian, an impoverished rural county in the coastal Chinese province of Zhejiang, Chen had arrived in Madrid on 10 November 1998. The date was etched on his memory 'like a second birthday', he said. It was the first time he had left his home country. The decision to depart had been a family one: his high-school grades had not been good enough for him to go to university, and earning money without a higher education would be tougher in China than in Europe. Besides, his older brother was already living in Madrid, part of a fast-growing migrant community from Chen's home region. On the way from the airport, his first impression was that of a country not much richer than the one he had left behind: 'The houses I saw along the way looked pretty bad. In China the houses are covered with tiles so they are pretty but here all you see are the bricks. I realised only later that Spaniards take greater care of the inside than the outside. Inside, their houses are always tidy, clean and pretty.'

Like most Chinese migrants in those years, he came without money and spoke no Spanish. Just eighteen years old, he earned his first cash waiting tables in a Chinese restaurant and selling plastic toys and cheap clothes at funfairs in villages across Spain. The only Spanish words he knew at the time were numbers, so he could haggle over prices, along with *hola*, *gracias* and *adiós*. Determined to save as much as possible, Chen shared a single room with his brother. 'The only thing to do was to work, work, work. In the beginning, we didn't even have a television. When we bought one, we bought a small one, so we could easily carry it with us when we had to move,' he recalled. Four years after his arrival, Chen joined forces with his brother and uncle to set up their own business. His partners had savings, but they had to ask for loans from two other family members to reach the €20,000 they needed to buy their delivery van. 'We worked every day from 8 a.m. in the morning to midnight. Once, I made a whole round trip just to take a kilo of peanuts to one of our customers,' he said.

The hard work paid off. As the number of Chinese-owned shops soared, so did the business of supplying them. Don Pin reported sales of €220,000 in its first year. Within little more than a decade, its annual turnover was more than €60m, and the company boasted a fleet of 35 trucks and employed 110 workers. Many of the men and women who worked in the offices and warehouses came from the same part of China as Chen. Most spoke to each other in Mandarin, but many conversations took place in the regional dialect spoken in Qingtian. This concentration highlighted a crucial feature of the Chinese migration pattern – the influence of family and regional networks. The vast majority of Chinese living in Spain arrived in the country because a brother, cousin, husband or uncle had made the same journey. Estimates vary, but some believe that as many as 70 to 80 per cent of Chinese migrants in Spain came not just from the same province, but from the same small county, Qingtian. Their dominance is reflected not least on the walls of Chinese restaurants up and down the country, which often boast framed pictures of Qingtian city.

'When you move abroad,' Wang told me, 'you always ask yourself: "Do I have a friend or family member there or not?" If you do, everything is easier. If not, it is so much more difficult.' But family networks were not just crucial in deciding what country the Chinese chose as their destination. They also played a critical role in helping the new arrivals to get started in business – by providing the all-important access to finance. 'If you want to open a bar or start a corner shop, you don't go to the bank to ask for €20,000, you just ask ten friends and family members for €2000 each,' Wang explained. 'One month after opening, you pay back the first person. The second month you pay back the next. The system works very well.' It worked, above all else, on the basis of personal trust and mutual dependency. 'You never sign a contract. And you never ask for interest,' said Chen, adding: 'This is not a system or an application. It is all about human trust.' It was possible to refuse requests, but by doing so a Chinese businessman would shut himself out of the intricate web of favours taken and favours owed that underpinned the community. 'Today I help you with a loan so you can open your shop. But tomorrow you help me to open my shop,' Chen said.

It was a system that was born, at least in part, out of necessity. Like most migrants, the Chinese arriving in Spain typically lacked the assets, credit history and financial guarantees sought by banks. Even if they had wanted to take out a loan from Banco Santander or BBVA, they would most likely have been turned down. But the approach also reflected a broader mistrust of the official banking sector. 'The Chinese know that the bank always wins. So if we don't have to ask for money from the bank, we don't,' said Mao Feng, a Madrid-based businessman and president of the Association of Chinese in Spain.

This cheap, flexible system of financing was one of the main reasons why the Chinese were able to weather the crisis better than most. Unlike their Spanish counterparts, the Chinese were largely insulated from the vagaries of the country's tottering retail banking system and when lenders stopped the flow of credit to small and medium-sized companies, the Chinese were unaffected. Also when a Chinese business was having trouble repaying a loan, or paying salaries, it was usually easy to find a swift and flexible solution. Its main creditors, more likely than not, were not twitchy banks but family members and friends. Its workers, typically, were similarly close – and usually ready to accept a temporary wage cut.

'Who survives in a crisis? Those who have capital or who have easy access to capital. And when the crisis came, the Chinese had their family network to fall back on,' explained Mario Esteban, an analyst at the Real Instituto Elcano in Madrid.

Other migrant groups were not as fortunate, or as well prepared. Indeed, the Chinese were the exception. Migrants from Latin America, North Africa and other countries were among the biggest losers during the crisis. With no job, no savings, and little prospect of finding new employment quickly, many had no choice but to head back.

One evening in early 2014, I found myself talking to Juan López, the owner of a small bar in Aluche, a working-class district in the south of Madrid that was popular with Latin American migrants. He told me he had bid farewell to hundreds of friends and patrons since the start of the crisis. 'Half the people I know have already left, and people are still leaving,' the bulky forty-four-year-old explained, leaning close to make himself heard. The neon-lit bar was shaking to the sound of Colombian dance music but the place was empty save for one table occupied by a sullen group of Latino drinkers. 'I ask them: "Why are you leaving Spain?" The answer is always the same: "There is nothing left here for me. If I have to be hungry, I would rather be hungry at home."'[9]

López came to Madrid from his native Peru more than two decades before. In the years that followed, millions more arrived in Spain in search of work and a better life. What they found was a country in the midst of an economic upswing, and in desperate need of workers. What they didn't know was that their arrival had helped inflate a housing bubble that would ultimately prove ruinous. As Spain's population rose, so did predictions of future housing demand. The new migrants, after all, needed, somewhere to live. So Spain built more houses and flats, creating the need for more workers to build those houses and flats, who in turn needed houses and flats themselves. It was a strange, seemingly virtuous circle that was destined to crunch to a halt sooner or later.

When the property bubble burst in 2008, the recession left thousands of migrants without a job. In many cases, their economic situation was made worse by the fact that they had taken on large mortgages themselves. Like so many other Spanish traits, the local penchant for home ownership had quickly been copied by the migrant community. By 2012, the demographic tide was flowing out once again, as hundreds of thousands decided to head back to their former countries. From his vantage point behind the bar, López had followed the decline in his customers' fortunes. 'When the crisis hit, people started spending less money. Then unemployment started affecting people. Then they stopped getting unemployment benefits.' In 2008, one year after the start of the crisis, Spain still recorded 310,000 more migrant arrivals than departures. That number fell to just 13,000 the following year before turning negative in 2010. In 2012 there were just over 140,000 more departures than arrivals, and the following year the deficit exceeded 210,000. For a country the size of Spain, these were large and painful numbers.

A short walk from the bar, I found a so-called *locutorio*, a quaint fixed-line telephone centre full of plywood booths that offered cheap long-distance calls to Latin America, Africa and Asia. To Liliane Díaz, the Ecuadorian owner, it had once seemed a rock-solid investment. 'I bought this place in 2007. At that time we had twelve phone booths. Now we have four,' she told me.[10] 'Sunday nights used to be so busy it was terrible. Now it's also terrible but because there are so few customers.' Her experience mirrored that of Spain's large mobile phone providers, who were also struggling to extract more revenue from an ever-decreasing market. According to data from the national telecoms regulator, the number of mobile phone contracts in Spain dropped by more than two million between 2012 and 2014.[11]

Speaking to economists and analysts at the time, the picture that emerged was bleak. Just as Spain's housing market had once been propped up by migrant arrivals, the steady outflow of people now seemed to condemn an already moribund property sector to years of further decline. The country's creaking public pension system, meanwhile, needed more workers to pay social security contributions, not less. A falling population also meant fewer consumers, lower tax revenue, and fewer shoulders to bear the nation's towering debt. The future looked inescapably gloomy. In 2013 the national statistics office put out a medium-term estimate predicting that the number of people living in Spain would fall by 2.7 million over the next decade, equivalent to a 5 per cent drop in population.[12]

Today we know that the demographic panic was exaggerated. The statisticians had fallen into the classic trap of assuming that the current – extraordinary – trend would continue unabated in the years ahead. Just as Spain's population was never going to grow for ever at the speed it did during the height of the boom, it was also not going to contract at crisis-era velocity for a decade and more. Instead, migrants did what migrants always do – they nimbly responded to changing economic and political patterns. As soon as Spain's economy returned to growth, the trend shifted. In 2014 the net migration loss fell to just 55,000, and by 2015 the balance had turned positive once again. In 2016 there were 112,000 more migrants arriving in Spain than leaving. Here, in fact, was one of the clearest signs that the country had turned a corner: its population was growing larger – and more diverse – once again.

Even at the height of the crisis, and despite the sudden rise in departures, there were plenty of signs that many of Spain's migrants were putting down roots. I became aware of this while waiting outside the church of the Holy Virgin Mary in central Madrid one icy Sunday morning in January, as the air around me filled with the smell of incense and the deeply melodic sound of

Romanian hymns. The simple red-brick church was packed with worshippers, who had come from all over the Spanish capital to celebrate mass in the Romanian Orthodox style. On the pavement outside, prams jostled for space with a stand selling icons and religious books, a large noticeboard and two glass boxes filled with electric candles, one for the living and one for the dead. A decade earlier, the sight of hundreds of Romanians worshipping in a Spanish church would have caused wonderment. Now it was simply part of a normal Sunday in close to a hundred parishes across the country.

The Romanian Orthodox Church in Spain had grown in leaps and bounds since the turn of the millennium, closely tracking the remarkable rise of the Romanian population. As noted above, their numbers had soared from a few thousand in 1999 to almost 900,000 in 2012, making Romanians the largest minority in the country at the time. To the surprise of many, Spain's Romanian population continued to rise even after Spain plunged into economic crisis. They were free to leave and find work in other, more prosperous European countries, but not many seemed to want this. 'The majority is happy to stay,' Viorica Sologan told me outside the church.[13] The fifty-nine-year-old Romanian had decided to leave mass early, and was busy sticking advertisements on trees and lampposts in the vicinity. Sologan had just lost her job as a carer and cleaner, but wanted to stay put rather than build a life in yet another country. 'It's too big a risk. I would have to learn a new language and learn how everything works. Not everyone can do that.'

That view was widely shared among Spain's Romanian community. 'I have yet to see any Romanian desperate to swim across the Channel,' said Miguel Fonda Stefanescu, the president of the Federation of Romanian Associations in Spain. 'People live here with their families and children. Their children go to school here. Unless things become even more difficult, they will spend the rest of their working life here and then go back home.'

Ion Vîlcu, the Romanian ambassador to Spain, made a similar point when I caught up with him at his office in a plush part of Madrid. 'You have to understand that a migrant community that is well integrated does not start packing its suitcases when times get difficult. You weather the storm and hope that the storm will pass,' he said. Vîlcu was echoing a widespread feeling in the community when he argued that Spain could teach some of its northern European partners a lesson in how to make migrant workers feel welcome. 'Spain has never engaged in the kind of populist and xenophobe discourse that we now see in other European countries, even though Spain was hit so hard by the crisis,' he told me. His comments offered a thinly veiled critique of the political fury that was erupting in the UK at the time, stoked by warnings from politicians and parts of the media that the removal of the last remaining restrictions on migrant workers from Romania and Bulgaria would trigger an influx of low-skilled workers and put a fresh strain on the welfare system. Such concerns never gained much traction in Spain, even though the Romanian population was about eight times as large as that of the UK. Cultural affinity and the similarity of the two languages clearly helped, the ambassador argued. Romanians can typically reach some level of fluency in Spanish after a few weeks of study, making it easier to take part in everyday life. 'Romanians have found in Spain a society that was open, that did not discriminate against them and that allowed them to integrate,' he told me.

The Chinese also did not feel under any economic pressure to leave. They had their networks, but they also had the savings to see them through the crisis. Thriftiness, I heard again and again, lay at the heart of the Chinese expat business culture. 'When a Chinese earns €1000 he will never spend it all. He will always set aside €500 or so to make provisions for the future or to invest,' Mao, president of the Association of Chinese in Spain, told me. Austere, hardworking, utterly committed to success – this was how the Chinese saw themselves. Indeed, as much as they claimed to admire Spain and the Spaniards, some Chinese found it hard to hide their disdain for some of the more carefree local habits. 'When I tell a Chinese worker I need someone to work on a Saturday, he will do it and I'll pay him,' Chen remarked. 'With a Spaniard, when I ask him to work on the weekend I have to negotiate. It is almost like I am asking him a favour!'

The Chinese community in Spain kept growing long after the economic collapse, but there was a subtle change nonetheless. Newcomers told me that the more recent wave of Chinese migrants was different from Chen's generation. Many arrived by choice, not out of economic necessity. They came to see something of the world and to improve their skills. But they admitted that they were also a little less driven than the early entrepreneurs.

Yun Ping Dong, twenty-seven, came to Spain in 2009 to study but she told me she had no immediate plans to return to China. 'Life is freer here, and calmer,' she said. 'We want to enjoy life a little bit more.' Work visas were harder to come by and – after decades of relentless economic growth in China – the economic gain of moving to Europe was not as clear-cut as it had been previously. Data showed that the number of new arrivals from China was finally tailing off: migrants were still coming, but they were fewer and better educated, and often came for a specific job or to study a particular course. 'There is no reason to come

229

to Spain any more. You live very well in China now,' remarked Mao, the association president.

Yet just as the wave of migrants had begun to ebb, a new wave started building – this time bringing money and investment from China rather than workers and entrepreneurs. It was an extraordinary trend that seemed to gather strength with every year that passed. At first, Spaniards seemed bemused when they heard that wineries and sausage-makers were falling into the hands of the Chinese. But the deals kept on growing. Soon enough, one of the country's largest hotel chains was the target of a successful takeover bid from China. Then it was the turn of the famous Edificio España, that hulking Franco-era skyscraper in downtown Madrid that had been boarded up and empty for so long. As the correspondent for the *Financial Times*, I chronicled many of the deals. Occasionally I would find myself listening to general managers or vice-presidents sent over from China to announce the latest transaction in broken Spanish or English. The mismatch between the vastness of their own business and the smallness of the Spanish target was often evident. Like most Spaniards, I had never heard of Changyu Pioneer, the group that bought up a medium-sized Spanish winery in the Rioja region in 2015. My eyes widened as their representative pulled out a series of postcards showing their gigantic Chinese vineyards – typically with a faux Bordeaux-style castle in the middle – and began to explain. Changyu, it turned out, controlled vineyards the size of Burgundy. The company was now hoping to import millions of bottles a year from Spain and France, in a bid to quench the nation's ever-growing thirst for wine.[14] To raise its profile in the old world, Changyu had just agreed to sponsor the Spanish football league. That deal, too, was no isolated case: in 2015 the Dalian Wanda group had bought a 20 per cent stake in Madrid's second team – Atlético de Madrid

– underlining Chinese interest in one of Spain's most successful exports.[15] When the club moved from the atmospheric but
decrepit Calderón stadium to a new arena in late 2017 (a move
that aroused mixed feelings among Atleti supporters such as
myself), its new home was christened the Wanda Metropolitano.
It was yet another symbol of Chinese success in Spain, as visible
as those little orange Don Pin trucks zooming across the capital
at all hours of the day.

Elsewhere, visibility remained a challenge. In certain places,
the new Spaniards *were* visible – indeed, they were omnipresent,
impossible to ignore. You saw their children in classrooms up
and down the country, though much more rarely in the fee-
paying, well-run schools favoured by middle-class Madrilenians.
You saw them in their neon vests and overalls, sweeping streets
and cleaning windows. You saw them congregating in parks
and playgrounds, looking after children that weren't their own.
But you rarely saw them on television, reading the news or
presenting quiz shows. You rarely saw them in parliament, in
editorial conferences, in boardrooms or on stage. Very few of
them were writing books or making movies or telling their
story in any other way. The Ecuadorians, the Romanians and
the Moroccans – they all played their role in keeping the country
running, but they were mostly not running anything themselves.
Whether in culture or politics, business or finance, their voices
were rarely raised or heard. It took until 2016 for the first black
and the first Muslim members of parliament to take their seats
in the Madrid legislature. In both previous general elections,
in 2009 and in 2011, immigrants had accounted for less than
1 per cent of members of parliament in Spain, one of the worst
under-representations in all of Europe.[16]

Was this a problem? Or was it just a matter of time? I had to
think of other countries – such as Germany, France and Britain

– and how long it took there for migrants and their descendants to break through. The mayor of London is the son of a Pakistani bus driver. One of Germany's brightest film directors is the son of Turkish migrants. Britain, France and Germany have all seen Muslims enter parliament, and eventually ministerial office, too. This happened many decades after the first wave of immigrants arrived. Indeed, most tales of high-profile immigrant success in Europe are tales about the second generation. They are written by the sons and daughters of parents from Turkey, Pakistan and Algeria, who grabbed the educational possibilities on offer and battled their way up the social ladder. In Spain, that generation is mostly still in school. Eventually, however, the halting, thickly accented Spanish spoken by the Chinese shop traders will give way to their children's mastery of Castilian, Catalan and Basque. The sons and daughters of Ecuadorian builders and cleaning ladies will have access to better schools and universities than their parents did back home. If anything, Spain's still formidable commitment to public services and a strong egalitarian mindset should make the breakthrough happen sooner rather than later.

There is another reason why I think there is cause to be hopeful about the prospects for the new Spaniards. That reason was brought home to me one October afternoon, when the street outside my apartment building was suddenly filled with the solemn, beautifully melodic sounds of a Peruvian marching band. I rushed to the balcony with my toddler son, who exclaimed with delight: 'Papa, they are making music in the street.' He ran to fetch his little toy trumpet and we headed downstairs to join a rapidly swelling march of worshippers. It turned out that the church on our street was one of several that celebrated the feast of the Señor de los Milagros (the Lord of Wonders), an image of Jesus Christ that is widely venerated in Peru. The Peruvians in Madrid had decided to replicate the feast in their new home:

they held a mass in the little church across the road from my apartment building, followed by a colourful procession that included men and women clad in purple robes, a young couple in traditional Peruvian dress dancing in the street, much waving of Peruvian flags and a battalion of Peruvian women selling home-made sweets and snacks along the way. There was a lot of shouting and eating and chatting as the procession made its way up Calle Fuencarral before turning right onto Calle Genova. Both are important traffic arteries in central Madrid, and both had been closed for the occasion. As we let the crowd carry us along, I marvelled at the decision: this was surely a significant inconvenience for thousands of drivers, yet it had been taken all the same. What mattered was that this was a Peruvian tradition that clearly meant a lot to the local community. So it was done. To me, the procession was emblematic of one of the outstanding features of immigration in Spain: the fact that – despite the eventual emergence of the far right in 2018 – the majority of Spaniards seemed so relaxed about it. The Madrilenians I saw in the street that day looked quite untroubled by the foreign flags and the noise, and by the fact that a string of public roads had been handed over to a small group of migrants. Spain's reward was on full display as the march went on, slowly looping back to the church where the procession had started. Again and again, the marchers erupted into shouts of 'Viva Peru!' But this was followed, almost always, by another shout: 'Viva España!' It was a gesture, nothing more, but I found the whole experience strangely moving: the migrants were celebrating their old and new home in equal measure. No one was questioning their loyalty to one nation or the other. They cherished both. Here they were, right outside my front door, showing everyone who watched that immigration, that most toxic issue of contemporary Western politics, could be a happy thing as well.

*

The Chinese, too, seemed optimistic. 'The first generation of Chinese migrants had a lot of difficulty with the language and with communication. They had no time to study. But their children study here in Spanish schools, they speak Spanish perfectly and they know Spanish culture very well. So I think things are getting better,' Mao said. He echoed a common sentiment when he argued that most Chinese living in Spain were here to stay. 'Many of us feel like the Spanish. The family is here, the kids are studying here. I think only a few Chinese are thinking about returning. They like life in Spain.'

Chen, the founder of Don Pin, told me there were countless things he liked about life in his adopted country. But he, for one, had no desire to grow old in Madrid. 'When I die, I want to die in my village. I arrived here when I was eighteen but I still feel my roots very strongly. But it is different for the children. My children will be Madrilenians.'

CHAPTER TEN

The Spanish exception

The Palacio Vistalegre is a vast, covered arena on the outskirts of Madrid that – depending on the event – can pack as many as 15,000 spectators under its circular roof. A rock band has to be pretty confident in its fan base to book a night in the hall. The same is true for a political party. At the height of its popularity, Podemos proudly showed off its mass appeal by filling the Vistalegre for its founding congress. It was from the stage of this arena that Podemos leader Pablo Iglesias made his famous promise in October 2014 to 'storm the heavens' of political power in Spain.

Four years later, almost to the day, the huge auditorium was in the hands of an altogether different political movement.

The far-right Vox party was another child of the Spanish crisis, founded by a group of disgruntled politicians from the conservative Popular party around Santiago Abascal, its Basque leader. Vox was formally established in December 2013, just weeks before Podemos itself saw the light of day. Unlike its left-wing rival, however, Vox struggled to gain attention – let alone votes – in the years that followed. At the 2016 general election, it suffered a crushing failure, winning just 0.2 per cent of the vote. The result seemed to confirm a widely-held belief that Spain was immune to the far-right surge sweeping Europe in the post-crisis years. Indeed, except for a handful of local councillors, Vox had no political presence to speak of when it set its sights on Vistalegre. What the party's leaders had, however, was confidence – confidence that their time had finally come, and confidence that Vox's support was large enough and passionate enough to fill the arena. They were not mistaken. On 7 October 2017, some 9000 followers crammed into the mighty hall, many of them proudly waving the banner of Spain.[1] '*España viva* [the living Spain] has awoken – thanks to God,' declared Abascal as he opened his speech. Vox, he said, was an instrument in the service of Spain. He lashed out at the 'cowards' of the Spanish centre-right, at the 'treason' in Catalonia, at the 'moral dictatorship imposed by political correctness' and at the waste of hard-earned Spanish money on 'illegal migrants'. He denounced the bureaucratic 'globalists' running the European Union, while hailing Spain's singular contribution to Europe: 'We saved it from the advance of Islam in seven centuries of *reconquista*!' Turning to the country's recent past, Abascal suggested that sympathisers and supporters of the Franco regime had nothing to be ashamed of. Without mentioning the dictator by name, he declared that freedom also meant 'the freedom to think what we want about the past'. No one, he added, should expect right-wing Spaniards 'to sit in the corner and ask for forgiveness'.

It was the issue of Catalonia, however, that Abascal returned to again and again. He called for independence leaders to be jailed, for independence parties to be banned, and for Catalonia's regional police force to be abolished. The only solution to the Catalan crisis, he argued, was to return all the rights and powers devolved to the Spanish regions back to Madrid – 'one government and one parliament alone for all of Spain'. The Vox leader closed his speech with a rousing declaration: 'Vox lives so that Spain may live. Viva España!' The hall returned his salute with a thunderous 'Viva!' of its own.

I was surprised to see Abascal on the big political stage, and even more surprised by the size of the crowd cheering him on. I had interviewed the Vox leader in early 2017, at a time when the party still looked like an abject failure. Abascal told me at the time that the party's poor performance was – at least in part – due to the rise of Podemos, which he claimed had encouraged right-leaning voters to rally round the flag of the PP. But he was convinced that Vox's moment would come: 'We have far more sympathies than votes. It is a question of time.' I asked him to explain what the new party was about. 'We don't identify with extreme labels but we share a lot of positions with parties on the alternative right – [we agree] that countries need borders and security, for example,' he told me.[2] Abascal also called for the closure of mosques funded by 'extremist' regimes such as Saudi Arabia, and argued that Vox and like-minded parties had to fight back against 'political correctness'. The biggest issue by far for the party and its voters, however, was 'national unity'. Thinking back to our conversation, I was struck by how similar his arguments and promises were to the ones he made in Vistalegre. The main difference was that – this time – Spain was listening.

Abascal's speech introduced a new tone into Spain's political discourse. Many of the themes he raised in Vistalegre – migration, the EU and Spain's recent past – were not among the typical speaking points of the Spanish right. Whatever the private views of members and voters of the Popular party, the centre-right party had never made criticism of migration or the EU a central plank in its election campaigns. Nor was there much appetite to get involved in debates about the legacy of the Civil War and the Franco regime. The PP had opposed the historical memory movement and its demand to finally prosecute the crimes of the Franco regime. But neither was it inclined to publicly defend – let alone glorify – the dictator's rule. If nothing else, such a stance would have made for bad politics. For as long as anyone could remember, far-right nostalgics had no one aside from the PP to vote for anyway. It was the voter in the political centre who would determine whether the party could win elections or not – the kind of voter, in other words, who had no time and no sympathy for open displays of Francoist sentiment. Vox, however, made clear from the outset that it was operating under a different set of rules. In some policy areas – such as Catalonia – its demands often seemed like a more radical version of those espoused by the PP and Ciudadanos. In other fields, however, the party made a conscious effort to do and say things that its rivals would never even think of – let alone say out loudly. Perhaps the best example of this was Vox's determined stance against feminism, which included harsh criticism of measures designed to combat violence against women and the frequent use of terms such as 'feminazis'. Perhaps unsurprisingly, more than 70 per cent of Vox voters turned out to be men. 'Vox is all about breaking the consensus and finding new political spaces,' Guillem Vidal, an expert on Spanish politics at the Geschwister Scholl Institute of Political Science in Munich, told me. The image Abascal and his colleagues were trying to conjure up was that of 'the great Spanish nation divided by nationalism and feminism'.

The event in Vistalegre made headlines – and raised questions: where had all those flag-waving Madrilenians come from? How many Vox supporters were there in other parts of the country? And would the enthusiasm that flooded the giant hall in the capital carry through to the next electoral contest, the regional ballot in Andalusia two months later?

The polls struck a cautious note: most surveys suggested Vox would win only a few percentage points, and no more than a handful of seats in the regional parliament, if they managed to enter the chamber at all. Andalusia was, of course, the last-remaining bastion of Socialist support in the country, a fiefdom that had been under the rule of the PSOE for four decades. But the region had also been at the sharp end of the migration crisis in recent years: the beaches and ports of Andalusia had long served as disembarkation points for migrants who crossed the Strait of Gibraltar in flimsy boats. The proximity between Europe and Africa – at the narrowest point the two continents are separated by only 14 kilometres of clear blue water – meant that the region and its people bore the brunt of the refugee surge that gathered pace throughout 2018.

There was another reason why Vox leaders looked to Andalusia as an inviting target for its hardline rhetoric: after all, the region had more reason than most to fear a Catalan breakaway. As the largest region in Spain, and one of the poorest to boot, Andalusia would be first in line to suffer the financial consequences of secession. For years, it had been the beneficiary of the country's generous system of fiscal transfers from the prosperous north to the poorer south. Losing Catalonia meant losing one of the system's main contributors. Money worries aside, Andalusians had a special reason to deplore the separatist discourse in Catalonia, where some independence activists liked to point to the poorer southern region as a symbol of Spanish backwardness. No matter what the polls said, Vox leaders had every right to look to the December ballot with hope.

Their hope would not be disappointed. On an election night that embarrassed pollsters and shocked the political mainstream, Vox obtained 11 per cent of the vote and 12 seats in the 109-seat parliament of Andalusia. The political upstart had not only managed to enter the regional legislature, but it was also assured a crucial role in the formation of the next government. Without the support of Vox, the PP would not be able to form a new administration. Spain's once-invisible far right had become the political kingmaker in Andalusia. Inside the Seville hotel where Vox supporters and leaders gathered to celebrate, the mood was jubilant. 'Long live the resistance!' was one of the chants that rose up from the crowd.[3] 'We will lead the *reconquista!*' declared Francisco Serrano, the regional party chief. There was also warm praise from European allies such as Marine Le Pen, the leader of France's National Front, who congratulated Vox in a Twitter message on the night. After four decades in the shadows, the Spanish far-right had staged a triumphal comeback.

The Andalusian result gave a boost to Vox that would carry well into the next year – and into Spain's critical general election in April 2019. Lingering hopes that the far-right resurgence might be limited to Andalusia dissolved with every new poll. No less alarming, at least from the standpoint of the Spanish left, was that Vox managed to pull both the PP and Ciudadanos further to the right, deepening the traditional rift between the country's opposing political camps. In February 2019, the leaders of Vox, Ciudadanos and the PP stood side-by-side at a mass demonstration in the centre of Madrid that called for Spanish unity and denounced the government of Pedro Sánchez. Feeling the pressure from the right, Albert Rivera, the leader of Ciudadanos and a former ally of the Socialist prime minister, went into the election campaign vowing not to make common cause with Sánchez. He made no such promise with regard to Abascal and Vox.

As the election drew nearer, it became clear that only the size of the Vox presence in Spain's parliament was in doubt. In the end, the party won 10.3 per cent of the vote and 24 seats in the national legislature. The result was not enough to secure an overall victory for the right, and slightly worse for Vox than many had expected and predicted. But looking at the faces of Abascal and his colleagues, there was little sign of disappointment. The Andalusian result, it turned out, was no fluke: Vox had battled its way onto the big stage as well.

To understand the importance of Vox's political breakthrough one must first understand why Spain resisted the rise of the far right for so long. For much of my time in the country, the fact that Spain was hostile terrain for parties with a xenophobic, anti-immigration or anti-European message was taken almost as a given. Political scientists even had a term for it: the Spanish exception. To find out what they meant, I drove down to the small Castilian town of Villacañas in early 2017, for an article that sought to explain Spain's status as a political outlier.

Like so many places in Spain, Villacañas still bore the scars of the recent crisis. Driving into town, the first thing I saw was a row of vast, silent factories. Some were plastered with faded 'for sale' signs. Others faced a gradual, losing battle against the weeds and bushes that encroached from all sides. These factories were once the pride of Villacañas. Although home to just over 10,000 people, the town used to be known as the 'door capital' of Spain. Before the collapse of the country's housing boom, it had boasted ten large manufacturers that produced millions of doors a year. Local unemployment was minuscule and workers had money to burn: luxury cars became a common sight, fancy overseas holidays a regular treat.

When the property bubble burst, six of the main manufacturers were forced to close. Some 3,000 workers lost their jobs. Unemployment in the area increased more than tenfold, eventually peaking at 28 per cent in 2012. So jolting was the transformation that Villacañas became famous once again: as a symbol of Spain's crisis and its economic woes. Reporters flocked to the little town south of Madrid to tell the tale of a nation's malaise, and explain how it had all gone so horribly wrong for Villacañas.

To me, however, the more interesting story was what happened next – or, to be more precise, what didn't happen. For all the obvious parallels with the rust-belt states in the US or the hard-hit industrial heartlands of England and France, there was no sign that Villacañas had experienced a populist backlash, an anti-immigration wave or a revolt against globalisation. There was hardly any clamour to leave the EU, and only sparse demand for a campaign to keep out the migrants. Despite the brutal economic decline and years of mass unemployment, the political centre seemed to hold – in towns like Villacañas, and across the country. At the time of my visit in January 2017, Spain had yet to see the rise of a populist far-right party like the National Front in France, an anti-immigration platform like the Alternative for Germany, or an anti-EU movement like the UK Independence party. Outside Spain, only a handful of smaller European countries, such as Portugal and Ireland, had been able to resist the tide. Among the big nations of the West, Spain appeared to stand alone. Polls and election results all pointed to the same conclusion: Spaniards were overwhelmingly in favour of EU membership, and mostly remained untroubled by immigration. 'People here worry about jobs, not about migrants,' explained José Manuel Carmona, a member of the Villacañas local council for the centre-right Popular party. 'If they blame anyone for the crisis, it is the politicians.'[4]

Locals did not see Brussels as the villain, either. Instead, they looked to the EU and its institutions for support – and they were not disappointed. Like many rural towns in Spain, the people of Villacañas had been grateful recipients of farm subsidies for decades. Now, in the middle of the crisis, they saw the EU provide financial aid to help retrain workers who had been laid off as a result of the downturn. 'I think locals here understand that the EU is an institution that has provided funds and help,' Santiago García Aranda, the town's Socialist mayor, told me.

The absence of the far right in Spain was remarkable in part because the country had long seemed like an inviting target for a party like Vox. The recent crisis had forced Madrid to slash spending and raise taxes – measures that were blamed at least in part on pressure from the European Commission and foreign leaders such as Germany's Angela Merkel. Trust in the political elite was shattered by corruption scandals. Moreover, the economic crisis erupted at the end of a decade that saw un-precedented numbers of migrant arrivals, including from Muslim countries such as Morocco. Yet somehow, the economic crisis and the political humiliations that followed were not enough to help Vox break through. Before heading out to Villacañas, I had looked up the local results of the 2016 general election. Vox had won just 10 out of 5771 votes in town, less than the local offshoot of the animal rights party. After my conversations with the mayor of Villacañas and other local leaders, I left the town convinced that the next election would not be any different.

Spanish political scientists and commentators provided plenty of reasons to back up my hunch. They argued that memories of the Franco era were too fresh, the sense of Spanish national-ism too weak, and sympathies for the EU and the migrant population too strong to allow space for a far-right surge. Their conclusion was that there was nothing fleeting or coincidental about Spain's rejection of far-right politics, but that the country was – in this sense at least – truly exceptional. All over the world, countries were succumbing to authoritarian strongmen, far-right parties and ultra-nationalist movements. Wherever one looked, voters were lending their support to political leaders promising to build walls, throw out the foreigners, end foreign entanglements and make their nations great again. The year 2016 brought us Brexit and Trump; 2017 brought us the rise of the Alternative for Germany, and put the far-right Freedom party into government in Austria. In March 2018 it was Italy's turn to demonstrate the strength of populist and anti-European sentiment, as the far-right Lega and the euro-sceptical Five Star Movement emerged triumphant in parliamentary elections. The contrast offered by Spain never looked starker than in June 2018, when prime minister Pedro Sánchez offered sanctuary to a boat drifting in the Mediterranean with more than 600 refugees on board, after Italy and other EU countries had refused to let the vessel dock. It was only a gesture – but a gesture that few European leaders could offer without inviting a political backlash at home. At the time, Sánchez had no reason to share that fear.

Four months later, Vox flooded the Palacio Vistalegre with flags and people, and Spanish politics would never be the same again. Villacañas, too, was eventually caught up in the far-right surge. Local support for Vox increased more than sixtyfold since my visit in 2017; with almost 11 per cent of the vote, the Villacañas branch of the party came fourth in the 2019 general elections.

Some weeks after the Andalusian election I spoke to one of the founders of Vox to find out why the party was riding high – and where it might go from here. Iván Espinosa de los Monteros, a US-educated former consultant and businessman who was now in charge of the party's international relations, insisted that the recent success should not have come as a surprise. 'Catalonia was the inflection point,' he told me. In the weeks and months that followed the October 2017 independence referendum, Vox leaders noticed that local rallies were drawing an ever greater number of people. The mood in the country had plainly, visibly changed: angered by the separatist challenge, more and more Spaniards had started hanging the national flag from their windows and balconies. Many of them were ready for a new message and a harsher tone: enough with the talk of compromise and constitutional reform. Catalonia had to be taught a lesson about loyalty and about the law – the sooner the better. Spaniards, Espinosa told me, had a tendency towards following political events with a certain degree of 'passivity'. They took care of 'what happens in their home, not what happens in the street'. In the case of Catalonia, he argued, the Spanish public had been content for years to watch events from the sidelines: 'As long as the unity of Spain was not seriously threatened, Spaniards thought that this was an issue for the politicians to deal with. But when they had the sense that the threat was real, it was like waking a sleeping giant.'

I asked Espinosa about the party's relations with other far-right parties in Europe, and how Vox differed from the likes of Le Pen's anti-immigration and anti-EU National Front. 'It is very difficult to compare us to other parties because the situation of Spain is very difficult to compare to other countries,' he responded. 'We have to defend things that were never even called into question in other countries.' States like France and Germany, he argued, faced many challenges, but a national break-up was not among them. It was that danger, more than anything else, that guided the politics of Vox.

Like many of his counterparts in the rest of Europe, Espinosa rejected the far-right label: 'We touch themes that are outside the left–right axis. The issue of Catalonia is the best example of this. But then you also have the issue of personal freedom – when it comes to hunting, for example, or the preservation of a certain model of rural life, the ability to enjoy bullfighting and other traditions. I am talking about the real lives of many people who are far from the reality of urban elites that want to tell everyone how we should live our lives.'

Where precisely all this left Vox within the universe of Europe's new far right was not easy to tell. The party was young – much younger than its peers in France, Italy, Austria and the UK – and had little experience of political campaigns, successful or otherwise. What was not in doubt, however, was Vox's ambition. 'We want to overtake the PP,' Espinosa told me. 'We want to leave them to be forgotten.'

The sudden rise of Vox in 2018 showed that a far-right party could indeed succeed in Spanish politics. This came as a surprise to many, though perhaps it ought not to have been. Looking back, I realised that there had been no shortage of warning signs. I had to recall a series of encounters over the years, not least with members of the Franco foundation, that hinted at the far-right potential still lurking in pockets of Spanish society.

I met Melisa Ruiz one Sunday in June 2016 in the run-down but still imposing halls of the former headquarters of Spain's public television news service. The building had stood vacant for years, but was now illegally occupied by Ruiz and her organisation, which called itself Hogar Social Madrid (HSM), or Social Home Madrid. Her appearance was as striking as the vast murals covering the entrance rotunda of the building, which depicted a Franco-era vision of Spain, with farmers, workers, soldiers and priests all working in harmony. Just twenty-seven years old, she had long bleach-blonde hair, and sported extensive tattoos, heavy make-up and oversized neon ear studs. Dressed in a dark-blue hoodie emblazoned with a castle and a bear, the official HSM logo, she presented – visually if not ideologically – an obvious break with the crusty image of Spain's old-school Francoist far right. Ruiz and her comrades had broken into the building a few months before, and had since converted it into the centre of their social and political activities. They knew they would be evicted sooner or later, as indeed they were. In the meantime they had set up a library and food bank that offered hand-outs to impoverished Madrilenians every Sunday – provided they were Spaniards.

There was not a migrant face in sight when the iron gate was flung open around midday to let in a few dozen people drawn by the Hogar's offering. I watched them shuffle up the stairs with their empty trolleys and bags, patiently waiting their turn. Ruiz would call them into the food storage room one by one, cheerfully enquiring how they were doing and what they needed. She knew many of them by name. The handouts offered were basic – a loaf of bread, sausages, rice, pasta, beans, biscuits, oil and milk – but gratefully received. There was no talk of politics, but the message was clear enough: this was Spanish aid for Spanish people. Any migrant who turned up asking for help would be politely turned away, Ruiz explained. The group wanted refugees to leave Spain, and Spain to leave the EU, and it had launched a string of high-profile stunts and demonstrations to publicise its cause. Here, indeed, was a raw expression of far-right political opinion in Spain.

'Our main concern is the sheer number of migrants living in Spain now and the huge social benefits they receive,' Ruiz told me after the daily distribution was done. 'For Spaniards who are going through hard times, this is a massive injustice.'[5] It was the same political pitch that had entered conversations – and parliaments – across much of the EU. In Spain, at the time, it remained a minoritarian cry, as Ruiz herself was quick to accept. She pointed to the historical legacy of Spain's Civil War and the four decades of right-wing dictatorship that had lasted until the late 1970s. 'This has left behind a revanchist mindset. The politically correct and socially acceptable thing in Spain is to be on the left,' she claimed. The country's past, Ruiz added, had also led many of her fellow right-wingers to look backwards, not forwards. 'Far-right parties in Spain have always been about nostalgia and melancholia. They have not created a new model that is adapted to the new times. We have started making a new model. We want to create something new,' she said.

Ruiz saw it as her mission to change the cultural hegemony of the left, in part through politically tinged social work and in part through headline-grabbing protest. Her group had developed a talent for making the news despite its small size and limited resources (Ruiz told me the HSM had no more than a hundred members at the time). HSM demonstrators would light massive flares outside mosques, creating a dramatic backdrop to chants and banners that would otherwise be easily ignored. It would piggyback on other events, disturbing the election rallies of Spain's mainstream parties, for example, or interrupting a protest held by Catalan independence activists. It also had a flair for slogans: on one occasion, it staged a protest outside the headquarters of Spain's Socialists. PSOE stands for Spanish Socialist Workers' party, and the HSM was keen to denounce the embattled centre-left as a group of aloof, academic internationalists. Their placards read: 'PSOE – not Socialist, not workers, not Spanish'. As Ruiz explained to me, this was all part of a protracted effort to change the conversation – and seed the ground for more structured political activity. It was, she argued, simply too early to think about launching a real political party and entering parliament. Her blend of social work and in-your-face protest, alongside her opposition to mass migration, economic liberalism and what she defined as 'radical feminism', made for an idiosyncratic political mix. Ruiz pointed to Greece's ultra-right Golden Dawn movement as a model, but was quick to acknowledge that Spain remained a political outlier in Europe, at least for the moment. Spanish society, she told me, 'does not yet see us as a political alternative'.

Around the same time as my meeting with Ruiz, I made a trip to Alcalá de Henares, a small university town north of Madrid that is famous above all else for being the birthplace of Cervantes. It was also one of only a handful of Spanish towns in which voters had – long before Vox's breakthrough – elected a far-right politician to their local council. Rafael Ripoll was the leader of a party that called itself Europa 2000, and had been a member of the Alcalá council since 2011. His style, speech and political approach were less provocative than that of Ruiz, but their analysis and proposals seemed broadly compatible. 'Migrants? They have the right to come when we want but they should leave when we want,' he told me in his small office in the town hall.[6] Much like his bleach-blonde counterpart back in Madrid, Ripoll railed against the excesses of free-market capitalism, and the social injustices wrought by globalisation. When I asked him about the EU, he gave me a solemn lecture on how Spain had been forced to sacrifice its shipyards and heavy industry in order to join the European trade bloc. Spain, he added, was now simply 'a country for tourists'. Ripoll said he agreed with much of the anti-establishment critique offered by Podemos, though not with its solutions: 'We want the nation state to be a wall against globalisation. Podemos wants to dissolve the nation state,' he said.

Ripoll also saw Spain's far right as a prisoner of the country's past. 'There is a simple reason [for the movement's weakness]: there has been a lack of self-criticism on the patriotic, nationalist side. We have been more preoccupied with reviving the past than with building the future. I think it's time to close the chapter of the past and time for the patriots in Spain to open a new chapter.'

Political scientists and sociologists, too, would often turn to the Franco legacy in trying to explain the conspicuous absence of a far right. In a well-argued report that was released in early 2017, researchers from the Real Elcano Institute in Madrid and the Demos think-tank in London pointed out that Spaniards' sense of identity continued to be shaped by the memory of the dictatorship: 'The overuse of national symbols and of references to national identity during Francoism caused a countermovement which still persists,' the paper said. 'The pro-democratic opposition to the regime rejected the exhibition of national symbols, the flag and the anthem, and Spanish nationalism was completely absent from their discourse. Instead, they looked to Europe.'[7] Carmen González Enríquez, the lead author, told me at the time: 'The main difference between Spain and other European countries is that, here, people see no link between immigration and national identity... The sense of national identity is generally rather weak in Spain. You sometimes hear local complaints. People will say: "All the local shops have gone." Or: "This village has changed so much." But it is never expressed in any political form,' she said.

According to a poll conducted for the Elcano/Demos study, only 10 per cent of Spaniards said they wanted to leave the EU, compared with 22 per cent in France and 45 per cent in the UK (though more than half of British voters chose to leave in the 2016 Brexit referendum). That level of support clearly reflected Spain's historic status as a net recipient of EU funding, but also less tangible factors. For many Spaniards, the EU still represented modernity and progress, while Spanish membership of the union offered reassurance that the country had finally joined the European mainstream.

That sentiment, moreover, remained strong despite the successes of Vox in late 2018 – so strong, in fact, that not even Vox itself could entirely ignore it. The far-right party was critical of the EU, and certainly more hostile to Brussels than other political groups in Spain. But it was also careful not to labour the point. 'We are not anti-European,' Espinosa told me. 'We are demanding of Europe. We have ideas about reforming Europe not because we want to destroy Europe but because we like Europe and we want to improve it.' Vox did not call for a Spanish exit from the EU, or from the euro. It campaigned against elitist bureaucrats in Brussels, but not against the European institutions as such. Whatever else it was, Vox did not look like the Spanish equivalent of the UK Independence party.

Vox was bolder on the issue of migration, an issue that did play a significant role in the party's discourse and programme. But Vox also made clear that its rhetoric was not aimed at the vast majority of migrant groups in Spain, namely those from Latin America and the rest of Europe. Abascal took aim at 'illegal migrants' and at migrants who he claimed were not willing to adapt to the Spanish way of life. To his listeners, it was quite clear who he meant: refugees from sub-Saharan and northern Africa who entered the country by boat or by crossing the fearsome border barriers that surrounded the Spanish enclaves of Melilla and Ceuta in Morocco. Espinosa drew much the same distinction when I spoke to him a few weeks after the Andalusian elections: 'We have nothing against immigration and we have nothing against the European Union. What we want is immigration that is legal, regulated and meets the interests of Spain.' Migrants from Latin America, who shared a language and culture with Spain, were like 'brothers', he said. Vox would look less kindly on those migrants, however, whose culture was 'incompatible' with that of Spain.

As Vox leaders honed their message on migration, they knew they had to tread carefully – more carefully, in any case, than their far-right counterparts in other European countries. Despite the party's recent successes, the fact remained that Spanish attitudes towards migrants and migration were markedly friendlier than elsewhere. One typical poll from 2018, the year that saw Vox finally break through at the ballot box, found that only 26 per cent of Spaniards described immigration as a 'problem'.[8] That was significantly lower than the European average; in Italy, for example, 51 per cent of respondents saw immigration as a problem. Another comparative survey, again from 2018, asked respondents in twenty-seven states around the world whether they wanted fewer or more migrants to come to their countries. In Spain, only 30 per cent said they wanted fewer migrants – the lowest by far for any European country – while 28 per cent said they wanted more migrants – the highest of any country in Europe included in the survey.[9]

Looking at these numbers, I wondered what role Spain's own experience of poverty and migration had to play. The country had, after all, been a nation of migrants itself not so long ago. In the leaden years of the Franco dictatorship, between the 1950s and 1973, some 2.75 million Spaniards had moved to Germany, France, Switzerland and elsewhere in search of work.[10] Virtually everyone in the country had a family member or relative or neighbour or acquaintance who had earned their money in those northern factories. For those left behind, the experience was chronicled not just in letters and stories, but also in the hugely popular 1971 film *Vente a Alemania, Pepe* (Come to Germany, Pepe). The film follows the journey of Pepe from a poor village in Aragón to Munich, where he hopes to make his fortune and – perhaps more importantly – get into bed with one of those famously uninhibited German girls. It is a comedy, but a bittersweet one, and sometimes the bitterness breaks through undiluted. Like the Spanish migrants in real life, Pepe arrives in cold, busy Germany clutching a cardboard suitcase. He struggles to understand and make himself understood. He pines for home. That experience of dislocation and estrangement is one that countless Spaniards still carry today, as a distant recollection or a much-repeated family story. To some, indeed, the memory is not so distant. The post-2008 crisis drove tens of thousands of Spanish workers abroad once again. This time, it was mainly the young and better-educated who headed north, but the pain of separation – and the sense that Spain had failed them – was not so different.

Curiously, just as in the 1960s and 1970s, the experience was again reflected in films and popular culture. In 2015 I watched a fresh comedic take on the experience of Spaniards looking for work in Germany. It was called *Perdiendo el Norte*, a title that literally means 'Losing the North', but is better translated as 'losing one's bearings'. This time it was not Pepe, the manual labourer, but Hugo and Braulio, two twenty-something university graduates struggling to find work in their home country. They, too, made the trip to Germany (Berlin, this time) where they met the same teutonic coldness that had confounded poor Pepe four decades earlier. The film was a forgettable assembly of slapstick scenes and overacted clichés but it seemed to strike a chord. More than 1.5 million tickets were sold, making *Perdiendo el Norte* one of the most successful films of the year. It was clear that part of its success rested on the simple fact that it depicted a reality that many Spaniards were familiar with. As I sat watching the screen, I wondered what was going through the heads of the Madrid cinemagoers sitting next to me. I was sure that many of them knew from personal experience that tough times force people to leave their loved ones behind and seek work across the border. And I was equally sure that many of them saw something familiar in the Ecuadorian bricklayer, the Moroccan fruit picker and the Romanian lorry driver trying to make ends meet in Spain now. Some might have seen their grandfather, writing letters home from the cold North in the 1960s. Others might have remembered a son or daughter, waiting tables in London half a century later.

For a large majority of Spaniards, the new migrants might have been foreigners, but they were certainly not strangers. The survey mentioned above,[11] released in April 2018, found that two-thirds of Spaniards 'interacted' with immigrants in their neighbourhood – in shops, restaurants, parks and streets – at least once a week. Close to 40 per cent said they had contact with immigrants in their neighbourhood on a daily basis. Only two countries in Europe – Greece and Italy – boasted more interactions. The Mediterranean climate and way of life evidently played a key role: so much of social life in Spain (and Italy, Greece, Portugal) takes place outdoors, in bars and on terraces, in parks and streets. I had only to think of Plaza del Dos de Mayo, the small, atmospheric square close to my apartment in Madrid. On summer nights in particular, it would be packed with people of all ages and origins, drinking beers, smoking, talking and listening to music until the early hours. Chinese and Moroccan kids would play football in the corner with Latinos and Spaniards, or jostle for space on the climbing frame in the crowded playground. Everyone mingled and talked. This one square in Madrid, I thought, probably offered migrants and locals more opportunities to meet in one night than they would have had in a normal German, Dutch or English city in a whole year. Climate and custom meant that southern Europeans socialised in the open, while northern Europeans met behind closed doors. The result was that Spaniards knew their relatively new neighbours better than other Europeans knew their far more established communities. And, more often than not, they liked what they saw: the 2018 survey also asked Europeans whether they would be comfortable with having an immigrant as a friend, work colleague, neighbour, doctor, family member or manager. No fewer than 83 per cent of Spaniards said they would feel comfortable with all of the above – the highest figure in the entire EU.[12]

That sense of familiarity was clearly in part the result of the peculiar nature of migration to Spain: a high proportion of the migrants who arrived in Spain before the crash of 2008 were from Latin America – people who were foreigners by passport, but who spoke the same language, followed the same sports and worshipped at the same church as the locals. Another large group of migrants came from Romania and, as mentioned, their language was closely related to Spanish. 'The experience of ethnic diversity for the average Spaniard has not been the same as for the French and British. It was less shocking,' said Sergi Pardos-Prado, a political scientist at the University of Oxford. Pardos-Prado made another good point when I spoke to him in the summer of 2016: Spaniards simply had other – more obvious – targets to blame for their economic misery. 'The blame for the crisis fell on the economic elites, on the banks, the IMF, the Troika [of international financial institutions that included the European Central Bank, the European Commission and the IMF] and on the austerity measures. But not on migrants and foreigners,' Pardos-Prado argued.[13]

*

That was true at the height of the economic downturn, and
for the years that followed. But was it still true in 2018? Had
the success of Vox not shown that Spaniards were starting
to worry about migration after all? Jorge Galindo, a political
analyst and columnist, seemed to think so. 'It was always said
that immigration is not a contentious aspect in Spanish politics.
I am afraid that is not true any more,' he told me in early 2019.
Galindo had looked at the voting patterns in the Andalusian
regional elections, and emerged with an important insight: Vox
had been especially successful in areas where the proportion of
migrants – and African migrants in particular – was especially
high. 'Immigration is becoming an issue, and some voters regard
the position of the PP on this matter as too soft,' Galindo told
me. What is more, he sensed that some of the stigma that had
previously been attached to anti-immigrant comments and
views had disappeared. 'The social norm has broken down,' he
concluded.

The success of Vox suggested that something had indeed
changed. Yet some felt that it was too early to bury the idea of a
Spanish exception. José Fernández-Albertos, a political scientist
at Spain's CSIC research institute, believed that the issue of
migration was only a minor factor in the rise of the far right.
'Immigration is not the centrepiece of what they are selling,' he
told me. 'Of course they are xenophobic and anti-immigrant but
when you compare them to the National Front [in France] and
the Alternative for Germany their emphasis is different: most
of their positions have to do with Catalonia, and with fighting
a cultural war against the left,' he added. 'Compared to other
European countries, immigration is still much less of an issue
in Spain than in other countries – especially when you look at

the number of migrants in Spain and the speed at which they arrived.'

In his view, one of the most important reasons why Vox broke through in 2018 – aside from the conflict in Catalonia – was the weakness of the PP. For decades, the centre-right party had managed to remain a catch-all movement for all strands of conservative voters, from free-market liberals to crusty old authoritarians. That alliance held for decades, largely because there was a political reward for compromise between those factions – namely, the chance to shape the policies of a powerful governing party. As the PP's share of the vote plunged, and the party eventually lost its grip on government, that reward no longer looked so enticing. 'Many voters no longer see the PP as the big house of the right. That means they are now ready to express their political views in a much more open way,' Fernández-Albertos argued.

Spain's lingering sense of sympathy for both the EU and for the migrant population had clearly not been strong enough to prevent the emergence of Vox. But could it ensure that the far right would remain, at least for the foreseeable future, a much smaller force in Spanish politics than it had become in other European countries? Both the Andalusian ballot in 2018 and the general election in 2019 seemed to suggest precisely that: for Spain, a far-right party winning 10 or 11 per cent of the vote was shocking. In the wider European context, however, Vox's results were very much at the low end of the nationalist spectrum. The polls mentioned above – highlighting the proximity between locals and migrants – also gave me hope that the vast majority of Spaniards would continue to resist the xenophobic tide. And if that was already the prevailing mood among the Spanish population, there was nothing in the media to push them in a different direction. The country's television channels, radio stations and newspapers – whether online or in print – were prone to flip into hysteria and hyperbole when it came to Catalonia or Podemos. But even the right-wing press kept a remarkably sober tone on issues such as the EU and migration. There was tough criticism of the way the European institutions had handled the eurozone debt crisis. But no one questioned the value of the EU as a whole. Nor was there a market for those dubious stories beloved by parts of the British press that chronicle Brussels' apparent plans to ban curved bananas or establish a European army. In part, the absence of such absurd tales reflected the peculiar nature of Spain's media: there was simply no such thing as a tabloid newspaper dealing in low-brow sensationalism. There was no Spanish equivalent of Britain's *Daily Mail* or *Sun*, or Germany's *Bild*. There was, of course, no shortage of poor reporting, errors, bias and manipulation. There was also a vast supply of gossip journalism, detailing the jealous escapades of bullfighters' wives and the dream weddings of Spain's nobility. But the outlets and television programmes that specialised in this kind of material stayed out of politics. Spain's biggest-selling newspapers maintained – or tried to maintain – a serious tone that simply did not lend itself to huge, jokey headlines about the idiocy of Brussels bureaucrats and Strasbourg fat cats. I do not wish to absolve the Spanish media of criticism: the country's public-sector broadcaster, for example, was all too often guilty of parroting the government line on everything from party corruption scandals to the conflict in Catalonia. The three largest Madrid dailies – *El País*, *El Mundo* and *ABC* – often failed to separate opinion from news sufficiently clearly. But their coverage of Brussels was unfailingly serious, and largely free of trumped-up trivia.

The same was true of issues surrounding migration. As the

UN refugee agency noted in an exhaustive report, comparing the way European news organisations covered stories about refugees and migrants, 'reporting in all three newspapers was broadly sympathetic to their plight'.[14] The report noted that the Spanish press rarely referred to refugees and migrants as threats, and that they were more likely to explain why those people were fleeing their home countries in the first place. Such conclusions chimed with my own impressions. In all my time in Spain, I cannot remember reading a single scaremongering story about foreign criminals or work-shy migrants. Such articles were a staple of big-selling newspapers in Britain and Germany, in part because they reflected the tastes and prejudices of readers and editors, but also because there was often genuine scope for competition between migrants and natives for government resources. In Spain, by contrast, the welfare system was structured in a way that made such tensions much less likely. The state grants generous access to core services such as health and education, but offers little in the way of social housing and direct support payments. 'You don't have this conflict between natives and non-natives over welfare that you have in other countries,' Fernández-Albertos, the political analyst, explained to me. 'Spain has pretty good public services but when it comes to housing and cash benefits it's very weak,' he said. 'And those are precisely the areas where it becomes visible that the state is making transfers from one sector of the population to another.' As a result, headlines about foreigners claiming benefits and migrant families living off welfare were and are rare in Spain. 'Part of this is always about competition for resources. When there are no resources to compete for, the potential for conflict decreases,' argued Pardos-Prado.[15] That argument went hand-in-hand with another feature of Spain's crisis: the fact that migrants were usually much harder hit than the native population, who could rely on family networks to cushion the blow. Foreign workers had no safety net to fall back on, and often had little choice other than to move back to their original countries. It was, as Fernández-Albertos pointed out, 'objectively difficult to argue that Spain treated its migrants too well during the crisis'.

Back in Villacañas, that was certainly the impression of hard-hit locals. At the height of the boom, migrants accounted for 5 per cent of the town's population – but that share decreased markedly in the years that followed. 'When the crisis came, most of them just left,' recalled García Aranda, the mayor.

To be clear: life in Spain can be difficult if you have a foreign accent, a darker skin or worship a different God. That was true before the arrival of Vox, and remains true today. Racism exists in Spain, and is – if anything – expressed with greater openness than in other European countries. Black football players, for example, are still greeted with monkey chants in some Spanish football arenas. Spaniards are, in my experience, also far more casual when it comes to voicing stereotypes and clichés about other nations than northern Europeans. I have seen perfectly reasonable and educated people jokingly pull their eyes into slits when the conversation turns to China or Japan. I have heard seemingly liberal acquaintances explain that Jews are good with money and have a lot of influence. Words, expressions and jokes that would strike the average Briton or American as unquestionably racist are thrown about without any awareness that they could hurt or insult. When Antoine Griezmann, a French striker playing for Atlético de Madrid, posted photos of himself in December 2017 as a blacked-up member of the Harlem Globetrotters, it caused shocked headlines in the British press. In Spain, no one seemed to understand what the fuss was about.

I do not wish to belittle these words and gestures. Racism, anti-semitism and hatred of Muslims exist everywhere, and Spain is certainly no exception. But, despite the rise of Vox, it is striking how rarely these attitudes have translated into threats and violence. Hate crimes and physical attacks against foreigners are extremely rare. I have already written that I never personally encountered instances of verbal abuse or insults directed at migrants. That impression is broadly confirmed by the official data. According to Spain's interior ministry, the police recorded 416 racial hate crimes in all of 2016 – a decline of 18 per cent compared to the previous year.[16] Cross-border comparisons are difficult because countries define and register such incidents differently. But Germany, for example, recorded more than 23 racial hate crimes every day, or 8530 in total, over the same period;[17] according to official data, there were no fewer than 995 attacks on refugee centres alone in 2016.[18]

I found much to admire about the way Spain dealt with the crisis. Nothing, however, impressed me more than the country's overwhelming refusal to turn against the foreigners living in their midst, or to blame outside forces such as the EU for the nation's economic troubles. Spain's politicians, for all their apparent weaknesses and foibles, deserve credit for this, as does the media. But it was ultimately the country's voters who decided to turn their fury on the elites in politics and business, and not on the more vulnerable recent arrivals from Latin America and North Africa, Eastern Europe and China.

That restraint started to unravel in late 2018, largely in response to the Catalan crisis, and it may unravel further in the years ahead. Experience suggests that a far-right party – once it has managed to gain a foothold – is very hard to dislodge. The mere presence of Vox is likely to legitimise far-right arguments and policies, and could further erode social taboos that existed for decades. Spain can expect to hear much more about treasonous Catalans and unwanted migrants in the near future. Indeed, it is possible that the far right will grow and grow, as it has done in other countries, and ultimately eclipse the traditional centre-right. But I very much doubt it. In its current configuration, Vox appeals to an important but ultimately limited group of voters. Crucially, the party's hardcore economic liberalism makes it an unappealing choice for the disenfranchised and the poor – a crucial component of the far-right alliance in other countries. Its strident anti-feminism, meanwhile, has antagonised a large section of the electorate. At the same time, one of the most important drivers of far-right sentiment in other countries, namely hostility towards the EU, is still largely absent in Spain, even on the political right. Another critical driver, migration, has indeed become a greater concern for some Spaniards, but it remains much less of an explosive theme than in other European societies.

The idea of the Spanish exception was always about more than just the absence of the far right. It captured the exceptional nature of a country where the vast majority of citizens – for all their economic troubles and social tensions – refused to give in to irrational hatreds or to look for scapegoats among minority groups. In that sense, despite the electoral breakthrough made by Vox, I believe the Spanish exception remains intact.

EPILOGUE

Towards a new Spain

There is a dimly lit room in the south corner of the Prado museum in Madrid that contains some of the most harrowing works of art ever made. The walls of Room 67 are grey, as is the floor. The paintings themselves are chillingly dark: the colours that predominate are black and brown, allowing the red of blood and the white of the eyes to stand out with piercing clarity. The fourteen works on display here were painted by Francisco de Goya from 1820 to 1823, and are known as the *pinturas negras*, or black paintings. They are the works of an old man, marked by war and illness, who had only recently lost his hearing. Goya painted these images directly onto the walls of his country house outside Madrid, and they were never meant to be seen by the public. In the Prado today, the first painting that comes into view is a high, rectangular canvas that is almost entirely abstract – except for the head of a small dog who appears to be half-buried or drowning. On the left wall is a depiction of Saturn devouring his own son, his gaping mouth tearing away at the arm of a headless body. There are pictures of witches and madmen, murderers and ghosts – a beautiful, terrifying assembly of misfits and monsters that seems daring even two centuries later.

The picture I find hardest to forget hangs right next to that wretched little dog. It is called *Fight with Cudgels*, and shows two men battering each other with primitive wooden weapons. The man on the left has been struck already; blood pours from his face, staining his white shirt. His opponent is trying to shield his face with his left arm, in anticipation of the blow that is about to come. His own club is raised for the inevitable counter-strike. The raw violence of the scene is startling, but the true horror of this fight only becomes clear as you look towards the bottom of the painting: both men's legs are buried in the ground up to the knees, only inches apart. There is no escape, no place for cowardice, no chance to run away. This truly is a fight to the death – merciless, senseless and desperate.

Over the years, the painting has become something of a metaphor for Spain, even a cliché. It is the first image that comes to mind when Spaniards speak of the *dos Españas*, the two Spains that are forever bound in combat. The idea dates back to the nineteenth century, and has been debated, analysed and criticised ever since. As the poet Antonio Machado wrote at the beginning of the twentieth century:

> Little Spaniard who comes
> into this world, God help you!
> one of the two Spains
> will freeze your heart.

Machado wrote his poem more than two decades before the outbreak of the Civil War but the seeds of that conflict were starting to sprout already. The two Spains that Machado alludes to were there long before the terrible conflict, and many believe they are still here today. Then as now, the fight is thought to pit right against left, reaction against reform, religious against secular, tradition against modernity. One might add, with a nod to today's political discourse: a clash between closed versus open.

What Goya would have made of all these posthumous inter-
pretations no one can say. But I had reason to recall this painting
on more than one occasion during my time as a reporter in
Spain: in the Basque country, of course, where senseless violence and unbearable proximity went hand-in-hand for so long.
I thought of it as I chronicled the rise of Podemos, which drew
heavily and consciously on the intellectual tradition that splits
society into good and bad, friend and enemy. And I thought of
Goya in Catalonia, where the two sides have remained firmly
dug in, refusing to cede an inch, despite more than a decade of
political blow and counter-blow.

There are, of course, not just two Spains – not even in
Machado's poem. The first lines of his work, which are quoted
much less frequently, speak of a little Spaniard being born 'between a Spain that dies, and a Spain that yawns'. Machado, in
other words, was describing not so much a clash between old
and new, but between two Spains that are both obsolete. One is
tired, the other already dying. The question he raises is whether
Españolito, the newborn, can chart a fresh course – towards a
third Spain, perhaps – or whether he will be crushed by the
conflict between the old rivals.

A decade after the start of the great crisis, that question seems
as pertinent as ever. The longing for a new beginning is evident,
but so are the divisions that continue to plague Spain today.
What is more, the *dos Españas* of Machado have morphed and
multiplied over time, leaving Spain with fissures that run along
political, social, economic, regional and even national lines. These
fissures have widened notably over the course of the great crisis,
and have yet to be healed by the recent recovery. The crisis has
destroyed trust in the elites, and sown bitterness among the millions left behind. Their anger and economic frustration remain
palpable. The crisis also helped inflame separatist sentiment in

Catalonia, convincing millions that the region's only hope of advancement lies in a break with Spain. At times, the clash has been violent, at others it has carried – at least rhetorically – a faint echo of conflicts past. Catalan separatists have become increasingly fond of drawing parallels between the actions taken by the Spanish government and judiciary today and those taken by the Franco dictatorship. Unsurprisingly, such poisonous accusations have met with outrage in Madrid.

There is no easy solution to the Catalan crisis, and there may be no solution at all. At the same time, it remains hard to see how Spain can move forward – or return to some semblance of normality – without such a solution. The conflict has further corroded a political system already worn down by the crisis and a series of corruption scandals. Much like Brexit in the UK, it has consumed so much time and energy that politicians have had little time to think about other challenges, let alone take steps towards solving them. Turmoil in Catalonia has also made it harder for Spain to overcome the protracted deadlock in its national parliament – the place where all the country's troubles and divisions lie open as if placed on a dissection table. Effective government has been all but impossible. None of the major Spanish parties can put together a coherent coalition government. The fragmentation is made even worse by the presence of nationalist deputies from Catalonia and the Basque country, some of whom wish to have nothing to do with the Spanish state altogether.

Spain is not the only country in Europe to have seen its party system fragment. Yet it is only in Spain that party leaders have stubbornly refused to take the only plausible path out of this impasse: coalition government. At times, they have been happy to strike agreements across party lines on specific issues (the ousting of Mariano Rajoy in May 2018 being a notable example). But they have shown themselves strangely resistant to forming an actual coalition – to sitting down week after week at a cabinet table with former rivals, and implementing a political programme that is the product of a genuine compromise. That reluctance, moreover, is not just limited to parties on opposing sides of the left–right divide, or the split between Catalonia and Spain. It extends even to political groups that share at least some ideological overlap, such as the Socialists and Podemos on the one side, or the PP and Ciudadanos on the other.

Why should this be so? Why this reluctance to cross the political divide?

The obvious answer is that there remains something of Goya's peasant fighters in the silver-tongued, sharp-suited Spanish politicians of today. Even after all these years of peace, democracy and prosperity, they struggle to escape the brutal zero-sum logic of the country's violent past. The legacy of Spain's bloody twentieth-century history is a deep sectarianism that turns rivals into enemies, and compromise into betrayal. Listen to the speeches in parliament, read the insults on social media: Fascist. Terrorist. Traitor. They will not pass. Not one inch. To resist is to win.

I remember a friend telling me that you can walk into a party in Madrid and know instantly what political affiliation the overwhelming majority of attendees will have. This is true. Spain's different political tribes like to stay with their own. There is also a distinctly hermetic quality to much of the political debate in the country, as evidenced by the endless radio debates between like-minded left-wingers on one channel, like-minded separatists on the other, and like-minded conservatives on the third. Spain's politicians are reluctant to cross the political divide, because Spanish voters themselves are reluctant to cross it.

And yet, amid all the conflict and division, there are signs of change. Many have been chronicled and examined over the preceding pages, but some are worth repeating all the same. First and foremost, the past few years have brought a striking change in the political make-up of the country. The generation that masterminded Spain's *transición* from dictatorship to democracy has exited the stage, and a new cast of actors is jostling for position. Mariano Rajoy is likely to have been the last Spanish prime minister with direct experience of the Franco era. His successor, Pedro Sánchez, was three years old when the dictator died. All of his rivals – the leaders of Spain's other main parties – are younger still.

The same changing of the guard can be observed in the world of business and finance. Men like Emilio Botín at Santander and César Alierta at Telefónica have gone, drawn away by death or the allure of a sumptuous retirement package. Spanish business has become younger, more female, more transparent, less obsessed with empire-building – and is all the better for it. At the same time, both Barcelona and Madrid are home to a lively technology and start-up scene that has the potential to disrupt the country's corporate sector even more than any generational change. Spain's media landscape has also been through significant upheaval. Gone are the days when the terms of public debate were set exclusively by *El País* on the left, *El Mundo* on the right, and *ABC* further to the right still. All three flagship papers have lost circulation and influence, especially among the young. Today, some of the most consequential voices in Spanish journalism are to be found on private television channels, or among the raft of punchy new online papers. The nation's media, like the nation's politics, has become fragmented, more unruly, harder to control. The scope for cosy deals between politicians and journalists has been reduced. One way or another, the scandal will out. This is good news for Spanish democracy.

In some ways, the fragmentation of Spain's political scene, too, is a cause for hope. The shattering of the stable two-party system has made it much harder to form a government, and harder still for that government to take decisive action. When, and if, the next economic crisis hits, Spaniards may yet rue the country's new fashion for minority government. But the fragmentation of parliament – both on the national and the regional level – is also evidence of a healthy shift in the country's political culture. Elections and opinion polls all point towards the same conclusion: voters have grown fed up with the political monocultures of old. Mindful of the waste and corruption that flourish in the midst of absolute majorities, voters are no longer willing to grant unrestrained political power to any single party. They also appear to have discovered the value of occasionally booting out a long-serving ruling party, or at least reducing its majority to a level where other parties can exercise effective control. The PP no longer governs in Valencia, the Socialists lost power in Andalusia, political bastions and strongholds are falling up and down the country. These shifts are recent and remain incomplete, but their impact is clear already. Spanish politics has become more responsive, less willing to ignore the mood of the public, and less able to withstand political pressure caused by scandal and underperformance. Standards of conduct have become higher. The threshold for public disgrace has fallen markedly.

Just how far it has fallen became evident after Pedro Sánchez took office as prime minister in May 2018. Remarkably, his cabinet suffered its first resignation just a week after ministers were sworn in. Máxim Huerta, the minister in charge of culture, was forced to step down after it emerged that he had paid a substantial fine for tax evasion.[1] The next resignation came less than three months later. This time it was the turn of Carmen Montón, the health minister. She was accused of having committed plagiarism – along with other academic irregularities – in the thesis she wrote for her master's degree at a Madrid university seven years before. Part of her work, it emerged, had simply been copied and pasted from Wikipedia.[2] Within days, scrutiny turned to the 2012 doctoral thesis of Sánchez himself. He defended himself vigorously against allegations that he had copied material without correct attribution, allowing his work to be unsealed for the public and releasing the result of two separate software tests designed to detect plagiarism. In his case, the cloud of suspicion drifted away, but the affair sparked a race to scrutinise the academic credentials of a host of other leading politicians.

To veteran observers of Spanish politics, this all seemed remarkable. I recalled the grim bemusement with which Spanish friends and colleagues greeted a similar wave of plagiarism scandals in Germany at the height of the crisis. You see, they would tell me, in Germany they resign because of a bunch of footnotes in a doctoral thesis. In Spain, our politicians lie and steal, and they always get away with it. It was a charge that – for all the hyperbole – rang painfully true at the time. All over the country, politicians seemed to be clinging to office despite daily revelations about corruption or malfeasance. Five years later, they were clinging no more. Majorities in Spain had become too fragile, and voters too fickle, for any party to defend errant leaders. This, too, is good news for Spanish democracy.

There is, of course, more to a functioning political system than clean government. Spain's recent turn towards greater political transparency and democratic control is welcome, but it has arrived, to some degree, as a by-product of debilitating political fragmentation. One way or the other, Spain has to become governable again – and for that to happen the country's political class needs to shed some of its tribal instincts.

Will it happen? The harsh and bitter tone of the 2019 election campaign gave little hope for change. Yet the chances of a new approach may not be as small as one might think, if only for reasons of naked self-interest. We should not forget that until recently there was simply no need for the country's parties and politicians to co-operate. For almost four decades, Spain's electoral pendulum swung from right to left and left to right, always delivering handsome majorities to one camp or the other. The country's political class knew only the comfortable glories of government or the frustrating depths of opposition – nothing in between. Today, they must navigate a much more ambivalent political space. In the years ahead, the path to political power will depend not solely on the result a party obtains at the ballot box, but also on the ability of its leaders to forge a coalition after election day. As Mariano Rajoy and the PP learnt in 2018, being the biggest bloc in parliament is of limited use when that bloc holds only a little more than a third of the seats in the legislature. A party that cannot strike deals across the aisle, in other words, will have little hope of ever leading the Spanish government. It may take time for that conclusion truly to sink in, but it is hard to imagine a stronger incentive for Spain's new breed of political leaders to change their stance.

Am I too optimistic? Perhaps. On Catalonia, in particular, I struggle to envisage a happy ending. But I would dearly like to see one. I spent more than four years criss-crossing Spain's multiple divides, and I did so with great curiosity and genuine affection. To me, as to so many foreigners, the cultural, social, political and linguistic differences that mark Spain were never a cause for frustration or anger. They were an integral part of the country, an important reason why I loved living there, and why I love going back there today. I also felt that, for all the evident divisions, there was much that Basques, Galicians, Andalusians, Castilians and Catalans had in common. At the risk of sounding mawkish, I found a friendliness and warmth towards strangers that never ceased to surprise me. I found a willingness to speak, ask, comment, explain and share stories that is hard to find elsewhere. The old couple that cannot stop talking, the raucous table on the restaurant terrace that keeps on adding chairs and drinkers, the booming noise you hear when you enter a bar, the crowd of well-wishers that surrounds every hospital bed, the hundreds of thousands of demonstrators marching and chanting in the street – they all point towards the same conclusion: Spain is a social country. It is not for people who want to be left alone. For everyone else, there are few better places in the world than Spain. It is a country that gets under your skin, and occasionally on your nerves, but that will always offer a respite from the illness that so many in the West have most come to fear: loneliness.

I also encountered, again and again, a basic human decency that cut across the prejudices and preconceptions people held. Even at the height of the economic crisis, and despite the anger and frustration swirling around Spanish society, the country remained tolerant, helpful, open, vibrant, creative and endlessly surprising.

I spent some of my happiest years in Spain, living with my family in Madrid, and travelling the length and breadth of the country. Our base was an apartment in the capital's Malasaña district, in the very heart of the city. Among older Madrilenians, the neighbourhood has a rather poor reputation, dating from the 1980s, when it was known for its wild nightlife and savage drug problem. Some of the bars and clubs from that era survive, but today they are non-smoking and frequented by a happy blend of veterans and youngsters. In recent years, Malasaña has emerged as something of a hipster heaven: if you are looking for vinyl records, vintage racing bikes or limited edition trainers, this is the place to go. The general feel extends to the local playground, where toddlers play in the sand dressed in tiny Ramones T-shirts.

In the summer – which by northern European standards is most of the year – we would go to the square several times a week to play with our son, or to read the newspapers in the corner café, or to have a few beers with friends after work. On scorching summer nights, the public fountain would provide ammunition for extended water balloon fights. Introductions were easily made, especially when you arrived with a decent football. 'Are you friends from school?' I once asked a couple of boys who had kindly let my much-younger son kick a ball with them. '*No, somos amigos de la plaza,*' came the reply – 'We are friends from the square.' It summed up everything that is right about Madrid – a big, sprawling city but also a village where children can still make friends in the street.

I miss many things about Spain: the food, of course, and the sun. The wide open landscapes as you head out from Madrid, the turquoise waters of the Balearics, and the wild, sweeping northern coast. I miss the raucous village feasts in Castile, when the air is thick with the smell of fireworks and pork crackling, and I miss the solemn excitement of Easter week in Andalusia, when thousands crowd into the streets at night to watch the local procession by candle-light. I miss the little restaurant next to my office, with its cheap, delicious food and serious old waiter. I miss racing through the Madrid dawn en route to Atocha railway station, and from there onwards to Valencia, Málaga or Seville for my next assignment. I miss the long nights in the bars and restaurants of Barcelona, weighing the next chapter of the Catalan drama with friends over plates of *escalivada* and sausage, and plenty of dark red wine.

I miss the noisy Sunday afternoon lunches with friends in the Sierra above Madrid, and the austere landscapes and villages of Extremadura. I miss the long walk down the hill to the old Calderón stadium, the roar of the fans of Atlético de Madrid growing louder with every step, as my son grips my hand a little tighter. And I miss coming home long after midnight, and finding my neighbourhood still throbbing with people, the narrow lanes of Malasaña crowded with noisy, friendly, happy faces, determined to keep going until the night is over and – damn this crisis – the morning comes.

Acknowledgements

This book would not have been written had I not met a Spanish journalist by the name of Ana Carbajosa in a bar in Luxembourg one day. We were Brussels correspondents at the time – she for *El País*, me for the *Financial Times* – and different in almost all ways except for one: a shared passion for the life of the foreign correspondent. Ana is a brave and subtle journalist, a tenacious reporter and a perpetual firework of ideas and inspiration. She is also, more importantly, a wonderful partner and a loving mother to our son Tom. After Brussels, Jerusalem and Madrid, we are now on our fourth joint assignment in Berlin, still arguing over who goes reporting and who stays home to cook dinner, still reading each other's stories before publication, still swapping ideas and sources on a daily basis. It can be tiring, it can be tense, and it often is frantic. But I would not change our life for any other in the world.

Starting a new posting in a foreign country can be a daunting challenge. For me, arriving in Madrid was almost like coming home. From the first day, I was able to tap into Ana's vast network of friends and family, and the knowledge and insights they brought with them. Aside from covering the political and economic events of the day, all correspondents strive to under-stand what really makes a country tick. It is, of course, an elusive goal. But, thanks to Ana, I felt I understood Spain better than any of the countries I had covered before.

Ana has also been involved from the first day in the making of this book: we did some of the original reporting together, she read the draft stories at the time, and went through numerous versions of the book later on. My agent, Toby Mundy, offered wise counsel and warm encouragement from the outset. I was also very fortunate to have two superb journalists and friends read through early drafts of the book: Daniel Dombey, of the *Financial Times*, and Guillermo Altares, of *El País*. Dan and I have been friends and colleagues since we shared an office at the *FT*'s Brussels headquarters more than fifteen years ago. To this day, I trust his judgement on almost all matters – except, perhaps, on the wisdom of eating four-day-old oysters. Guillermo is one of Spain's most respected journalists, editors and critics, as well as the author of a splendid book on European history. Both provided invaluable advice and numerous corrections. Any errors of fact or analysis that remain are entirely my own.

I had the privilege of interviewing most of Spain's senior leaders in politics, business and finance, often on multiple occasions. These interviews and background conversations were a vital source for this book, and I would like to thank my interlocutors for their time. They include: Mariano Rajoy, Luis de Guindos, Cristóbal Montoro, José Manuel García-Margallo, José Ignacio Wert, José Manuel Soria, Íñigo Méndez de Vigo, Alfonso Dastis, Pablo Casado, Álvaro Nadal, Carmen Martínez Castro, Pedro Sánchez, Josep Borrell, Miquel Iceta, Eduardo Madina, Manuel de la Rocha, Albert Rivera, Inés Arrimadas, Luís Garicano, Antonio Roldán, Pablo Iglesias, Carolina Bescansa, Juan Carlos Monedero, Ada Colau, Manuela Carmena, Artur Mas, Oriol Junqueras, Carles Puigdemont, Carmé Forcadell, Jordi Sánchez, Mónica Oltra and Andoni Ortuzar.

I have only ever had one proper job and one real employer in my life: as foreign correspondent for the *Financial Times*. Since I joined the paper as a graduate trainee in 2002, I have been posted to Brussels, Jerusalem, Madrid and now Berlin – and I have benefited at every turn from friendly, helpful, meticulous and immensely clever colleagues. This book is based to a large degree on reporting I did for the *FT* during my stint in Spain – reporting that would not have been possible without the commissioning, editing, help and encouragement of my friends and collaborators on the paper. In Madrid, I had the pleasure of working with two wonderful *FT* colleagues, Miles Johnson and Ian Mount. On the world desk in London, I am supremely indebted to Ben Hall, Joshua Chaffin and James Wilson – three calm, intelligent and ever-helpful editors who steered European coverage during my time in Spain. In the analysis section of the *FT*, I was lucky to find three excellent editors in Chris Grimes, Geoff Dyer and Tom O'Sullivan. Several of the preceding chapters are based on reporting I did for the *FT*'s splendid weekend magazine, where Alice Fishburn and her team have been a joy to work with all these years. Roula Khalaf, the former foreign editor and now the deputy editor of the *FT*, has been endlessly supportive over the past decade and more, as has Alec Russell in his roles as world news editor, news editor and weekend editor. My editor-in-chief, Lionel Barber, runs the best newspaper in the world, and I will be forever grateful that he decided to take me along for the ride. It is hard to overstate what a privilege it is working for the *FT*, a place that manages to be both slightly anarchic and fiercely committed to journalistic excellence, that backs up its reporters in good times and in bad, and that harbours some of the cleverest and most entertaining people I have ever had the pleasure to meet.

In Madrid, I benefited from countless conversations (and drinks) with fellow correspondents Fiona Maharg-Bravo,

Raphael Minder, Jeannette Neumann, Michael Reid, Hans-Christian Rößler and Sarah White. Among Spanish colleagues, I am greatly indebted to Lluís Bassets, a wonderfully erudite columnist for *El País* and the former head of the paper's office in Barcelona, and to Pere Rusiñol, a journalist of rare passion and integrity, who opened countless doors for me in Catalonia, and was kind enough to read sections of my book that deal with Catalan politics. Alfredo Cáliz, a brilliant photographer and friend, accompanied me on reporting trips up and down the country. We ate some memorable dinners and listened to some lovely music along the way, and also managed to produce some magazine journalism that I look back on with genuine pride and satisfaction.

Like all correspondents in Madrid, I depended heavily on the wisdom of political and economic analysts, many of whom I pestered on a near-weekly basis. They include José María de Areilza, Oriol Bartomeus, Antonio Barroso, William Chislett, José Fernández-Albertos, Jorge Galindo, Carmen Gónzalez Enríquez, Manuel Arias Maldonado, Lluis Orriols, Alberto Penadés, Pablo Simón and José Ignacio Torreblanca. On economics and business, I learnt much from my conversations with Javier Andrés, Lorenzo Bernaldo de Quiros, Jordi Canals, José Ignacio Conde Ruiz, Rafael Domenech, Marcel Jansen, Santiago Lopez, Daragh Quinn, Antonio Rodríguez-Pina, Juan Rubio-Ramírez and Raymond Torres.

Last but not least, my heartfelt thanks go to Isabel Gutiérrez de la Cámara, who has managed the affairs of the *Financial Times* office in Madrid for more than a quarter of a century with energy, intelligence and charm. Over the course of my time in Madrid, I spent more time with Isa than with any person outside my close family – and I loved every minute of it.

Spain really was good to me. *Gracias a todos.*

Notes

Prologue: A crisis reveals

1 Tobias Buck, 'Severe recession leaves Spain bewildered', *Financial Times*, 5 November 2012, https://www.ft.com/content/47bfc3f4-236b-11e2-a46b-00144feabdc0

2 Banco de España, 'Evolución de los principales grupos bancarios españoles (2009–2014)', https://www.bde.es/f/webbde/INF/MenuHorizontal/SalaDePrensa/mapa_sector2014.pdf

3 Raymond Carr, *Spain – A History*, p. 5.

4 Ana Carbajosa, Serafí de Arco, 'España supera por primera vez a Italia en riqueza por habitante', *El País*, 18 December 2007, https://elpais.com/diario/2007/12/18/economia/1197932402_850215.html

5 Amparo González-Ferrer and Francisco Javier Moreno-Fuentes, 'Back to the Suitcase? Emigration during the Great Recession in Spain', *South European Society and Politics* 22 (2017), pp. 447–71.

6 Antonio Muñoz Molina, *Todo lo que era sólido*, p. 17.

7 Tobias Buck, 'Spain seeks to burnish its battered Brand', *Financial Times*, 11 April 2013, https://www.ft.com/content/a46b57dc-9f6f-11e2-b4b6-00144feabdc0

8 J. H. Elliott, *Scots and Catalans – Union and Disunion*, p. 227.

9 Fraga was one of several Franco-era leaders able to continue his political career after Spain's transition to democracy. He co-wrote the country's new constitution, and became one of the founders of the conservative Alianza Popular, the forebear of today's governing centre-right Popular party. Fraga himself served as the regional president of his home region of Galicia from 1990 to 2005.

[10] Jonathan Mayhew, *The Poetics of Self-Consciousness – Twentieth Century Spanish Poetry*, Bucknell University Press, Lewisburg, 1994, p. 101.

[11] José Ortega y Gasset, *La Pedagogía social como programa político* (1910), in *Obras Completas*, Volume One, Revista de Occidente, Madrid, 1967, p. 521, https://mercaba.org/SANLUIS/Filosofia/autores/Contempor%C3%A1nea/Ortega%20y%20Gasset/Obras%20completas/Tomo%201.pdf

Chapter One: Another country

[1] Tobias Buck, 'Catalonia's referendum exposes a divided Spain', *Financial Times*, 29 June 2017, https://www.ft.com/content/138164a6-5b8a-11e7-b553-e2df1b0c3220

[2] Europapress, 'Arenys de Munt celebra un dia "especial" tras 5 años de la primer consulta', 9 November 2011, https://www.europapress.es/catalunya/noticia-arenys-celebra-dia-especial-anos-primera-consulta-independentista-20141109122241.html

[3] Centre d'Estudis d'Opinió, 'Dossier de Premsa del BOP', 2da Onada 2012, http://upceo.ceo.gencat.cat/wsceop/4128/Dossier_de_premsa_694.pdf

[4] Centre d'Estudis d'Opinió, 'Dossier de Premsa del BOP', 3a Onada 2013, http://upceo.ceo.gencat.cat/wsceop/4688/Dossier%20de%20premsa%20-733.pdf

[5] Buck, 'Catalonia's referendum exposes a divided Spain'.

[6] Ibid.

[7] Jesús Sérvulo González, 'Cataluña aporta la mitad que Madrid a la solidaridad regional', *El País*, 7 September 2017, https://elpais.com/economia/2017/09/07/actualidad/1504799988_582658.html

[8] Mayte Alcaraz and Alberto Ruiz-Gallardón: 'La separación de Cataluña acabaría con la nación española', *ABC*, 15 October 2012, http://www.abc.es/20121014/espana/abci-entrevista-ruiz-gallardon-201210140040.html

[9] Buck, 'Catalonia's referendum exposes a divided Spain'.

[10] Elliott, *Scots and Catalans*, p. 10.

[11] Ibid., p. 26.

[12] Raphael Minder, *The Struggle for Catalonia*, Hurst, 2017, p. 21.

[13] Interview with the author, May 2017.

[14] Robert Hughes, *Barcelona*, p. 24.

[15] Buck, 'Catalonia's referendum exposes a divided Spain'.

Chapter Two: Autumn in Catalonia

[1] Tobias Buck, 'Catalan secession vote fosters tension, expectation, hope and fear', *Financial Times*, 6 October 2017, https://www.ft.com/content/29233056-aa67-11e7-ab55-27219df83c97

[2] Llàtzer Moix, 'Tomar partido', *La Vanguardia*, 5 October 2017, http://www.lavanguardia.com/politica/20171005/431798101286/tomar-partido.html

[3] Tribunal Constitucional de España, Ruling of 7 September 2017, https://www.tribunalconstitucional.es/NotasDePrensaDocumentos/NP_2017_074/2017-4334STC.pdf

[4] Speech by Mariano Rajoy at La Moncloa, 7 September 2017, http://www.lamoncloa.gob.es/presidente/intervenciones/Paginas/2017/prot20170907.aspx

[5] J. G. Albalat, 'Un herido por el impacto de una pelota de goma en Barcelona', *El Periódico*, 1 October 2017, https://www.elperiodico.com/es/politica/20171001/las-pelotas-de-goma-vuelven-a-catalunya-en-el-referendum-unilateral-del1-o-6323646

[6] Tobias Buck, 'The far-left separatists who took Catalonia to the brink', *Financial Times*, 5 October 2017, https://www.ft.com/content/4f0f3e46-a999-11e7-ab55-27219df83c97

[7] CUP, 'Programa Polític de la CUP-CC, Eleccions del 21 de Desembre de 2017', http://cup.cat/sites/default/files/programaelectoralcup21d.pdf

[8] *El País*, 'Anna Gabriel: "Me satisfaría tener hijos en grupo, en colectivo"', 12 May 2016, https://elpais.com/ccaa/2016/05/11/catalunya/1462966185_313983.html

[9] Fearing prosecution, Anna Gabriel did eventually flee to Switzerland.

[10] Michael Stothard, 'Catalan leader steps back from immediate independence declaration', *Financial Times*, 10 October 2017, https://www.ft.com/content/5c058fd2-add2-11e7-aab9-abaa44b1e130

[11] See Xavier Vidal-Folch and Miquel Noguer, 'Los tres días que conmocionaron Cataluña', *El País*, 27 November 2017, https://politica.elpais.com/politica/2017/11/25/actualidad/1511634052_767273.html

[12] La Sexta, Gritos de 'Puigdemont traidor' en la manifestación de estudiantes a favour de la DUI en Cataluña, 26 October 2017, https://www.lasexta.com/noticias/nacional/estudiantes-esperan-seguimiento-muy-mayoritario-huelga-aplicacion-155_2017102659f19a370cf2abf238810e85.html

[13] Michael Stothard, 'Puigdemont rules out elections as Catalan crisis deepens', *Financial Times*, 26 October 2017, https://www.ft.com/content/25700ea8-ba15-11e7-8c12-5661783e5589

[14] Francesc Macià proclaimed a Catalan republic on 14 April 1931 but vowed to integrate the new entity into a 'Federation of Iberian republics'. Four years later, Lluís Companys proclaimed the Catalan state of the Spanish federal republic. Neither proclamation led to independence, or to the creation of a federal republic in Spain. Companys was executed by the Franco regime in 1940.

[15] Interview with the author, Barcelona, November 2017.

[16] Article 155 of the Spanish constitution was finally lifted in June 2018, when the new Catalan regional government under Quim Torra took office.

[17] Tobias Buck, 'Disappointment in Girona after EU turns back on Catalan ambitions', *Financial Times*, 6 November 2017, https://www.ft.com/content/8983e762-c22f-11e7-b2bb-322b2cb39656

[18] Tobias Buck, 'Weary voters return for trial of strength in Catalonia', *Financial Times*, 20 December 2017, https://www.ft.com/content/0f1c3964-e577-11e7-8b99-0191e45377ec

[19] Centre d'Estudis d'Opinió, 'Enquesta sobre context polític a Catalunya, 2018', Taules estadístiques, http://upceo.ceo.gencat.cat/wsceop/6508/Taules%20estad%C3%ADstiques%20-874.pdf

[20] Buck, 'Catalonia's referendum exposes a divided Spain'.

Chapter Three: The great hangover

1 Joaquín Ferrandis, 'La Ciudad de las Artes ha costado cuatro veces lo que se presupuestó', *El País*, 16 March 2011, https://elpais.com/diario/2011/03/16/cvalenciana/1300306679_850215.html

2 Tobias Buck, 'Spain: Boom to bust and back again', *Financial Times*, 6 April 2017, https://www.ft.com/content/254bb8a8-1940-11e7-a53d-df09f373be87

3 Guillermo de la Dehesa, 'Spain and the Euro Area Sovereign Debt Crisis', conference paper, 13 September 2011, https://piie.com/sites/default/files/publications/papers/dehesa20110913.pdf

4 Martin Sandbu, *Europe's Orphan*, p. 2

5 William Chislett, *A New Course for Spain: Beyond the Crisis*, p. 21

6 De la Dehesa, 'Spain and the Euro Area Sovereign Debt Crisis'.

7 Jesus Fernandez-Villaverde, Luis Garicano and Tano Santos, 'Political Credit Cycles: The case of the Eurozone', Working Paper 18899, National Bureau of Economic Research, March 2013, http://www.nber.org/papers/w18899.pdf

8 Banco de España, 'Report on the financial and banking crisis 2008–2014', https://www.bde.es/f/webbde/Secciones/Publicaciones/OtrasPublicaciones/Fich/InformeCrisis_Completo_web_en.pdf

9 Thomas Catan and Jonathan House, 'Spain's Bank Capital Cushions Offer a Model to Policy Makers', *Wall Street Journal*, 10 November 2008, https://www.wsj.com/articles/SB122627447630612005

10 Banco de España, 'Report on the financial and banking crisis 2008–2014'.

11 Ibid.

12 Tobias Buck, 'La Caixa: Spain's quiet powerhouse', *Financial Times*, 9 April 2015, https://www.ft.com/content/4b3340f6-d63d-11e4-b3e7-00144feab7de

13 Fernandez-Villaverde et al., 'Political Credit Cycles: The case of the Eurozone'.

14 Victor Mallet and Miles Johnson, 'The bank that broke Spain', *Financial Times*, 21 June 2012, https://www.ft.com/content/d8411cf6-bb89-11e1-90e4-00144feabdc0

15 Tobias Buck, 'Spain launches criminal probe into ill-fated Bankia

flotation', *Financial Times*, 13 February 2017, https://www.ft.com/content/9647fdda-f1f6-11e6-8758-6876151821a6

16 Íñigo de Barrón, '"Tarjetas black": Rato, condenado a cuatro años y seis meses de cárcel y Blesa, a seis años', *El País*, 23 February 2017, https://elpais.com/economia/2017/02/23/actualidad/1487855184_159731.html

17 Lorena Ortega, 'Aterriza el primer vuelo comercial en el aeropuerto de Castellón', *El País*, 15 September 2015, https://elpais.com/ccaa/2015/09/14/valencia/1442266091_640563.html

18 Ferran Bono, 'La Ciudad (desértica y millonaria) de la Luz', *El País*, 30 July 2017, https://elpais.com/cultura/2017/07/29/actualidad/1501359409_492532.html

19 Joaquín Ferrandis, 'Infraestructuras millonarias, a precio de saldo', *El País*, 7 February 2015, https://elpais.com/ccaa/2015/02/07/valencia/1423337235_300650.html

20 Francisco D. González, 'CAM, una oficina en manos del PP', *El Mundo*, 12 January 2015, http://www.elmundo.es/comunidad-valenciana/2014/01/12/52d24e67e2704e20528b456b.html

21 For more detail on the story of Bancaja and the role played by Olivas, see: Fernandez-Villaverde et al., 'Political Credit Cycles: The case of the Eurozone'.

22 Nacho Herrero, 'Olivas, el expresidente de Bancaja, condenado a año y medio de prisión por una factura falsa', *El Periódico*, 13 January 2017, https://www.elperiodico.com/es/economia/20170113/olivas-expresidente-de-bancaja-condenado-prision-5741201

23 Banco de España, 'Report on the financial and banking crisis in Spain 2008–2014'.

24 Josep Torrent, 'Tierra de Saqueo', *El País*, 12 January 2012, https://politica.elpais.com/politica/2012/01/15/actualidad/1326649186_916777.html

25 Gema Peñalosa, 'Blasco, condenado a ocho años de prisión y 20 de inhabilitación', *El Mundo*, 28 May 2014, http://www.elmundo.es/comunidad-valenciana/2014/05/28/5384f54f268e3e42308b457c.html

26 Spanish Economy Ministry, 'Economic Policy and Funding Programme for 2018', Presentation, http://www.thespanisheconomy.com/stfls/tse/ficheros/2014/180307_Kingdom_of_Spain.pdf

27 Ibid.

28 Tobias Buck, 'Spain's car industry at heart of nascent recovery', *Financial Times*, 3 November 2013, https://www.ft.com/content/155f4564-42ec-11e3-8350-00144feabdc0

29 Banco de España, 'Informe sobre la crisis financiera', May 2017, https://www.bde.es/f/webbde/GAP/Secciones/SalaPrensa/InformacionInteres/ReestructuracionSectorFinanciero/Arc/Fic/InformeCrisis_Completo_web.pdf

30 There was one notable exception. Banco Popular, Spain's sixth-largest lender, suffered a dramatic bank run in May 2017 that forced European regulators to declare the bank 'failing or likely to fail'. Popular was placed into resolution in accordance with a new pan-European regime to deal with failing banks. Shareholders and junior bondholders were wiped out but depositors and senior bondholders were protected. In a hasty overnight auction, Popular was sold to Banco Santander for the symbolic price of €1. The process was not without controversy but, crucially, there was no spill-over effect into the larger banking sector. Markets concluded, rightly, that Popular was an isolated case. Unlike its domestic rivals, the bank had consistently underestimated its exposure to toxic real-estate loans and assets bought during the boom, and failed to make sufficient provisions.

Chapter Four: Left behind

1 Tobias Buck, 'Spain: Stuck on the sidelines', *Financial Times*, 24 April 2013, https://www.ft.com/content/fdfb8afe-a6ab-11e2-885b-00144feabdc0

2 Instituto Nacional de Estadística, 'Encuesta de Población Activa, Primer trimestre de 2013', https://www.ine.es/daco/daco42/daco4211/epa0113.pdf

3 OECD, 'Details of Tax Revenue – Spain', https://stats.oecd.org/Index.aspx?DataSetCode=REVESP

4 OECD, 'The 2012 Labour Market Reform in Spain: A Preliminary Assessment', OECD Publishing, 2014, http://dx.doi.org/10.1787/9789264213586-en; José Ignacio García Pérez and Macel Jansen, 'Assessing the impact of Spain's latest labour market reform', *Spanish Economic*

and Financial Outlook, May 2015, http://www.spanishreforms.com/documents/10180/105418/019art02_labour_assessment_igp_mj.pdf/3743ec80-c83c-4b8d-9885-5f538bad311a; Rafael Doménech, 'The Spanish Labor Market: Reform Achievements and Challenges', BBVA Research presentation to the International Monetary Fund, 2 October 2017, https://www.bbvaresearch.com/wp-content/uploads/2017/10/Domenech_IMF_2oct2017.pdf

5 OECD, 'Pisa 2015 – Results in focus', p. 5, http://www.oecd.org/pisa/pisa-2015-results-in-focus.pdf

6 Eurostat, 'Early leavers from education and training by sex', http://ec.europa.eu/eurostat/tgm/table.do?tab=table&init=1&language=en&pcode=t2020_40&plugin=1

7 Ibid.

8 Tobias Buck, 'The fear and despair of Spain's young jobseekers', *Financial Times*, 1 March 2014, https://www.ft.com/content/c12e01d2-dbc4-11e5-98fd-06d75973fe09

9 Marcel Jansen, Sergí Jiménez-Martín, Lucía Gorjón, 'The Legacy of the Crisis: The Spanish Labour Market in the Aftermath of the Great Recession', Fedea 2016, http://www.fedea.net/nsaw/descargas/NSAW01en.pdf

10 OECD, 'Youth unemployment rate', https://data.oecd.org/unemp/youth-unemployment-rate.html

11 OECD, 'Youth not in employment, education or training', https://data.oecd.org/youthinac/youth-not-in-employment-education-or-training-neet.html

12 Observatorio de Emancipación, Nota Introductoria 1er semestre 2017, http://www.cje.org/descargas/cje7252.pdf

13 Buck, 'The fear and despair of Spain's young jobseekers'.

14 Banco de España, 'Survey of Household Finances (2014)', 24 January 2017, https://www.bde.es/f/webbde/SES/Secciones/Publicaciones/InformesBoletinesRevistas/ArticulosAnaliticos/2017/T1/files/beaa1701-art2e.pdf

15 Tobias Buck, 'Spain wakes up to risk posed by long-term joblessness', *Financial Times*, 8 December 2016, https://www.ft.com/content/e582f902-bbac-11e6-8b45-b8b81dd5d080

Chapter Five: Storming the heavens

1 Patricia Ortega Dolz, 'Las cuatro esquinas de Podemos', *El País*, 12 November 2014, https://elpais.com/politica/2014/11/11/actualidad/1415734745_829674.html

2 Jairo Vargos, 'Pablo Iglesias consigue en un día los 50.000 apoyos que pedía para seguir adelante con Podemos', *Público*, 18 January 2014, http://www.publico.es/politica/pablo-iglesias-dia-50-000.html

3 Luis Gómez and Manuel Viejo, 'Las redes de arrastre de Podemos', *El País*, 30 May 2014, https://elpais.com/politica/2014/05/28/actualidad/1401305050_166293.html

4 Giles Tremlett, 'The Podemos revolution: how a small group of radical academics changed European politics', *Guardian*, 31 March 2015, https://www.theguardian.com/world/2015/mar/31/podemos-revolution-radical-academics-changed-european-politics

5 Aitor Riveiro, 'Pablo Iglesias abre la Asamblea de Podemos: "El cielo no se toma por consenso: se toma por asalto"', eldiario.es, 18 October 2014, https://www.eldiario.es/politica/Pablo-Iglesias-Asamblea-Podemos-toma_0_314968669.html

6 Tobias Buck, 'Spain's surging Podemos party rushes to get to the top', *Financial Times*, 21 November 2014, https://www.ft.com/content/697bfd1c-70dc-11e4-85d5-00144feabdc0

7 Tobias Buck, 'Podemos' populist surge', *Financial Times*, 19 February 2015, https://www.ft.com/content/ecca8824-b7a3-11e4-981d-00144feab7de

8 Lasse Thomassen, 'Hegemony, populism and democracy: Laclau and Mouffe today', *Revista Española de Ciencia Política* 40, March 2016, pp. 161–76.

9 Ernesto Laclau, *On Populist Reason*, Verso, London and New York, 2005, p. 18.

10 Tremlett, 'The Podemos revolution'.

11 Interview with Pablo Iglesias, 'Spain on Edge', *New Left Review* 93, May/June 2015.

12 Pablo Iglesias, *Politics in a Time of Crisis*, p. 12

13 Buck, 'Spain's surging Podemos party rushes to get to the top'.

14 Tobias Buck, 'Lunch with the FT: Pablo Iglesias', *Financial Times*,

27 November 2015, https://www.ft.com/content/e65e7aae-9362-11e5-94e6-c5413829caa5

15 Joaquín Gil, 'Monedero cobró 425.000 euros por asesorar a Venezuela y sus socios', *El País*, 21 January 2015, https://politica.elpais.com/politica/2015/01/20/actualidad/1421789190_331983.html

16 Pablo Iglesias, 'Understanding Podemos', *New Left Review* 93, May/June 2015.

17 David Ruiz Marull, '¿Qué falló en los sondeos a pie de urna?', *La Vanguardia*, 27 June 2016, https://www.lavanguardia.com/politica/elecciones/20160627/402794314538/sondeos-elecciones-generales-26j-fallo.html

18 Buck, 'Podemos' populist surge'.

19 La Sexta, 'Pablo Iglesias: "Tarde of temprano Unidos Podemos gobernará España. Es cuestión de tiempo"', https://www.lasexta.com/noticias/nacional/elecciones-generales-2016/pablo-iglesias-tarde-o-temprano-unidos-podemos-gobernara-este-pais-es-cuestion-de-tiem po_201606285772813c6584a81a3361b5c6.html

20 Tobias Buck, 'Spain's Podemos mourns losses at 2016 election', *Financial Times*, 28 June 2016, https://www.ft.com/content/3e354aa2-3d3e-11e6-8716-a4a71e8140b0

21 Tobias Buck, 'Podemos still waiting to conquer Spain', *Financial Times*, 18 October 2016, https://www.ft.com/content/8bd3bc20-91ea-11e6-a72e-b428cb934b78

22 Ibid.

23 Interview with La Cafetera, Radiocable, 2 February 2017, https://www.eldiario.es/la-cafetera-de-radiocable/Carolina-Bescansa-explica-renuncia-Podemos_6_608299167.html

24 Luis Alegre, '¿Qué está pasando en Podemos?', eldiario.es, 5 February 2017, https://www.eldiario.es/tribunaabierta/pasando-Podemos_6_609349060.html

Chapter Six: The quiet Galician

1 Europa Press, 'Pedro Sánchez inicia la próxima semana una ruta por toda España para "escuchar a los militantes"', 18 January 2017, https://

www.europapress.es/nacional/noticia-pedro-sanchez-inicia-proxima-semana-ruta-toda-espana-escuchar-militantes-20170118210323.html

2 Tobias Buck, 'Mariano Rajoy plays patient election game', *Financial Times*, 14 December 2015, https://www.ft.com/content/e1dcc936-a02d-11e5-beba-5e33e2b79e46

3 Metroscopia poll in *El País*, 30 November 2015, https://politica.elpais.com/politica/2015/11/28/actualidad/1448730399_666049.html

4 Ibid.

5 Tobias Buck, 'Mariano Rajoy plays the long game as opponents burn out', *Financial Times*, 28 October 2016, https://www.ft.com/content/65592584-9c4f-11e6-a6e4-8b8e77dd083a

6 Pilar Marcos, 'Aznar cede a Rajoy todo su poder en el PP', *El País*, 2 September 2003, https://elpais.com/diario/2003/09/02/espana/1062453601_850215.html

7 Luis R. Aizpeolea and Pilar Marcos, 'Aznar comunicó el viernes por la noche a Rajoy que le propondría como sucesor', *El País*, 2 September 2003, https://elpais.com/diario/2003/09/02/espana/1062453606_850215.html

8 Buck, 'Mariano Rajoy plays patient election game'.

9 Mariano Rajoy, *En Confianza*, 2011, p. 24.

10 Interview with Cadena Ser radio station, 28 September 2016, http://cadenaser.com/programa/2016/09/27/hoy_por_hoy/1474992493_870585.html

11 Tobias Buck and Lionel Barber, 'FT Interview: Mariano Rajoy', *Financial Times*, 15 January 2013, https://www.ft.com/content/4304f0ba-5efc-11e2-9f18-00144feab49a

12 Esteban Urreiztieta and Eduardo Inda, 'Bárcenas pagó sobresueldos en negro durante años a parte de la cúpula del PP', *El Mundo*, 20 January 2013, http://www.elmundo.es/elmundo/2013/01/18/espana/1358536985.html

13 Francisco Mercado, Miguel Jiménez, Carlos E. Cué and José Manuel Romero, 'Las cuentas secretas de Bárcenas', *El País*, 31 January 2013, https://politica.elpais.com/politica/2013/01/30/actualidad/1359583204_085918.html

14 Tobias Buck, 'Spanish PM Mariano Rajoy admits mistake over

slush fund', *Financial Times*, 1 August 2013, https://www.ft.com/content/8581451e-fa89-11e2-87b9-00144feabdc0

[15] Centro de Investigaciones Sociológicas, 'Tres problemas principales que existen actualmente en España', http://www.cis.es/cis/export/sites/default/-Archivos/Indicadores/documentos_html/TresProblemas.html

[16] Comunicación Poder Judicial, 'La Audiencia Nacional condena a penas de hasta 51 años de prisión a 29 de los 37 acusados en el "caso Gürtel"', 24 May 2018, http://www.poderjudicial.es/cgpj/es/Poder-Judicial/Audiencia-Nacional/Noticias-Judiciales/La-Audiencia-Nacional-condena-a-penas-de-hasta-51-anos-de-prision-a-29-de-los-37-acusados-en-el--caso-Gurtel-

[17] Eduardo Inda and Esteban Urreiztieta, 'Los SMS entre Rajoy y Bárcenas', *El Mundo*, 14 July 2013, http://www.elmundo.es/elmundo/2013/07/14/espana/1373779073.html

[18] Tobias Buck, 'Spaniards ready to give us a chance, says Socialist leader', *Financial Times*, 21 December 2014, https://www.ft.com/content/4db39ba6-8777-11e4-8c91-00144feabdc0

Chapter Seven: A history of violence

[1] Tobias Buck, 'After Eta: Spain's history of violence', *Financial Times*, 27 January 2017, https://www.ft.com/content/8ad74460-e350-11e6-8405-9e5580d6e5fb

[2] The acronym stands for Euskadi Ta Askatasuna, or Basque Homeland and Liberty.

[3] Informe Foronda, 'Los contextos históricos del terrorismo en el País Vasco y la consideración social de sus víctimas 1968–2010', December 2014, p. 165, https://www.ehu.eus/documents/1964362/3976964/Informe-Foronda.pdf/02af1dec-6d32-7759-f233-90777b0e8db4

[4] Tobias Buck, 'Basque voters revel in new kind of politics', *Financial Times*, 22 September 2016, https://www.ft.com/content/245d46e0-801c-11e6-bc52-0c7211ef3198

[5] Ibid.

[6] Ikerfell poll, cited in *El Correo*, 'La mayoría de los vascos quiere más autogobierno pero rechaza romper con España', 17 September 2016,

http://www.elcorreo.com/elecciones/vascas/201609/17/solo-vascos-reivindica-independencia-20160916232457.html

7 eldiario.es, 'Documento: La carta en la que Eta anuncia su disolución', 2 May 2018, https://www.eldiario.es/norte/DOCUMENTO-carta-ETA-anuncia-disolucion_0_767123640.html

8 Ibid.

9 *El País*, ETA asesina a Miguel Ángel frente al clamor por salvar su vida, 13 July 1997, https://elpais.com/diario/1997/07/13/portada/868744801_850215.html

10 Buck, 'After Eta: Spain's history of violence'.

11 Ibid.

12 Ibid.

13 Informe Foronda, 'Los contextos históricos del terrorismo'.

14 Buck, 'After Eta: Spain's history of violence'.

15 Jesús Rodríguez, 'El silencio de Hernani', *El País*, 20 July 2007, https://elpais.com/diario/2007/07/22/eps/1185084946_850215.html

16 Buck, 'After Eta: Spain's history of violence'.

17 Informe Foronda, 'Los contextos históricos del terrorismo', p. 164.

18 'Proyecto de investigación de la tortura en el País Vasco (1960–2013)', 27 June 2016, http://www.eitb.eus/multimedia/documentos/2016/06/27/1987310/Memoria%20Proyecto%20tortura%202016.pdf

19 'Civil and political rights, including the question of torture and detention. Report of the Special Rapporteur on the question of torture, Theo van Boven, Visit to Spain', 6 February 2004, https://documents-dds-ny.un.org/doc/UNDOC/GEN/G04/107/16/PDF/G0410716.pdf?OpenElement

20 Buck, 'After Eta: Spain's history of violence'.

21 Pedro Gorospe, 'El gobierno anuncia que acercará más presos de Eta antes del fin del verano', *El País*, 8 August 2018, https://elpais.com/politica/2018/08/08/actualidad/1533728901_300746.html

22 Buck, 'After Eta: Spain's history of violence'.

23 José Yoldi, 'La prueba biológica confirma que los cadáveres hallados en Alicante son los de Lasa y Zabala', *El País*, 11 April 1995, https://elpais.com/diario/1995/04/11/espana/797551213_850215.html

24 Buck, 'After Eta: Spain's history of violence'.

[25] Interview with the author, Madrid 2016.

[26] Fernando Aramburu, *Patria*, p. 462 (translation by the author).

Chapter Eight: Spain's cross to bear

[1] Soledad Gallego-Díaz and Carloe E. Cué, 'Aprobaremos un plan contra la explotación laboral' (interview with Pedro Sánchez), 24 June 2018, https://elpais.com/politica/2018/06/23/actualidad/1529773600_203119.html

[2] Isabel Woodford, 'Spanish parliament votes to exhume remains of dictator Franco', Reuters, 13 September 2018, https://www.reuters.com/article/us-spain-politics-franco/spanish-parliament-votes-to-exhume-remains-of-dictator-franco-idUSKCN1LT2C9

[3] Olga R. Sanmartín, 'El 54% opina que no es el momento de exhumar a Franco', *El Mundo*, 15 July 2018, http://www.elmundo.es/espana/2018/07/15/5b4a2a39ca4741d7728b45ce.html

[4] Centro de Investigaciones Sociológicas, 'Estudio 2760 Memorias de la guerra civil y el franquismo', April 2008, http://www.cis.es/cis/export/sites/default/-Archivos/Marginales/2760_2779/2760/e276000.html

[5] Isabel Rubio, 'Franco, Primo de Rivera y otras figuras del franquismo conservan 1.143 calles en España', *El País*, 10 May 2018, https://elpais.com/politica/2018/05/09/actualidad/1525863933_856305.html

[6] Tobias Buck, 'Facing up to Franco: Spain 40 years on', *Financial Times*, 8 May 2015, https://www.ft.com/content/5e4e6aac-f42f-11e4-99de-00144feab7de

[7] Hugh Thomas, *The Spanish Civil War*, p. 133.

[8] Ibid.

[9] Paul Preston, *Franco*, p. 29.

[10] Antony Beevor, *The Battle for Spain*, p. 50.

[11] Thomas, *The Spanish Civil War*, p. 498.

[12] Beevor, *The Battle for Spain*, p. 406.

[13] Paul Preston, *The Spanish Holocaust*, p. xi.

[14] Jeremy Treglown, *Franco's Crypt: Spanish memory and culture since 1936*, pp. 201–15.

[15] Preston, *The Spanish Holocaust*, p. xii.

16 Conferencia Episcopal, 'Orientaciones morales ante la situación actual de España', Instrucción Pastoral, 23 November 2006, http://www.conferenciaepiscopal.es/documentos/Conferencia/Orientaciones SituacionActual.html

17 *El País*, 'Rouco sobre la Memoria Histórica: "A veces es necesario saber olvidar"', 24 November 2008, https://elpais.com/sociedad/2008/11/24/actualidad/1227481202_850215.html

18 Iñigo Aduriz, 'Casado asegura que la exhumación de Franco es "una cortina de humo" del gobierno y confirma la abstención del PP', eldiario.es, 27 August 2018, https://www.eldiario.es/politica/Casado-PP-abstendra-exhumacion-Franco_0_808069361.html

19 Tobias Buck, 'Spain fails to turn page on legacy of Franco's dictatorship', *Financial Times*, 23 September 2016, https://www.ft.com/content/dbb4f3d6-80e6-11e6-8e50-8ec15fb462f4

20 Tobias Buck, 'Madrid steps closer to banishing Franco tributes', *Financial Times*, 22 July 2016, https://www.ft.com/content/297b09ca-4fff-11e6-88c5-db83e98a590a

21 Luca Constantini, Madrid paraliza el cambio de nombres de calles franquistas hasta que se resuelvan tres recursos, *El País*, 26 July 2017, https://elpais.com/ccaa/2017/07/24/madrid/1500894593_625183.html

Chapter Nine: The new Spaniards

1 Tobias Buck, 'China's migrants thrive in Spain's financial crisis', *Financial Times*, 9 October 2014, https://www.ft.com/content/f8d02554-3e93-11e4-a620-00144feabdc0

2 Instituto Nacional de Estadística, 'Estadística del Padrón Continuo', https://www.ine.es/prensa/padron_tabla.html

3 Instituto Nacional de Estadística, 'Población extranjera por Nacionalidad, sexo y año', http://www.ine.es/jaxi/Tabla.htm?path=/t20/e245/p08/l0/&file=02005.px&L=0

4 Lucía Abellán, 'Council of Europe urges Spain to create independent anti-racism body', *El País*, 27 February 2018, https://elpais.com/elpais/2018/02/27/inenglish/1519734872_101885.html

5   Somtoseeks.com, 'The truth about racism in Spain: Advice for black travelers', 25 February 2018, https://www.somtoseeks.com/what-black-travelers-should-know-about-racism-in-spain/

6   Rosa Aparicio and Alejandor Portes, 'Growing up in Spain: The integration of the children of immigrants', Social Studies Collection No. 38, 'la Caixa' Welfare Projects 2014, https://obrasociallacaixa.org/documents/10280/240906/vol38_en.pdf/518ea9c0-9ca0-4df8-b62f-d262cfee0f18%20

7   Jason DeParle, 'Spain, like US, grapples with immigration', 10 June 2008, *New York Times*, https://www.nytimes.com/2008/06/10/world/europe/10migrate.html

8   Ana Carbajosa, 'Cuidar los hijos de otras', *El País*, 29 September 2016, https://elpais.com/cultura/2016/09/28/actualidad/1475075894_811141.html

9   Tobias Buck, 'Migration: The drain from Spain', *Financial Times*, 20 February 2014, https://www.ft.com/content/f7bdd5ce-995e-11e3-91cd-00144feab7de

10 Ibid.

11 Comisión Nacional de los Mercados y la Competencia, 'Informe Económico Sectorial de las Telecomunicaciones y el Audiovisual 2015', p. 93.

12 Instituto Nacional de Estadística, 'Proyección de la Población de España a Corto Plazo 2013–2023', Nota de Prensa, http://www.ine.es/prensa/np813.pdf

13 Tobias Buck, 'Romanians in Spain plan to put down roots', *Financial Times*, 16 January 2014, https://www.ft.com/content/6d293362-7d49-11e3-a579-00144feabdc0

14 Tobias Buck, 'Changyu Pioneer accelerates wine imports into China', *Financial Times*, 30 October 2016, https://www.ft.com/content/6a55a130-9cf8-11e6-a6e4-8b8e77dd083a

15 Tobias Buck and Josh Noble, 'Dalian Wanda scores 20% stake in Atletico Madrid', *Financial Times*, 21 January 2015, https://www.ft.com/content/687428ee-a076-11e4-8ad8-00144feab7de

16 Miguel Ángel Criado, 'El Congreso español es el que tiene menos miembros de origen inmigrante', *El País*, 15 February 2016, https://elpais.com/elpais/2016/02/15/ciencia/1455521726_813402.html

Chapter Ten: The Spanish exception

1 Constanza Lambertucci, 'Far-right political party Vox attracts 9,000 people to Madrid rally', *El País*, 8 October 2018, https://elpais.com/elpais/2018/10/08/inenglish/1538983913_173766.html

2 Tobias Buck, 'No right turn for Spanish politics', *Financial Times*, 17 January 2017, https://www.ft.com/content/414246f6-dbe4-11e6-86ac-f253db7791c6

3 J. J. Gálvez, 'La extrema derecha emerge en Andalucía: Vox obtiene 12 diputados', *El País*, 3 December 2018, https://elpais.com/politica/2018/12/02/actualidad/1543765846_278055.html

4 Buck, 'No right turn for Spanish politics'.

5 Tobias Buck, 'Spanish far-right seeks to break beyond the political fringe', *Financial Times*, 12 June 2016, https://www.ft.com/content/250d09e2-2bf6-11e6-bf8d-26294ad519fc

6 Ibid.

7 Carmen González-Enríquez, 'The Spanish Exception: Unemployment, inequality and immigration, but no right-wing populist parties', 14 February 2017, http://www.realinstitutoelcano.org/wps/wcm/connect/e9e0d7c1-7c71-4335-a2fb-15b219e62c5e/WP3-2017-GonzalezEnriquez-Spanish-Exception-unemployment-inequality-immigration-no-right-wing-populist-parties.pdf?MOD=AJPERES&cacheid=1487009991261

8 European Commission, Special Eurobarometer Report 469, 'Integration of immigrants in the European Union', April 2018, p. 58.

9 Pew Research Center, 'Many worldwide oppose more migration – both into and out of their countries', 10 December 2018, http://www.pewresearch.org/fact-tank/2018/12/10/many-worldwide-oppose-more-migration-both-into-and-out-of-their-countries/

10 William Chislett, 'Forty years of democratic Spain: political, economic, foreign policy and social change 1978–2018', Report for the Elcano Royal Institute, October 2018.

11 European Commission, Special Eurobarometer Report 469, p. 28.

12 Ibid., p. 38.

13 Buck, 'Spain's far-right seeks to break beyond political fringe'.

14 UNHCR, 'Press Coverage of the Refugee and Migrant Crisis in the

EU: A Content Analysis of Five European Countries', December 2015, https://www.unhcr.org/56bb369c9.pdf

15 Buck, 'No right turn for Spanish politics'.

16 Ministerio del Interior, 'Informe sobre la evolución de los incidentes relacionados con los delitos de odio en España', http://www.interior. gob.es/documents/10180/5791067/ESTUDIO+INCIDENTES+DEL ITOS+DE+ODIO+2016.pdf/c5ef4121-ae02-4368-ac1b-ce5cc7e731c2

17 Bundesministerium des Innern, 'Straf- und Gewaltdaten im Bereich Hasskriminalität 2015 und 2016', https://www.bmi.bund.de/SharedDocs/ downloads/DE/veroeffentlichungen/2017/pmk-2016-hasskriminalitaet. pdf?__blob=publicationFile&v=1

18 Bundeskriminalamt, 'Kriminalität im Kontext von Zuwanderung', file:///C:/Users/stefan.wagstyl.ADFT/Downloads/kernaussagenZu KriminalitaetImKontextVonZuwanderungI-IIIQuartal2017.pdf

Epilogue: Towards a new Spain

1 Reuters, 'Spanish minister resigned over tax fine', 13 June 2018, https:// www.reuters.com/article/us-spain-politics/spanish-minister-resigns- over-tax-fine-idUSKBN1J92JQ

2 Sam Jones, 'Spain's health minister quits over degree scandal', *Guardian*, 12 September 2018, https://www.theguardian.com/world/2018/ sep/12/spain-health-minister-carmen-monton-resigns-masters-degree- irregularities

Further reading

Alonso, Sonia & Rovira Kaltwasser, Cristóbal. 'Spain: No country for the Populist Radical Right?', *South European Society and Politics* 20 (2015), pp. 21–45

Aramburu, Fernando. *Patria* (Barcelona, 2016)

Bassets, Lluís. *Lecciones Españolas* (Barcelona, 2017)

Beevor, Antony. *The Battle for Spain* (London, 2006)

Brenan, Gerald. *The Spanish Labyrinth* (Cambridge, 1943)

——. *The Face of Spain* (London, 1987)

Carr, Raymond (ed.). *Spain – A History* (Oxford, 2000)

Cercas, Javier. *The Anatomy of a Moment* (London, 2011)

——. *Soldiers of Salamis* (London, 2003)

Chislett, William. *Spain – What everyone needs to know* (Oxford, 2013)

——. *A New Course for Spain: Beyond the Crisis* (Madrid, 2016) *Forty years of democratic Spain: political, economic, foreign policy and social change 1978-2018* (Madrid, 2018)

Del Molino, Sergio. *La España vacía – Viaje por un país que nunca fue* (Madrid, 2016)

Elliott, J. H. *Scots and Catalans – Union and Disunion* (New Haven and London, 2018)

Fernández-Albertos, José. *Los votantes de Podemos – Del partido de los indignados al partido de los excluidos* (Madrid, 2015)

Ferrándiz, Francisco. *El pasado bajo tierra* (Barcelona, 2014)

González-Enríquez, Carmen. *The Spanish Exception: Unemployment, inequality and immigration, but no right-wing populist parties* (Madrid, 2017)

González-Ferrer, Amparo & Moreno-Fuentes, Francisco Javier. 'Back to the Suitcase? Emigration during the Great Recession in Spain', *South European Society and Politics* 22 (2017), pp. 447–71

Hughes, Robert. *Barcelona* (London, 2001)

Iglesias, Pablo. *Politics in a Time of Crisis – Podemos and the Future of Democracy in Europe* (London, 2015)

Minder, Raphael. *The Struggle for Catalonia – Rebel Politics in Spain* (London, 2017)

Muñoz Molina, Antonio. *Todo lo que era sólido* (Barcelona, 2013)

Ortega y Gasset, José. *Invertebrate Spain* (London, 1937)

Orwell, George. *Homage to Catalonia* (London, 1938)

Preston, Paul. *Franco* (London, 1995)

——. *¡Comrades! Portraits from the Spanish Civil War* (London 1999)

——. *The Spanish Holocaust* (London, 2013)

Rajoy, Mariano. *En confianza* (Barcelona, 2011)

Sandbu, Martin. *Europe's Orphan – The Future of the Euro and the Politics of Debt* (Princeton, 2015)

Thomas, Hugh. *World Without End – The Global Empire of Philip II* (London, 2014)

——. *The Spanish Civil War* (London, 2001)

Treglown, Jeremy. *Franco's Crypt – Spanish Culture and Memory since 1936* (New York, 2013)

Tremlett, Giles. *Ghosts of Spain – Travels through a Country's Hidden Past* (London, 2006)

Index